GRAMMAR OF COLLOQUIAL TIBETAN

GRAMMAR OF COLLOQUIAL TIBETAN

C. A. BELL

THIRD EDITION

GYAN

Published by

Gyan Publishing House
5, Ansari Road
Daryaganj, New Delhi-110002
Phone: 011-47034999, 9811692060
E-mail: books@gyanbooks.com

Distribution Network
gyanbooks.com
India, USA, Canada, UK, Australia, France

ISBN :-978-81-212-4381-0 (PB)
First Published, Calcutta, 1939 (Third Edition)

2nd Impression 2020

Printed at: Gyan Press, Delhi.

Grammar of Colloquial Tibetan
Author: C. A. Bell

Government of Bengal

Grammar of Colloquial Tibetan

By

C. A. BELL, C.M.G., C.I.E.

Late of Indian Civil Service, Late Political Officer Sikkim

THIRD EDITION

Superintendent, Government Printing
Bengal Government Press, Alipore, Bengal
1939

"It is only from its roots in the living generation of men that language can be reinforced with fresh vigour for its seed. What may be called a literate dialect grows ever more and more pedantic and foreign till it becomes at last as unfitting a vehicle for living thought as Monkish Latin."

JAMES RUSSELL LOWELL.

PREFACE TO SECOND EDITION.

In the first edition this Grammar was published as the first part of a "Manual of Colloquial Tibetan," the second part consisting of an English-Tibetan Colloquial Dictionary. In this second edition both parts have not only been revised, but have also been considerably enlarged. The map accompanying this edition —the latest from the Indian Survey Department—is bulkier than the Royal Geographical Society's map of 1904, with which the first edition was furnished. It has therefore been found best to bring out the Grammar and Dictionary as separate books. The map accompanies the Grammar.

2. The Tibetan words have been romanized throughout the Grammar, for the convenience of those who lack either the time or the inclination to master the Tibetan character. Many additions have been made, especially in the Chapters on the Verb and in the Conversational Exercises, which latter number thirty-two as against eighteen in the first edition.

3. As Political Officer in Sikkim I was in charge of the diplomatic relations of the British Government with Tibet and Bhutan also. Much material for framing rules and illustrations has therefore been gleaned from my Tibetan friends of all classes, High Priests, Cabinet Ministers, civil and military officers, shop-keepers, mule-drivers, peasants, etc., etc., during my fifteen years' service in Tibet and on the borderland. Among all these my thanks are especially due to Rai Sahib Kusho Pahlese of the noble family of Pahla in Lhasa. And Mr. David Macdonald, British Trade Agent at Yatung, Tibet, has again rendered valuable assistance.

4. In addition to the grammars formerly consulted I have examined Mr. Hannah's careful work, which was not published until some years after my first edition had seen the light. My

acknowledgments are also due to the Government of Bengal, who have defrayed the cost of this edition also in return for the copyright which I have made over to them.

5. This Grammar has been adopted as one of the text-books in the High Proficiency examination in the Tibetan language, held under the auspices of the Government of India.

6. In conclusion I must express my pleasure at finding that a second edition was called for owing to the first edition being sold out—a rare occurrence among books on Tibet—for it may be hoped that some have found it useful.

DARJEELING :
November 1919.

C. A. BELL.

PREFACE TO FIRST EDITION OF "MANUAL OF COLLOQUIAL TIBETAN."

1. The object of this little work is to provide a practical handbook for those who wish to acquire a speedy knowledge of Colloquial Tibetan. It, therefore, does not deal with the written language, which differs widely from the colloquial, and is useless for conversational purposes.

2. Notwithstanding the political and commercial importance of Tibet it is remarkable that so few Europeans are able to converse with the people in their own tongue. The language is undoubtedly a hard one to acquire on account of the complexity of the grammar, the intricacy of the spelling, the fine shades of pronunciation, the different terminology, known as the honorific, employed in addressing the higher classes, the variety of dialects, and the distinction, already noted, between the literary and spoken language. To minimise these difficulties and to make the approach to the colloquial as easy as possible, is the aim of this handbook. It seeks to do so by giving a minimum of grammatical notes, fully explained by examples, a clear statement of the rules of pronunciation, a simple system of phonetic spelling in the Roman character, a set of conversational exercises and a sufficiently full vocabulary of both common and honorific words to meet the ordinary requirements of conversation with all classes.

3. Tibet is essentially a country of dialects. A well-known proverb says—

། ལུང་པ་རེ་རེ་སྐད་ལུགས་རེ།
། བླ་མ་རེ་རེ་ཆོས་ལུགས་རེ། །

"Every district its own dialect ;
Every lama his own doctrine."

Under these circumstances it was necessary to select the dialect most widely spoken, and that of Lhasa has been chosen accordingly. It is not only the dialect of the Central Province but may be said to be also the *lingua franca* of the whole of Tibet. It is more generally spoken than any other, and is recognized as the most correct form of speech by all.

4. The Vocabulary contains somewhat less than ten thousand Tibetan words, the number of separate English words being some seven thousand or about twice as many as those contained in any colloquial Tibetan vocabulary up to date. The remaining three thousand words are made up of about two thousand honorific words and one thousand extra Tibetan words. Where two or more Tibetan words are given for one English equivalent, all are in common colloquial use and the one placed first is the commonest. It is hoped that the honorific words given may be found useful. Existing vocabularies give but few. A knowledge of honorific words is essential for talking to or of Tibetans of good position. It is hoped also that the exercises in Tibetan handwriting given in Part I, Chapter XVII, may assist any student, who so desires, to learn how to write Tibetan letters and other documents in a clear and correct style.

5. It is recommended that the grammar be used as follows: The rules of each Chapter should be perused and their accompanying examples learnt by heart. The *Words* at the end of the Chapter should then be committed to memory as far as possible, and the exercise (for reading and copying) should be read aloud to the teacher to ensure correct pronunciation, and every word should be understood. After this the other exercise (for translation) should be translated *viva voce* and then written down, care being taken, when writing, to verify the spelling, as very few Tibetan teachers can spell correctly. On the following day the Tibetan half of the reading exercise should be covered up, and the English half re-translated into Tibetan, first *viva voce* and then in writing. If the above plan is followed the student will gain the

soundest possible knowledge of the language. But if the student has not time for the above thorough system, he should omit the writing of both exercises and limit himself to the *viva voce*.

6. As regards teachers it is best to obtain at first one who speaks English. If the teacher can speak the Lhasa language also, so much the better, but very few of the English-speaking Tibetans in the Darjeeling district or in Sikkim are really proficient in the latter. As soon as he can converse a little, the student should change to a Lhasa man that speaks Tibetan only, so as to be certain of always speaking in Tibetan. When the teacher knows English or Hindustani there is always a tendency for the conversation to drop into the latter languages. The Lhasa teacher should of course be as well educated a man as is procurable. The student should also, when he is able to understand and converse a little, call in Tibetans of the Lhasa province to talk to him, one at a time, changing them every two or three weeks. Tibetans are generally ready to talk; they have not the formal constraint of manner which characterizes so many of the Indian races. The more he calls in thus, the better will he be able to understand and reply to any chance Tibetan he meets.

7. A word as to the system of romanization. In this, which is believed to be as phonetic as possible, I had reluctantly to differ from the various systems of my predecessors, as none of them seemed to me to reproduce the sounds in the dialect of Lhasa, though some reproduced those in the Sikkimese and other dialects. The system followed in this book is nearly the same as that recommended to Government for official reports, etc., by Captain O'Connor, C.I.E., Trade Agent at Gyangtse, and the author, but distinguishes the different sounds with greater accuracy than was considered necessary in the Government system.

8. The Tibetan words and syllables in brackets are those used in the simple form of book-language. Where the pronunciation

of the literary and spoken form of a word is the same, the literary form alone is given, since the sole object of entering the spoken form is to show the exact pronunciation of the word.

9. In conclusion, I must acknowledge my obligations to the Government of Bengal for their patronage, to the Grammars of the Rev. Graham Sandberg, the Rev. H. A. Jäschke and the Rev. Father A. Desgodins, and especially to Mr. Henderson's Tibetan Manual, which marks a great advance in the Tibetan colloquial over any of its predecessors. And most of all are my thanks due to Mr. David Macdonald, who has revised this book throughout, and to whose unrivalled knowledge of both colloquial and literary Tibetan are largely due whatever merits the work may possess.

CHUMBI, TIBET:
March 1905.

C. A. BELL.

CONTENTS.

			Page
CHAPTER	I.	The Alphabet and its Pronunciation ...	1-19
,,	II.	The Indefinite and Definite Articles ...	20-23
,,	III.	The Noun	24-30
,,	IV.	The Adjective	31-35
,,	V.	The Auxiliary Verb	36-42
,,	VI.	The Verb	43-55
,,	VII.	The Verb continued	56-66
,,	VIII.	Numerals	67-79
,,	IX.	Pronouns	80-92
,,	X.	Adverbs	93-98
,,	XI.	Postpositions, Conjunctions and Interjections.	99-106
,,	XII.	The Order of Words in a Sentence ...	107-108
,,	XIII.	The Honorific Language	109-117
,,	XIV.	Miscellaneous; Monetary System, Weights and Measures, Lineal Measurements, Divisions of Time, Years, Seasons, Dates, Days of the Week and the Time of Day.	118-126
,,	XV.	A Conversation Transliterated, Translated and Paraphrased.	127-130
,,	XVI.	Conversational Exercises—	
		1. General conversation ...	131-132
		2. The same continued	132-134
		3. Talk with servants	134-135
		4. The same continued	135-136
		5. Food	137-138
		6. Time of the day, days of the week, dates, seasons, etc.	138-140
		7. The same continued	140-141

		Page
8.	The weather	141-142
9.	Conversation with the teacher, *hon.*	143-144
10.	Relatives	144-145
11.	On the march	145-147
12.	The same continued	147-149
13.	The same continued	149-151
14.	Crossing a river	152-154
15.	Talking to persons on the road ...	154-155
16.	General enquiries by an interpreter in the field.	156-157
17.	The same continued	157-158
18.	Buying supplies for troops ...	158-159
19.	The same continued	159-160
20.	The same continued	160-161
21.	Buying meat in the bazaar ...	161-162
22.	Buying a turquoise	163-164
23.	Buying silk	164-166
24.	A small trader calls at a gentleman's house with some wares.	167-169
25.	Deciding a dispute	169-171
26.	Paying a visit	171-172
27.	The same continued	173
28.	Receiving a visit from a Tibetan Official.	174-176
29.	The same continued	176-178
30.	The same continued	178-180
31.	A visit to the Dalai Lama by a Tibetan General.	180-182
32.	Diplomatic intercourse, *hon.* ...	182-184

CHAPTER XVII. Exercises in Tibetan handwriting ... 185

ABBREVIATIONS.

Adj.=adjective.
Adv.=adverb.
Art.=article.
Ch.=Chinese.
Conj.=conjunction.
C.T.=Central Tibet, i.e., the provinces of U and Tsang.
Def.=definite.
Do.=ditto.
E.G.=for instance.
F.=female, feminine.
Hin.=Hindi.
Hon.=honorific.
H. hon.=high honorific.
Imp.=imperative.
Inf.=inferior.
Interj.=interjection.
Interr.=interrogative.
Lit.=literally.
M.=male, masculine.
Mon.=Mongolian.
Neg.=negative.
Opp.=opposed.
Post.=postposition.
Pron.=pronoun.
Rel.=relative.
S.=substantive.
Sik.=Sikkimese.
Sup.=superior.
Ts.=Tsang province.
V.I.=verb intransitive.
V.T.=verb transitive.
W.=with.

ERRATA.

Page	89 line	24	for	*te-ring-sang*	read	*te-ring-sang.*
,,	116 ,,	20	,,	ད་རང་	,,	དེ་རིང་
,,	143 lines	8-9	,,	*dra-tak-po*	,,	*dra-tak-po*
,,	151 line	23	,,	ཡག་པོ་	,,	ཡག་པོ་
,,	163 ,,	22	,,	སྐྱེར་བ་	,,	སྐྱེར་བ་
,,	165 ,,	10	,,	སྐྱགས་སེ་ (སེར་)	,,	སྐྱག་སེ་
,,	175 ,,	21	,,	*hle-sa*	,,	*hla-sa.*
,,	184 lines	8-9	,,	*tön-min*	,,	*tön-min.*

GRAMMAR OF COLLOQUIAL TIBETAN.

NOTE.—Where the colloquial and the literary form differ the latter is given in brackets in the Tibetan character. In the romanized Tibetan the colloquial forms alone are given.

CHAPTER I.

THE ALPHABET AND ITS PRONUNCIATION.

1. The Tibetan Alphabet was originally taken from the Sanskrit Devanagari in the 7th century A.D., but many of the letters, especially in Central Tibet, now represent sounds different from their prototypes. Both the Sanskrit and the Tibetan pronunciations have changed considerably during this period.

2. The Tibetan letters are as follows:—

Consonants and their romanized equivalents.

	Surds.	Aspirates.	Sonants.	Nasals.
Gutturals	ཀ་ *ka*	ཁ་ *kha*	ག་ *ḱa*	ང་ *nga*
Palatals	ཅ་ *cha*	ཆ་ *chha*	ཇ་ *ch́a*	ཉ་ *nya*
Dentals	ཏ་ *ta*	ཐ་ *tha*	ད་ *t́a*	ན་ *na*
Labials	པ་ *pa*	ཕ་ *pha*	བ་ *ṕa*	མ་ *ma*
Sibilants	ཙ་ *tsa*	ཚ་ *tsha*	ཛ་ *tśa*	
Semi-vowels	ཝ་ *wa*	ཞ་ *sh́a*	ཟ་ *śa*	འ་ (not romanized.)
	ཡ་ *ya*	ར་ *ra*	ལ་ *la*	
	ཤ་ *sha*	ས་ *sa*	ཧ་ *ha*	ཨ་ *a*

3. In this Chapter I endeavour to give as nearly as possible the sound represented by each Tibetan letter. The romanization throughout is intended only as a rough guide to the pronunciation for those who are unable to give the time for studying the exact pronunciation. The consonants when used as initials, i.e., when immediately preceding the vowel of a syllable, are pronounced as below :—

ཀ་ The *k* in the Hindustani word *kam*. To be pronounced with the tongue between the teeth and without breathing.

ཁ་ an aspirated *k*, e.g., *block-head*, pronounced in one breath. The same as the aspirated *k* in Hindustani words, e.g., *khana*.

ག་ also a *k* but pronounced through the throat and in a lower tone than ཀ་

ང་ like the *ng* in *coming*. Say *coming in*, eliminating the first four letters *comi*.

ཅ་ *ch* in *chin*. To be pronounced with the tongue between the teeth and without breathing.

ཆ་ *ch* aspirated, e.g., *touch-hands* pronounced in one breath, i.e., like the aspirated *ch* in Hindustani.

ཇ་ is also a *ch* pronounced through the throat and in a lower tone than ཅ་

ཉ་ as the initial sound in *nuisance*.

ཏ་ a Dental *t* to be pronounced with the tongue between the teeth and without breathing. This ཏ་ and ཉ་ differ from the English *t* and *n*, in that the English letters require the tongue to be placed against the roof of the mouth and so have a heavier sound.

ཐ་ aspirated *t*, e.g., *thora* in Hindustani; or—subject to the difference noted under ཏ་—*pat hard* pronounced in one breath. Not to be confused with the English *th* sound, in words like *the*.

ད་ is like ཏ་ but pronounced through the throat and in a lower tone than ཏ་

ན་ is like the English *n*, e.g., in *nest* subject to the difference noted under ཏ་

པ་ like English *p* as in *pear*, to be pronounced with the tongue between the teeth and without breathing.

ཕ་ aspirated *p*, e.g., *stop here*, pronounced as one word. Not to be confused with *ph* sound occurring in English words like *phantasy*, etc.

བ་ is also a *p* but pronounced through the throat and in a lower tone than པ་ If it forms the second syllable of a word whose first syllable ends with a vowel or with ང་འ་ར་ or ལ་ it is pronounced as *w*.

མ་ as English *m*, e.g., in *man*.

ཙ་ *ts* is pronounced like *weights* eliminating the letters *weigh*. To be pronounced with the tongue between the teeth and without breathing.

ཚ་ as *ts* aspirated, e.g., in *pats hard* pronounced as one word.

ཛ་ is also a *ts*, but pronounced through the throat and in a lower tone than ཙ་

ཝ་ like *w* in English, e.g., in *wing*.

ཞ་ Something like *sh* in English, but pronounced in a lower tone and more through the throat.

ཟ་ Something like *s* in English, but pronounced in a lower tone and more through the throat.

འ་ has no pronunciation of its own. When it precedes ག་ཇ་ད་བ་ or ཛ་; these letters are pronounced respectively like *g* in *gun*, *j* in *jam*, *d* in *den*, *b* in *bend*, and *ds* in *pads*. See also para. 23.

ཡ་ like *y* in English, e.g., in *yacht*.

ར་ is short like *r* in English, e.g., in *rat*. It is never rolled.

ལ་ like *l* in English, e.g., in *linger*.

ཤ་ like *sh* in English, but pronounced sharply and through the teeth.

ས་ like *s* in English, but pronounced sharply and through the teeth.

ཧ་ like *h* aspirated in English, e.g., in *hand*.

ཨ་ When a vowel is initial, either ཨ་ or འ་ is used as its base. The difference in pronunciation of these two is that the throat is opened for ཨ་ and kept closed for འ་ The result is that ཨ་ carries the ordinary vowel sound, whatever the vowel may be; while འ་ in the case of ུ or ོ gives a slight, but very slight sound of *w*; e.g., འུར་ *noise*=something between *ur* and *wur* though more like *ur*.

4. The five vowels are called དབྱངས་ལྔ་ *Yang-nga*: a ཨ་ i ཨི་ u ཨུ་ e ཨེ་ o ཨོ།

The four vowel signs are *i* ི *u* ུ *e* ེ *o* ོ.

Every consonant implies a following *a*, unless another vowel is attached. This *a* is sounded like the English *u* in *rub*.

ི named གི་གུ་ *ki-ku*, like *i* in *in* or *tin*, e.g., མི་ man=*mi*.

ུ named ཞབས་ཀྱུ་ *shap-kyu*, like *oo* in *root* when initial or final. Like *u* in *pull*, when medial, e.g., གྲུ་ boat=*tru* ; ནུབ་ west=*nup*.

ེ named འགྲེང་བུ་ *Deng-bu*, like *e* in *men*. But when final also often like *i* in *tin*, e.g., ལེན་པ་ to take=*lem-pa* ; ལྡེ་མིག་ key=*di-mi*.

ོ named ན་རོ་ *na-ro*, like *o* in hole ; e.g., ལོག་པ་ to come back=*lok-pa*.

5. The Tibetan letters with the four vowel-signs are as follow :—

ཀི་ *ki.*	ཁུ་ *khu.*	གེ་ *ke.*	ངོམས། *ngom.*
ཅི་ *chi.*	ཆུ་ *chhu.*	ཇེ་ *che.*	ཉོན། *nyön.*
ཏི་ *ti.*	ཐུ་ *thu.*	དེ་ *te.*	ནོར། *nor.*
པི་ *pi.*	ཕུ་ *phu.*	བེ་ *pe.*	མོས། *mö.*
ཙི་ *tsi.*	ཚུ་ *tshu.*	ཛེ་ *tse.*	ཝོལ། *wöl.*
ཞི་ *shi.*	ཟུ་ *su.*	འེ་ *e.*	ཡོད། *yö.*
རི་ *ri.*	ལུ་ *lu.*	ཤེ་ *she.*	སོང་། *song.*
	ཧེ་ *he.*	ཨོཾ། *Om.*	

(The *o* is named "*le-kor*," and represents the letter མ་).

The above set of examples is that ordinarily used in Tibetan schools and monasteries.

6. Final Consonants.—The preceding paragraph shows the ordinary pronunciation of the vowels which is, however, further affected by some of the final consonants. Of final consonants there are only ten; that is to say, though any consonant may begin a syllable only one of these ten consonants may end it. These ten final consonants are as follow:—

ག་ང་ད་ན་བ་མ་འ་ར་ལ་ས་ Let us briefly consider the pronunciation of each as a final, and its effect upon the pronunciation of the preceding vowel.

ག་ is pronounced so slightly as hardly to be heard and shortens the preceding vowel. When followed, however, by another consonant in a second syllable of the same word it is clearly pronounced, and does not affect the pronunciation of the preceding vowel, thus མིག་ eye=*mi*, but འཕོག་པ་ to hit=*phok-pa*.

ང་ is pronounced more sharply than when an initial. It does not affect the pronunciation of the preceding vowel, e.g., མིང་ name=*ming*, but sounded sharply. The sound of final ག་ and ང་ can be obtained from the teacher with but little practice.

ད་ }
ལ་ } These all modify the sounds of the preceding vowels, *a*, *u* and *o*; i.e., *a* into *e* (in French *les*); *u* into *ü* (in French *sur*); *o* into *ö* (e.g., *hören* in German or *eu* in French *peu*). These modified sounds will, therefore, be romanized into *e*, *ö*, *ü* respectively.
ས་ }

The final consonant itself is not pronounced; e.g., ལུད་ manure=*lü*, བལ་ wool=*pë*, བྲོས་པ་ to flee=*trö-pa*.

ད་ makes the preceding vowel short; ལ་ and ས་ make it long, thus ལུད་ manure=*lü* (short *u*); but ལུས་ body=*lü* (long *u*).

ན་ modifies vowels as ད་ལ་ and ས་ modify them, but is itself pronounced, e.g., ལན་ answer=*len*. When followed by པ་ཕ་བ་ or མ་ in the same word it is pronounced as *m*, e.g., རིན་པོ་ཆེ་ precious=*rim-po-chhe*.

བ་ མ་ ར་ } Do not affect the pronunciation of the vowel, and are themselves pronounced the same as when initial, e.g., ཚབ་ delegate=*tshap*, ཟམ་པ་ bridge=*sam-pa*, ཟུར་ corner=*sur*. But ར་ like ག་ is sometimes pronounced so lightly as hardly to be heard.

འ་ is not itself pronounced but lengthens the sound of the vowels preceding it. No vowel except the indirect *a* precedes it, e.g., ནམ་མཁའ་ sky=*nam-khā*.

7. **Affix.**—The letter ས་ also occurs as a second final consonant or affix after either of the four letters ག་ང་བ་མ་ It is not pronounced, but in the case of ག་ preceded by *a*, it has the effect of lengthening the *a*, e.g., ལགས་སི་ yes=*lā-si*. It is sometimes written in an incomplete form below the final consonant thus ལགྶ་སི་

8. **Sanskrit Letters.**—The following six letters taken from the Sanskrit are occasionally used in the Colloquial language, namely :—

ཊ་	ཋ་	ཌ་	ཎ་	ཥ་	ཀྵ་
tra	*thra*	*dra*	*na*	*kha*	*khya*

ཊ་ is known as *ta-lo-tra*, which means "*ta* reversed is *tra*";

ཎ་ as *na-lo-na*, "*na* reversed is *na*"; and so on.

9. **Examples.**

[The student is recommended to cover the romanized Tibetan letters with a piece of paper and thus to test his knowledge of the alphabet and its pronunciation.]

ཀོ་བ་ leather=*ko-wa*.	ས་ earth=*sa*.
སྒར་ encampment=*gar*.	ཟ་བ་ to eat=*sa-wa*.
ཤིང་ tree=*shing*.	དད་པ་ faith=*de-pa*.
ཆུ་ water=*chhu*.	དང་ and=*tang*.
ཨ་མ་ mother=*a-ma*.	ལས་ཀ་ work=*le-ka*.
འོད་ light, *s.*=*ö*.	ལུག་ sheep=*lu*.
ཕན་ profit=*phen*.	ལག་པ་ hand=*lak-pa*.
ཞོན་པ་ to ride=*shöm-pa*.	ཇོ་བོ་ lord=*cko-wo*.

10. **Diphthongs.**—There are no real diphthongs, but under this head may be classed the combination *ai*, *oi*, *ui*, occurring when the one syllable of a word ends in *a*, *o*, or *u*, and the next begins with *i*; e.g., རོ་ and འི་ of the corpse=*ro-ï*, pronounced almost like *rö*, but with a slight sound of *i*; similarly ཁ and འི་ of the mouth=*kha-i* and almost=*khĕ*; བུ and འི་ of the son=*ṕu-ï* and almost=*ṕü*. In fact the འི་ modifies the preceding vowels in practically the same way as ས་ would do.

The other combinations of vowels are *ao*, *io*, *uo*, *eo*, *oo*, *au*, *iu* *eu*; e.g., ཟའོ། ཤིའོ། དུའོ། ཚེའོ། ཉེའོ། ཀའུ། བྱིའུ། ཞེའུ། They are not often used in the colloquial and are not really diphthongs, as each vowel is clearly though rapidly pronounced.

Note that འ་ and not ཨ་ is always used as the base of the second vowel; that is, the letter over which the second vowel must be written; e.g., ཁ and འི་ and not ཁ་ and ཁི་

11. **Compound Consonants.**—These are of two kinds, namely Subjoined and Superadded. These subjoined consonants are:—

ཝ་ཡ་ར་ལ་ and ཧ་ They are known respectively as ཝ་ཟུར་ *wa-śur*, "*wa* on the edge"; ཡ་བཏགས་ *ya-ta*, "*ya* subjoined"; ར་བཏགས་ *ra-ta*, "*ra* subjoined"; ལ་བཏགས་ *la-ta* "*la* subjoined"; and ཧ་བཏགས་ *ha-ta* "*ha* subjoined."

12. **Wasurs.**—*Wasur* may be joined to sixteen consonants, viz.:—

ཀྭ་ ཁྭ་ གྭ་ ཅྭ་ ཉྭ་ ཏྭ་ དྭ་ ཙྭ་ ཚྭ་ ཞྭ་ ཟྭ་ རྭ་ ལྭ་ ཤྭ་ སྭ་ ཧྭ་

The effect on the pronunciation is to lengthen the sound of the vowel in the same way as final འ་ but not quite so much, e.g., ཚྭ་ salt=*tshā*.

13. Of *yatas* there are seven, which are joined to the following letters, thus—

ཀྱ་ *kya* ཁྱ་ *khya*, གྱ་ *kya*, པྱ་ *cha*, ཕྱ་ *chha*, བྱ་ *cha*, མྱ་ *nya*.

Note the pronunciation of the last four.

Thus སྐྱོང་པོ་ hard=*kyong-po*.

ཕྱིན་པ་ to go=*chhim-pa*.

བྱ་ bird=*cha*.

14. *Rala* is joined to thirteen consonants, namely:—

ཀྲ་ *tra*, ཁྲ་ *thra*, གྲ་ *tra*,

ཏྲ་ *tra*, དྲ་ *tra*,

པྲ་ pronounced *tra*, or *pa*, ཕྲ་ *thra*, བྲ་ pronounced *tra*, *pa* or *ra*.

Note that gutturals and labials take the sound of dentals.

Rata is also joined to ནྲ་ *na*, མྲ་ *ma*, ཤྲ་ *sha*, སྲ་ *sa* or

NOTE.—Several English grammars also give ཐྲ་ *thra*, but this is neither given in Tibetan primers nor used in the colloquial language.

tra or *hra*, ཧྲ་ *hra*, e.g., ཁྲག་ blood = *thra*, གྲུ་ boat = *tru*, དྲིལ་བུ་ bell = *tri-pu*, བྲིས་པ་ (འབྲི་བ་) to write = *tri-pa*, སྲས་ son = *se*, སྲབ་ bridle = *trap*.

Note that where any of the first nine *ratas* are followed by the vowels ི or ེ the *r* is pronounced less strongly than when followed by the other vowels. And in no case is the *r* pronounced as strongly as in English.

15. *Hata* in the colloquial language is not used except with ལ་ e.g., ལྷ་ a god=*hla*, the *h* being pronounced before the *l*. It is also joined to ག་ད་བ་ཛ་ and ཌ་ and is then written གྷ་དྷ་བྷ་ཛྷ་ and ཌྷ་ respectively, but these last five cases only occur in transcribing Sanskrit words, and are of little use for colloquial purposes.

16. *La-ta* is joined to six consonants, thus—

ཀླ་གླ་བླ་ཟླ་རླ་སླ་ These are all sounded as *la* in a high tone, except ཟླ་ which is pronounced *da*, e.g., གླུ་ song=*lu*; ཟླ་བ་ month=*da-wa*.

17. **Examples.**

བྲག་ rock=*tra*.

སྨྱུ་གུ་ reed-pen=*nyu-gu*.

སླེ་ཀོག་ basket=*Le-ko*.

ངའི་སྲབ་ my bridle=*nge-trap*.

ཁྱོད་ཀྱི་སྲོག་ your life=*khyö-kyi so.*

ཁོའི་གླུ་ his song=*khö lu.*

ཞབས་བྲོ་ dance=*sh̄aṗ-ro.*

བྲང་ཁོག་ chest (of body)=*h̄ang-kho.*

སྲང་འགག་ lane=*hrang-ga.*

18. **Superscribed Consonants.**—There are three of these, namely, ར་ལ་ and ས་ They are placed on the tops of other letters.

ར་ is placed on the top of twelve consonants, thus:

རྐ་	རྒ་	རྔ་	རྗ་	རྙ་	རྟ་	རྡ་	རྣ་	རྦ་	རྨ་	རྩ་	རྫ་
ka	*ga*	*nga*	*ja*	*nya*	*ta*	*da*	*na*	*ba*	*ma*	*tsa*	*dza.*

Note that the ར་ is written as ʳ; except with ཉ་ when the full ར་ is written. Note also that རྒ་ is pronounced as *ga*, རྗ་ as *ja*, རྡ་ as *da*, རྦ་ as *ba* and རྫ་ as *dza*. The others differ from the ordinary ག་ང་, etc., in that they are pronounced in higher tone.

19. **Examples.**

རྐང་པ་ foot=*kang-pa*, རྒད་པོ་ old man=*ge-po*, རྒྱན་ ornament=*gyen*, རྡོ་ stone=*do*, རྣོ་པོ་ sharp=*no-po*, རྩ་བ་ root=*tsa-wa*, ལུག་རྫི་ shepherd=*luk̄-dzi*. The ར་ itself is not pronounced except sometimes when occurring in the second syllables of words; e.g., རྡོ་རྗེ་ sacred thunder-bolt=*dor-je*. When ར་ surmounts a consonant as above, it is named ར་མགོ་ *rang-go*, i.e., ra-head, and the consonant is said to be "tied on" or "subjoined" as the *ya-tas*, *ratas*, etc., above. Thus རྐ་ is named *ra-ka-ta*, i.e., *ra* with *ka* subjoined, རྒ་ is named *ra-ga-ta*, and so on.

20. ལ་ similarly named ལ་མགོ་ *lang-go*, i.e., la-head, is superadded to ten consonants as follow :—

ལྐ་ ལྒ་ ལྔ་ ལྕ་ ལྗ་ ལྟ་ ལྡ་ ལྤ་ ལྦ་ ལྷ་

ལྷ་ is pronounced *ḥla*. The rest are pronounced in the same way as the corresponding consonants with superadded ར། ལྕ་ and ལྤ་ are pronounced in a high tone as *cha* and *pa* respectively.

21. ས་ similarly named ས་མགོ་ *sang-go*, i.e., sa-head, is superadded to eleven consonants as follow :—

སྐ་ སྒ་ སྔ་ སྙ་ སྟ་ སྡ་ སྣ་ སྤ་ སྦ་ སྨ་ སྩ་

These are pronounced in the same way as the corresponding consonants with superadded ར་ or ལ་ The consonants surmounted by ལ་ or ས་ are similarly said to be "tied on," e.g., ལྔ་ is named *la-nga-ta*, and སྡ་ is named *sa-da-ta.*

22. **Examples.**

ལྔ་ five=*nga.*

སྔ་དྲོ་ morning=*nga tro.*

ལྕགས་ iron=*cha.*

ལྡིང་བ་ to soar (in the air)=*ding-wa.*

སྡིག་པ་ sin=*dik-pa.*

སྨན་ medicine=*men.*

23. **Prefixed Letters.**—The five letters ག་ད་བ་མ་འ་ are found in many words before the initial consonant. These prefixes are not themselves pronounced, but affect the pronunciation in the same way as superadded ར་ལ་ or ས་

ག་ occurs before ཅ་ཉ་ཏ་ད་ན་ཙ་ཞ་ཟ་ཡ་ཤ་ས་

ད་ before ཀ་ག་ང་པ་བ་མ་

བ་ before ཀ་ག་ཅ་ཛ་སྐ་ཏ་ད་ཉ་ཙ་ཛ་ཞ་ཟ་ཟླ་ཤ་ས་

མ་ before ཁ་ག་ང་ཆ་ཇ་ཉ་ཐ་ད་ན་ཚ་ཛ་

འ་ before ཁ་ག་ཆ་ཇ་ཐ་ད་ཕ་བ་ཚ་ཛ་

Examples.

གཅིག་ one=*chi.*	གདན་ bolster=*den.*
གསར་པ་ new=*sa-pa.*	དངུལ་ silver=*ngü.*
བཏང་བ་ to send=*lang-wa.*	བདུན་ seven=*dün.*
མཁས་པོ་ skilful=*khe-po.*	འཛོམ་པ་ to assemble=*dzom-pa.*

24. Confusion might arise in the case of one of the prefixed letters making a word with one of the final consonants, the vowel being the inherent *a*, e.g., དག་ as to whether it represents *tă* or *gā*. The confusion is obviated as follows. If it is the initial ད་, the word is written དག་*tă.* If it is the prefix, འ་ is added thus, དགའ་=*gā.*

25. When བ་ as initial consonant follows ད་ as prefix, the combination is either sounded as *w* or not sounded at all. If accompanied by a *yata* or a vowel sign, it is not sounded at all; e.g., དབུགས་ breath=*u*, དབྱངས་ tune, melody=*yang*; དབྱུག་པ་ to

throw=*yuk-pa.* If accompanied by *rata* it follows the ordinary rule of *ratas* (para. 14) and prefixed ད་ (para. 23) and is pronounced *dr.* In other cases it is pronounced as *w*, e.g., དབང་ power, authority=*wang.*

26. **Sentences for Pronunciation.**

Bring some hot water. ཆུ་ཚ་པོ་འཁྱེར་ཤོག་ *chhu tsha-po khe sho.*

This water is not hot. ཆུ་འདི་ཚ་པོ་མི་འདུག་ *chhu di tsha-po min-du.*

It is cold. གྲང་མོ་རེད་ *trang-mo re.*

You can go now. ད་འགྲོ་ཆོག་གི་རེད་ *ta dro chhok-ki-re.*

27. **Irregular Sounds.**—In the following cases the pronunciation is modified for the sake of euphony.

(*a*) *m* and *n* sounds.—When one syllable is followed by another beginning with a prefixed letter the sound of *m* or *n* is often introduced. This occurs especially when the first syllable ends in ག་ e.g.

ཕྱག་ལྡེ་ key, *hon.=chhan-di.*

ཕྱག་འབྲུ་ grain, *hon.=chhan-dru.*

མི་འདུག་ is not=*min-du.*

ན་བཟའ་ clothes, *hon.=nam-sa.*

(*b*) *Reduplicated Sounds.*—When the following final consonants, or affixes, namely, ག་གས་ང་ངས་ར་ and ལ་ are followed by པ་ or བ་ the sound of the final consonant is reduplicated, e.g., བཀག་ (འགེགས་) པ་གནང་བ་ to hinder, *hon.=kak-ka nang-wa;*

གསུངས་པ་རེད་ he said, *hon.=sung-nga-re.* ཉར་བ་གནང་བ་ to take care of, *hon.=nyar-ra nang-wa;* ཚིལ་བུ་ fat=*tshil-lu;* དཔོན་པོས་ གནང་བ་རེད། the official has given, *pöm-pö naug-nga-re.*

(*c*) བ་ following a vowel or ལ་ When བ་ follows a vowel its sound is sometimes omitted altogether, e.g., སྦ་བ་ goitre =*ba-a.*

ཀ་བ་ pillar=*ka-a.*

བ་ after ལ་ is often pronounced as *r*, e.g.,—

རྒྱལ་བ་གནང་བ་ to conquer, *hon.=gye-ra nang-wa.*

(*d*) Other changed sounds.

བཞེས་ཐུར་ spoon=*ship-thu.*

རྒྱ་ར་ (རྒྱ་བྲ་) sweet buck-wheat=*gyap-ra.*

(*e*) There are also other irregular sounds, but it seems unnecessary to enumerate them all here. They will be picked up more easily in the conrse of conversation.

28. **The Tones.**—In Tibetan the tone, that is to say the pitch of the voice, varies, each word in this language having a tone in which it should be pronounced. It is very important for the student to render these tones with substantial accuracy; otherwise the pronunciation becomes uncertain and many of his words will assume meanings which he does not intend for them.

29. For practical purposes we must discriminate between three tones, viz., the high, the medium, and the low. The initial letter and the prefix govern the tone.

High Tone.—Use this in a word beginning with a prefix except when the initial letter is ཁ་ག་ཆ་ཇ་ཐ་ད་ཕ་བ་ཚ་ or ཛ་ Use it also with any of the following initials, viz., ཀ་ཅ་ཏ་པ་ཙ་ཤ་ས་ཧ་

Medium Tone.—Use this in a word beginning with ཁ་ཆ་ཐ་ཕ་ཚ་ as initials whether with or without prefixes.

Low Tone.—Use this in a word beginning with any of the following letters as initials ག་ང་ཇ་ཉ་ད་ན་བ་མ་ཛ་ཝ་ཞ་ཟ་ཡ་ར་ལ་འ་ also in words in which a prefix precedes the initials ག་ཇ་ད་བ་ or ཛ་ Such initials are in this case, as previously noted in paragraph 23, pronounced as *g*, *j*, *d*, *b* and *dz*, respectively. For effect of ག་ང་ད་བ་ལ་ས་ in lengthening or shortening the preceding vowel see above paras. 6 and 7.

Examples.

ཀོ་བ་ leather=*ko-wa*, high tone.

སྤོས་ incense=*pŏ*, high tone and lengthened.

པག་ brick=*pă*, high tone and shortened.

ཆམ་པ་ cold (in the head)=*chham-pa*, medium tone.

ཐབས་ opportunity=*thap*, medium tone.

ཐག་པ་ rope=*thak-pa*, medium tone and shortened.

ལ་ to (postposition) *la*, low tone.

ལགས་ yes (a polite affirmative)=*lā*, low tone and lengthened.

བོད་ Tibet=*pö*, low tone and shortened.

Note the difference in above examples between སྤོས་ and བོད་ and between ལ་ and ལགས་

30. **Punctuation.**—It will have been noticed from the examples that at the end of each syllable a dot is placed at the top right-hand corner. This dot is named ཚེག *tshe.* A comma, semi-colon or colon is indicated by a vertical line (|) called *she*, a full-stop by a double line (||) called *nyi-she*, and the end of a chapter by four lines (|| ||) called *s̄hi-she.* In hand-writing a mark (‹) is usually placed between each syllable instead of the *tshe*, but is sometimes incorporated with the last letter of the syllable.

31. **Spelling.**—The Tibetan method of spelling words should be acquired, as the teacher in common with all Tibetans will use it.

32. Pronounce the first consonant or compound consonant, add the vowel and pronounce the two together.

Thus, ཀོ་ ; *ka-na-ro, ko.* སྐི་ ; *sa-ka-ta, ka, kak̄i-k̄u, ki.* It is as if to say *sa* with *ka-ta* makes *ka*, *ka* with *k̄i-k̄u* makes *ki.*

33. If there is a final consonant, pronounce the whole word with it, then the consonant itself, and then the whole word again. Thus, ཀོང་ ; *ka-na-ro, ko, kong-nga-kong.* Again ཀྱོང་ ; *kaya-ta, kya, kya-na-ro, kyo, kyong-nga, kyong.*

34. If the vowel is the inherent *a*, pronounce the first consonant, then the whole word, then the final consonant, and then the whole word again e.g. ཀང་ ; *k̄a, k̄ang-nga, k̄ang.* སྒང་ ; *sa-ga-ta, ga, gang-nga, gang.* ལྟོགས་ ; *la-ta-ta, ta, ta-na-ro, to, tok̄-k̄a-sa, tok̄.*

35. When a prefixed letter begins the syllable, e.g., ག་ད་ etc., it is pronounced as *ka-wo, ta-wo*; e.g., གཉེན; *ka-wo-nya-deng-bu, nye, nyen-na, nyen*. དགག; *ta-wo-ga, gap-pa gap*. This *wo* is pronounced very shortly.

36. A syllable containing only a consonant and the inherent *a*, e.g., མ་ is called *ma-kyang*, i.e., "only *ma*," to distinguish it from the consonant accompanied by one of the other vowels. Thus, to enquire whether a syllable is སོ་ or ས་ you may say "Is it *sa-na-ro* or *sa-kyang?*"

36. **Examples.**

ལུང་ handle. *la shap-kyu, lu, lung-nga, lung.*

རས་ cotton. *ra, re-sa, re.*

བཏང་བ་ to send. *pa-wo-ta-tang-nga, tang; wa: tang-wa.*

འཁྱུད་པ་ to embrace. *a-wo-kha-ya-ta khya, khya shap-kyu, khyu, khyü-ta, khyü; pa: khyü-pa.*

དགྲ་ enemy. *tă-wo-ga-ra-ta, dra.*

ལྷ་ spirit. *la-ha-ta, hla.*

བསོད་ནམས་ good fortune. *pa-wo-sa-na-ro, so, sö-ta, sö; na, nam-ma-sa, nam: sönam.*

ཞྭ་མོ་ hat. *sha-wa-sur, sha; ma-na-ro, mo; sha-mo.*

དཔེ་ཆ་ book. *Ta-wo-pa-deng-bu, pe; chha: pe-chha.*

གློག་ lightning. *ka-la-ta, la, la-na-ro, lo, lo-ka, lo.*

རྒྱུག་པ་ to run. *ra-ga-ta, ga, ga ya-ta gya, gya shap-kyu, gyu, gyuk ka, gyuk; pa: gyuk-pa.*

རིགས་བརྒྱུད་ lineage. *ra-ki-ku, ri, ri-ka-sa, rik; pa-wo-ra-ga-ta, ga, ga ya-ta, gya, gya-shap-kyu, gyu, gyü-ta, gyü: rik-gyü.*

37. Sentences.

Where are you going to? ཁྱོད་ག་པ་འགྲོ་གི་ཡིན་པ་ *khyö ka-pa dro-ki yim-pa?*

I am going to Darjeeling, Sir. ལགས་ང་རྡོ་རྗེ་གླིང་ལ་འགྲོ་གི་ཡིན་ *lā nga Dor-je-ling lă dro-ki yin.*

What have you got in the bundle? རྡོག་ཁྲེད་ནང་ལ་ག་རེ་ཡོད་པ་ *dok-thre nang-la ka-re yö-pa?*

Different kinds of things, Sir. ལགས་ཆ་ལག་སྣ་ཚོགས་ཡོད་ *lā cha-lă na-tsho yö.*

Have you a tea-pot among them? དེའི་ནང་ལ་ཁོ་ཏིང་ཡོད་པས་ *te-ī nang-la kho ting yö-pē?*

Yes, Sir, I have. ལགས་ཡོད་ *lā-yö.*

What is its price? གོང་ག་ཚོད་ཡིན་པ་ *kong ka-tshö yim-pa?*

Twenty rupees. ལགས་སྒོར་མོ་ཉི་ཤུ་ཐམ་པ་ཡིན་ *lā gor-mo nyi-shu tham-pa yin.*

Will you let me have it for fifteen rupees? སྒོར་མོ་བཅོ་ལྔ་ལ་གཏོང་གི་ཡིན་པས་ *gor-mo che-nga la tong-ki yim-pē?*

No, Sir. ལགས་མེན་ *la-men.*

Well, good-day! ཨོ་ན་ག་ལེ་རྒྱུག་ *o-na kale-gyu.*

Good-day, Sir! ད་ཨོ་ན་ག་ལེ་འཆིབ་རྒྱུ་གནང་ *tao-na ka-le chhip-gyu-nang.*

CHAPTER II.

THE ARTICLE.

I. The Indefinite Article.

1. This is the same as the numeral ONE without the prefix གཅ་ namely ཅིག་ *chi.*

2. The final ག་ is very slightly pronounced (see above Cap. I, para. 6).

3. It is placed after the noun or adjective, which it qualifies; thus མི་ཅིག་ *mi-chi,* A MAN.

4. It also takes any case-inflection instead of its noun or adjective, which latter in such case are not inflected. The method of case-inflection will be dealt with later under the chapter relating to nouns.

5. ཅིག་ is often omitted where we should use "a" or "an" in English. *If there might otherwise be doubt as to whether more than one is meant* use ཅིག་

6. In the case of *weights* and *measures* or in other cases where something FULL is implied, ཀང་ *kang* is used instead of ཅིག་, e g., ཕོར་པ་ཀང་ *phor-pa kang,* A BOWL-FULL.

WORDS.

Man= མི་ *mi.*	Dog= ཁྱི་ *khyi.*
Woman= སྐྱེས་དམན་ *kyi-men.*	Cat = ཞི་མི་ *shimi.*

Please give = གནང་རོགས་གནང་ *nang-ro-nang.*

Rupee = སྒོར་མོ་ *gor-mo.*

To me = ང་ལ་ *nga-la.*

And = དང་ *tang.*

Noise = སྐད་ *ke.*

Do not make (of noise) = མ་རྒྱབ་ *ma-gyap.*

Country = ལུང་པ་ *lung-pa.*

Pleasant = སྐྱིད་པོ་ *kyi-po.*

Is = རེད་ *re.*

Wood = ཤིང་ *shing.*

Armful = པང་པ་གང་ *pang-pa kang.*

He = ཁོ་ *kho.*

To him = ཁོ་ལ་ *kho-la.*

Tibetan = བོད་པ་ *pö-pa.*

Note that the verb comes at the end of the sentence.

EXERCISE No. 1. (For reading and copying.)

A man = མི་ཅིག ། *mi-chi.*

A woman = སྐྱེས་དམན་ཅིག ། *kyi-men chi.*

A dog and a cat = ཁྱི་ཅིག་དང་ཞི་མི་ཅིག ། *khyi chi tang shi-mi chi.*

Please give me a dog. (*Lit.* To me a dog please give) ཁྱི་ཅིག་གནང་རོགས་ནང་། *nga-la khyi chi nang-ro-nang.*

Please give him a rupee ཁོ་ལ་སྒོར་མོ་ཅིག་གནང་རོགས་གནང་། *kho-la gor-mo chi nang-ro-nang.*

Do not make a noise སྐད་མ་རྒྱབ། *ke ma-gyap.*

It is a pleasant country. (*Lit.* country pleasant is) ལུང་པ་སྐྱིད་པོ་རེད། *lung-pa kyi-po re.*

Please give me an armful of wood. (*Lit.* To me wood an armful please give). ང་ལ་ཤིང་པང་པ་གང་གནང་རོགས་གནང་། *nga-la shing pang-pa kang nang-ro nang.*

He is a Tibetan. ཁོ་བོད་པ་རེད། *kho pö-pa re.*

Exercise No. 2. (For translation).

A dog. A man and a dog. A woman and a cat. Please give me a rupee. Please give him a cat.

II. The Definite Article.

7. As in the case of the indefinite article, so also in that of the definite article THE in English is often left unexpressed in Tibetan. Where expressed, འདི་ *di*, THIS and དེ་ *te*, THAT are used, though these represent demonstrative pronouns rather than the definite article. It follows therefore that འདི་ or དེ་ should not be used unless THE in the sentence really represents THIS or THAT.

8. Where THE refers to a noun previously mentioned, དེ་ is used.

9. As in the case of ཅིག་ so also both འདི་ and དེ་ are placed after the noun or adjective which they qualify and take the case-inflection instead of the noun or adjective.

10. The particles ཀ་ཁ་ and ག་ have the sense of THE when placed after numerals. Thus གཉིས་ཀ་ *nyi-ka*, THE TWO, BOTH; བདུན་ཁ་ *dün-kha*, THE SEVEN. The ཀ་ཁ་ག་ *ka*, *kha*, *ka*, take the case-inflection similarly to འདི་ *di*.

Words.

Who = སུ་ *su*.	Wind = ལྷགས་པ་ *hlak-pa*.
Boy = བུ་གུ་ *pu-gu*.	Strong (of wind) = ཚ་པོ་ *tsha-po*.
Good = ཡག་པོ་ *yak-po*.	Bring = འཁྱེར་ཤོག་ *khe-sho*.
Bhutanese = འབྲུག་པ་ *druk-pa*.	Food = ཁ་ལག་ *kha-la*.

EXERCISE No. 3.

The dog and the cat. ཁྱི་འདི་དང་ཞི་མི་འདི། *khyi di tang shi-mi di.*

Who is the man? (*Lit.* The man who is?) The man (i.e., the man just mentioned) is a Tibetan. མི་འདི་སུ་རེད། *mi di su re;* མི་དེ་བོད་པ་རེད། *mi te pö-pa re.*

The boy is good. བུ་གུ་འདི་ཡག་པོ་རེད། *pu-gu di yak-po re.*

Who is the boy? The boy is a Bhutanese. བུ་གུ་འདི་སུ་རེད། *pu-gu di su re;* བུ་གུ་དེ་འབྲུག་པ་རེད། *pu-gu te druk-pa re.*

The wind is strong. ལྷགས་པ་ཚ་པོ་རེད། *hlak-pa tsha-po re.*

Bring the wood (or *some* wood). ཤིང་འཁྱེར་ཤོག། *shing khe-sho.*

Bring the food. ཁ་ལག་འཁྱེར་ཤོག། *kha-la khe-sho.*

EXERCISE No. 4.

The man. The man is a Bhutanese. Please give me wood. *Lit.* (To me the wood please give.) The wind is good.

CHAPTER III.

The Noun.

1. **Abstract Nouns** though used in the literary language are frequently avoided in the colloquial by the phrase being turned and an adjective employed instead of the abstract noun. Thus, THE CLEVERNESS OF THIS DOCTOR IS KNOWN TO ALL, ཨམ་ཆི་འདི་མཁས་པོ་ཡིན་པ་སྒང་ཁས་ཤེས་ཀྱི་རེད། *am-chhi di khe-po yim-pa gang-khe shing-ki-re. Lit.* ཨམ་ཆི་ *am-chhi*, DOCTOR, འདི་ *di*, THIS, མཁས་པོ་ *khe-po*, CLEVER, ཡིན་པ་ *yim-pa*, THAT HE IS, སྒང་ཁས་ *gang-khe*, ALL, ཤེས་ཀྱི་རེད། *shing-ki-re*, KNOW.

When expressed ལོས་ *lö* is generally added to the adjectival root; e.g., ཆེ་ལོས་ *chhe-lö*, GREATNESS; སྦོམ་ལོས་ *bom-lö*, THICKNESS. Certain abstract nouns are formed by joining together two contradictory words, thus, SIZE = ཆེ་ཆུང་ *chhe-chhung*, lit. LARGE—SMALL; TEMPERATURE = ཚ་གྲང་ *tsha-trang*, lit. HOT—COLD; QUALITY = བཟང་ངན་ *sang-ngen*, lit. GOOD—BAD. Thus, WHAT IS THE SIZE OF THAT HOUSE? ཁང་པ་དེ་ཆེ་ཆུང་ག་འདྲས་རེད། *khang-pa te chhe-chhung kan-dre re*, lit. ཁང་པ་ *khang-pa*, HOUSE, དེ་ *te*, THAT, ཆེ་ཆུང་ *chhe-chhung*, SIZE, ག་འདྲས་ *kan-dre*, OF WHAT KIND, རེད་ *re*, IS.

2. **Nouns denoting membership of a certain country, religion, profession, etc.,** are formed by adding པ་པོ་བ་བོ་མ་ or མོ་ *pa, po, pa, po, ma* or *mo*, to the name of the country, religion, etc., concerned. Thus, BHUTANESE = འབྲུག་པ་ *druk-pa*; CARPENTER = ཤིང་བཟོ་བ་

shing-so-wa; INHABITANT OF CHUMBI VALLEY (TROMO)=གྲོ་མོ་བ་ *tro-mo-wa*; SERVANT=གཡོག་པོ་ *yok-po*; CHIEF=གཙོ་བོ་ *tso-wo*; མ་ and མོ་ when used in this connection sometimes denote the feminine gender, e.g., རྒྱལ་པོ་ *gye-po*=KING, རྒྱལ་མོ་ *gye-mo*=QUEEN. But, as noted below (para. 6), feminines are often denoted by one of the participles པ་བོ་བ་ or བོ་ thus, THIS WOMAN IS A TIBETAN, སྐྱེས་དམན་འདི་བོད་པ་རེད། *kyi-men di pö-pa re.* བ་ and བོ་ are used instead of པ་ and པོ་ respectively when the preceding syllable ends in a vowel.

3. **Nouns denoting the agent** are usually formed by adding མཁན་ *khen* to the root of the verb, e.g., ཡོང་བ་ *yong-wa*, TO COME, ཡོང་མཁན་ *yong-khen*, THE PERSON WHO COMES. This termination མཁན་ corresponds to the termination *wala* in Hindustani, e.g., *ane-wala*. More rarely མི་ *mi* is used.

4. **Diminutives.**—These are not only formed by the addition of the words ཆུང་ *chhung*, or ཆུང་ཆུང་ *chhung-chhung*, SMALL, to the noun, but in some cases also by the terminations ཨུ། གུ་ or ཕྲུག་ *u*, *ku*, or *thru*, e.g., རྡེའུ་ *di-u*, SMALL STONE from རྡོ་ *do*, STONE; བུ་གུ་ *pu-gu*, BOY from བུ་ *pu*, SON; བྱ་ཕྲུག་ *chap-thru*, CHICKEN from བྱ་ *cha*, FOWL. With the diminutive in ཨུ་ the inherent *a* and the vowel *o* are changed into *e*; e.g., རྡོ་ as above becomes རྡེའུ་ If the noun ends in ག་ this is sometimes cut off and with ུ forms the diminutive, e.g., ལུག་ *lu*, SHEEP, ལུ་གུ་ *lu-ku*, LAMB.

5. **Gender.**—Rules as to gender are but loosely observed in colloquial Tibetan. In names of animals, trees, etc., the genders

can be distinguished by the particles ཕོ་ *pho*, for masculine and མོ་ *mo*, for feminine. These precede the root of the noun, e.g., ཕོ་ཤིང་ *pho-shing*, MALE TREE, མོ་ཤིང་ *mo-shing*, FEMALE TREE. They are also used by themselves as nouns; e.g., ཕོ་མོ་ *pho-mo*, MALES AND FEMALES.

6. In a limited number of words པ་པོ་བ་བོ་ denote the masculine and མ་མོ་ the feminine, the particles in such cases following the noun, e.g., སྲས་པོ་ *se-po*=SON, སྲས་མོ་ *se-mo*= DAUGHTER. But in numerous cases these six particles are used without denoting gender at all: e.g., བླ་མ་ *la-ma*, PRIEST; ཝ་མོ་ *wa-mo*, FOX, both male and female; སྐྱེས་དམན་འདི་གྲོ་མོ་བ་རེད། *kyi-men di tro-mo-wa re*, THIS WOMAN IS AN INHABITANT OF THE CHUMBI VALLEY, གྲོ་མོ་བ་ *tro-mo-wa*, being used both for male and female.

7. **Declension.**—The declension is simple, and is effected as in Hindustani by means of postpositions. Thus the accusative is the same as the nominative, the genitive takes གི་ or when the noun ends in a vowel more usually འི་ the dative ལ་ the agentive གིས་ or when the noun ends in a vowel more usually ས་ and the ablative ནས། It will thus be seen that nouns ending in a consonant are declined somewhat differently from those ending in a vowel. One example of

each is therefore given :—

Nom. and Acc.	གཡག་	*ya*,	a yak.
Gen.	གཡག་གི་	*yak-ki*,	of a yak.
Dat.	གཡག་ལ་	*yak-la*,	to a yak.
Agent.	གཡག་གིས་	*yak-ki*,	by a yak.
Abl.	གཡག་ནས་	*yak-ne*,	from a yak.

8. With some verbs the accusative *may* be formed in ལ་ e.g., ཁོས་ང་ལ་ (or ང་) བརྡུངས་སོང་། *khö nga-la dung-song*, HE BEAT ME. Its use in these cases is optional. With other verbs ལ་ *cannot* be used, e.g., ཁོས་ལྟོ་ཆས་ (not ལྟོ་ཆས་ལ་) ཟ་གི་འདུག་ *Khö top-chhe sá-ki du*, HE IS EATING FOOD.

9. In the *literary* language, if the noun ends in ད་བ་ or ས་ the genitive is formed by ཀྱི་ and the agentive by ཀྱིས་; if the noun ends in ན་མ་ར་ or ལ་ the genitive is formed by གྱི་ and the agentive by གྱིས། It is only when the noun ends in ག་ or ང་ that the genitive is formed by གི་ and the agentive by གིས། But in the colloquial གི་ and གིས་ respectively are, as a rule, used for all, especially by the lower classes, though it is more elegant to give the forms used in the literary language.

10.	Nom. and Acc.	གཡོག་པོ་	*yok-po*,	a servant.
	Gen.	གཡོག་པོའི་	*yok-pö*,	of a servant.
	Dat.	གཡོག་པོ་ལ་	*yok-po la*,	to a servant.
	Agent.	གཡོག་པོས་	*yok-pö*,	by a servant.
	Abl.	གཡོག་པོ་ནས་	*yok-po-ne*,	from a servant.

11. The plural is formed by adding to the nominative ཚོ་ (sometimes pronounced ཚོ་) which, ending in a vowel, takes after it the postpositions of a noun that ends in a vowel. Thus :—

Nom. and Acc.	གཡག་ཚོ་	*yak-tsho,*	yaks.
Gen.	གཡག་ཚོ འི་	*yak-tshö,*	of yaks.
Dat.	གཡག་ཚོ་ལ་	*yak-tsho-la,*	to yaks.
Agent.	གཡག་ཚོས་	*yak-tshö,*	by yaks.
Abl.	གཡག་ཚོ་ནས་	*yak-tsho-ne,*	from yaks.

12. All plurals are declined as above. There are thus two forms of declension in the singular, but only one in the plural. It should be noted that when it is apparent from the context that the pural is intended, the singular form of the noun is used ; thus, མི་ཁ་ཤས་ཡོང་གི་འདུག་ *mi kha-she yong-gi-du,* SOME MEN ARE COMING, lit. མི MEN ཁ་ཤས་ SOME ཡོང་གི་འདུག་ ARE COMING ; མི་ not མི་ཚོ་ being used.

13. As regards the cases they are used in the ordinary way except that the agentive is employed in place of the nominative with *transitive* verbs, thus, གཡོག་པོས་ཁོ་རྡུང་གི་འདུག་ *yok-pö kho dung-gi-du,* THE SERVANT IS BEATING HIM, lit. གཡོག་པོས་ BY THE SERVANT, ཁོ་ HIM, རྡུང་གི་འདུག IS BEATING ; but སང་ཉིན་ གཡོག་པོ་འགྲོ་གི་རེད། *sang-nyi yok-po dro-ki-re,* THE SERVANT WILL GO TO-MORROW, lit. སང་ཉིན་ TO-MORROW, གཡོག་པོ་ THE SERVANT,

འགྲོ་གི་རེད། WILL GO (see also POSTPOSITIONS, Cap. XI, paras. 1 to 3).

WORDS.

Your ཁྱོད་རེའི་=*khyö-re.*	My ངའི་=*nge.*
Mother ཨ་མ་=*a-ma.*	Phari ཕག་རི་=*Phari.*
Lhasa ལྷ་ས་=*hla-sa.*	Thief ཀུན་མ་=*ku-ma.*
Father པ་པ་=*pa-pa.*	Are ཡོད་=*yö.*
To catch ཟིན་པ་=*śim-pa.*	Here མདས་ (འདི་རུ་)=*de.*
Trader ཚོང་པ་=*tshong-pa.*	Many=མང་པོ་=*mang-po.*
One who catches ཟིན་མཁན་=*śim-khen.*	Mule དྲེ་=*tre.*
	Name མིང་=*ming.*

EXERCISE No. 5.

Your mother's cat. ।ཁྱོད་རེའི་ཨ་མའི་ཞི་མི། *khyö-re a-me shi-mi.*

My servant will go. ངའི་གཡོག་པོ་ཕག་རི་ནས། *nge yok-po pha-ri ne.*

from Phari to Lhasa. ལྷ་ས་ལ་འགྲོ་གི་རེད། *hla-sa la dro-ki-re.*

My father is beating the dog. ངའི་པ་པས་ཁྱི་རྡུང་གི་འདུག། *ng pa-pe khyi dung-gi-du.*

The men who caught the thief are here. ཀུ་མ་ (ཀུན་མ) ཟིན་མཁན་ དེ་ཚོ་མདས་ (འདི་རུ་) ཡོད། *ku-ma śim-khen te-tsho de-yö.*

Many women are coming. སྐྱེས་དམན་མང་པོ་ཡོང་གི་འདུག། *kyi-men mang-po yong-gi-du.*

This is a male mule. འདི་ཕོ་དྲེ་རེད། *dipho-tre re.*

This man has done the work. མི་འདིས་ལས་ཀ་འདི་བྱས་པ་རེད།

mi di le-ka di cKe-pa re. Lit. མི་འདིས་ *by this man*, ལས་ཀ་འདི་ *the work*, བྱས་བ་རེད། *has done.*

Exercise No. 6.

My father's dog. Your mother's name. All the men are here (*lit.* men, the, all, here, are). That woman is beating your mule. Please give me food. He has taken service.

CHAPTER IV.

THE ADJECTIVE.

1. The adjective usually follows the noun and in this case takes the declension instead of the noun. If an article or demonstrative pronoun accompanies, it comes last of the three, and takes the declension, both noun and adjective in such case remaining in the nominative case. The declension of adjective, article or pronoun, follows the same rule as that of nouns. Thus, ཁང་པ་ཆུང་ཆུང་གི་ *khang-pa chhung-chhung-gi*, OF THE SMALL HOUSE, lit. ཁང་པ་ *house*, ཆུང་ཆུང་ *small* གི་ *of*; ཁང་པ་ཆུང་ཆུང་དེའི་སྟེང་ལ་བྱ་ཅིག་འདུག་ *khang-pa chhung-chhung, te-ï gang-la cha-chi du*, THERE IS A BIRD ON THE TOP OF THAT SMALL HOUSE; lit. ཁང་པ་ཆུང་ཆུང་དེའི་ *of that small house*, སྟེང་ལ་ *on the top*, བྱ་ཅིག་ *a bird*, འདུག་ *is*. Should the adjective be put before the noun, it takes the genitive case, and the inflection is then taken by the noun if alone with the adjective, but by the article or demonstrative pronoun if such accompany. Thus, བོད་པའི་སྐྱེས་དམན་ལ་ *pö-pe kyi-men la*, TO THE TIBETAN WOMAN. བོད་པའི་སྐྱེས་དམན་དེ་ལ་ཁ་ལག་གནང་རོགས་གནང་། *pö-pe kyi-men te la kha-la nang-ro-nang*, PLEASE GIVE SOME FOOD TO THAT TIBETAN WOMAN; lit. བོད་པའི་སྐྱེས་དམན་དེ་ལ་ *to that Tibetan woman*, ཁ་ལག་ *food*, གནང་རོགས་གནང་། *please give.*

2. Most adjectives end in པོ་ *po*, which is but seldom changed to མོ་ *mo*, when used with a feminine noun, e.g., རྣོད་མ་དཀར་པོ་ཅིག་ *gö-ma ka-po chi*, A WHITE MARE. Note that དཀར་པོ་ *ka-po*, WHITE is not changed to དཀར་མོ་ *ka-mo.*

3. Several adjectives are formed from nouns—the noun being put in the genitive case, thus: ཤིང་གི་སྣག་བུམ་ཅིག་ *shing-gi nak-pum chi*, A WOODEN INK-POT, lit. ཤིང་གི་ *of wood*, སྣག་བུམ་ཅིག་ *an ink-pot.* གསེར་གྱི་ག་ཝུ་ *ser-kyi kao*, A GOLDEN CHARM BOX. Also from adverbs, the adverb being similarly put in genitive form, thus, འོག་གི་ཁང་མིག་ *ok-ki khang-mi*, LOWER ROOM, འོག་ meaning BELOW.

4. Other adjectives are formed from words repeated, thus :—སྒོར་སྒོར་ *gor-gor*, ROUND.

Others from words repeated with this difference that the first word has the inherent vowel *a*, the second a different vowel; e.g., འཁྱར་རེ་འཁྱོར་རེ་ *khyar-re khyor-re*, SHAKY, TOTTERING. Such repeated words are in the colloquial usually dissyllabic.

5. Adjectives denoting a negative such as those which in English begin with IN—, UN—or end with—LESS are occasionally rendered in Tibetan by མེད་ *me* or མེད་པ་ *me-pa*, following the noun concerned, e.g., ཁྲིམས་མེད་ *thrim-me*, LAWLESS, i.e., WITHOUT LAW; དོན་དག་མེད་པ་ *tön-ta me-pa*, USELESS, lit. WITHOUT MEANING. They are however more frequently rendered by a negative. Thus: THIS IS UNFITTING=THIS IS NOT FITTING and is accordingly rendered འདི་འོས་པོ་མི་འདུག། *di ö-po-min-du.*

6. —ABLE,—IBLE are often expressed by ཉེན་པ་ e.g., ཁ་ལག་འདི་ཟ་ཉེན་པ་མི་འདུག། *kha-la di śa nyem-pa min-du*, THIS FOOD IS NOT EATABLE, i.e., IS NOT FIT FOR EATING, lit. ཁ་ལག་འདི་ THIS FOOD ཟ་ཉེན་པ་ EATABLE, མི་འདུག་ IS NOT. Where the meaning is

that of READY FOR, use ཚོག་ or ཚོག་ཚོག་ e.g., ཁ་ལག་འདི་ཟ་ཚོག་ཚོག་མི་འདུག། *kha-la di sá chho-chho min-du* THIS FOOD IS NOT YET READY TO BE EATEN.

7. The comparison of adjectives is formed by ལས་ *le=than, more than*, thus: རྟ་དེ་ལས་རྟ་འདི་ཆེན་པོ་རེད། *ta te-le ta di chhem-po re*, THIS HORSE IS BIGGER THAN THAT ONE, lit. རྟ་དེ་ལས་ *more than that horse*, རྟ་འདི་ *this horse* ཆེན་པོ་རེད་ *is big.* Note that the adjective itself remains unchanged. Some adjectives, e.g., ཡག་ག་ *yak-ka*, BETTER, མང་ང་ *mang-nga*, MORE; ཆེ་བ་ *chhe-wa*, GREATER; སྦོམ་པ་ *bom-pa*, THICKER have separate forms for the comparative. In such cases these are used with ལས་ in the same way as the adjective whose form does not change, thus: རྟ་འདི་ཡག་ག་འདུག་ *ta di yak-ka du*, THIS IS THE BETTER HORSE; དེ་ལས་འདི་ཡག་ག་འདུག་ *te-le di yak-ka du*, THIS IS BETTER THAN THAT. Frequently the adjectival root is conjugated like a verb, thus; དེ་ལས་འདི་སྦོམ་གྱི་རེད། *te-le di bom-kyi re*, THIS IS THICKER THAN THAT.

8. The Superlative Degree of adjectives is formed either by ཤོས་ *shö* or by the words "*more than all*," "*from among all.*" Thus: འདི་ཆེ་ཤོས་རེད། *di chhe-shö re*, THIS IS THE BIGGEST, སྐང་ཁའི་དཀྱིལ་ནས་འདི་ཡག་པོ་རེད། *gang-khe kyi-ne di yak-po re*, THIS IS THE BEST, lit. སྐང་ཁའི་ *all*, དཀྱིལ་ནས་ *from among*, འདི་ཡག་པོ་རེད། *this is good.* ཐམས་ཅད་ལས་རས་གོས་འདི་སྲབ་ཀྱི་རེད། *tham-che le re-gö di trap-kyi re*, THIS IS THE THINNEST COTTON CLOTH, lit. ཐམས་ཅད་ལས་ *more than all*

རས་གོས་འདི་ *this cotton cloth*, སྲབ་ཀྱི་རེད་ *is thin*. Again, ཚང་མའི་ནང་ནས་འདི་རིང་པོ་རེད། *tshang-me nang-ne di ring-po re*, THIS IS THE LONGEST, lit. ཚང་མའི་ *all*, ནང་ནས་ *from among*, འདི་རིང་པོ་རེད། *this is long.*

9. Note that སྒང་ཁ། *gang-kha*, ཐམས་ཅད་ *tham-che* and ཚང་མ་ *tshang-ma* each mean *all*, and that དཀྱིལ་ *kyi* and ནང་ *nang* mean *among* or *in*. They also govern the genitive case and follow it. (See below under Postpositions, Cap. XI).

Words.

Son བུ་ *pu.*

Parents ཕ་མ་ *pha-ma.*

Iron ལྕགས་ *cha.*

Things, goods ཅ་ (ཆ་) ལག་ *cha-la.*

Durable ཁྲོག་ཆེན་པོ་ *tro chhem-po.*

Fat ཤ་རྒྱགས་པ་ *sha gyak-pa.*

Talk, speech སྐད་ཆ་ *ke-chha.*

Foal ཏེག་གི་ (ཏེའུ་) *ti-gi.*

Brave སྙིང་ཆེན་པོ་ *nying chhem-po.*

སྙིང་ heart, ཆེན་པོ་ big.

Khampa, ཁམས་པ་ *kham-pa*, i.e., inhabitant of Kham (ཁམས་) large province in Eastern Tibet.

Exercise No. 7.

This man is the son of good parents. མི་འདི་ཕ་མ་ཡག་པོའི་བུ་རེད། *mi di pha-ma yak-pö pu re.*

Iron things are more durable than wooden things. ཤིང་གི་ཅ་ (ཆ་) ལག་ལས་ལྕགས་ཀྱི་ཅ་ (ཆ་) ལག་ཁྲོག་ཆེ་གི་རེད། *shing-gi cha-la le cha-kyi cha-la tro chhe-ki re.*

That fat woman is beating a foal. སྐྱེས་དམན་ཤ་རྒྱགས་པ་དེས་རྟེག་གི་ (རྟེའུ་) ཅིག་རྡུང་གི་འདུག། *hyi-men sha gyak-pa te ti-gi chi dung-gi du.*

It is my white mare's foal. འདི་ངའི་རྒོད་མ་དཀར་པོའི་རྟེག་གི་ (རྟེའུ) རེད། *di nge gö-ma ha-pö ti-gi re.*

The Bhutanese are braver than the Chumbi Valley men, *lit.* more than the Chumbi Valley men the heart of the Bhutanese is big. གྲོ་མོ་བ་ལས་འབྲུག་པ་སྙིང་ཆེན་པོ་རེད། *tro-mo-wa le druk-pa nying chhem-po re.*

The Khampas are the bravest Tibetans. བོད་པ་གངས་ཁའི་དཀྱིལ་ནས་ཁམས་པ་སྙིང་ཆེ་གི་རེད། *pö-pa gang-khe hyi-ne hham-pa nying chhe-ki-re.*

This is nonsense (*lit.* useless talk). འདི་དོན་དག་མེད་པའི་སྐད་ཆ་རེད། *di tön-tu-me-pe he-chha re.*

Exercise No. 8.

This is the thickest. He is that fat man's son. Please give me an iron ink-pot. Phari is colder that Lhasa. Many Bhutanese will go to Lhasa. The man who caught the dog is beating it.

CHAPTER V.

THE AUXILIARY VERB, "TO BE."

1. The conjugation of this verb is as follows:—

Present Indicative Tense.

Affirmative form.

ང་ཡིན་ *nga-yin* or ཡོད་ *yö*, I am.

ཁྱོད་ཡིན་ *khyö-yin* or ཡོད་ *yö* or རེད་ *re* or འདུག་ *du*, thou art.

ཁོ་ཡིན་ *kho-yin* or ཡོད་ *yö* or རེད་ *re* or འདུག་ *du*, he is.

ང་ཚོ་ཡིན་ *ngan-tsho yin* or ཡོད་ *yö*, we are.

ཁྱོད་ཚོ་ཡིན་ *khyön-tsho yin* or ཡོད་ *yö* or རེད་ *re* or འདུག་ *du*, ye are.

ཁོ་ཚོ་ཡིན་ *khon-tsho yin* or ཡོད་ *yö* or རེད་ *re* or འདུག་ *du*, they are.

2. ཡིན་ and རེད་ are used only in an *attributive* sense; ཡོད་ and འདུག་ are used primarily in the sense of *existing*, but are also sometimes used in an attributive sense. Thus: ཀུ་ (ཀུན་) མ་ཛིན་མཁན་ང་ཡིན། *ku-ma śim-khen nga yin*, I AM THE MAN WHO CAUGHT THE THIEF. *I am (exist) here*, ང་མདས་ (འདི་རུ་) ཡོད། *nga de yö*, never ང་མདས་ (འདི་རུ་) ཡིན། *nga de yin*. HE IS GOOD, ཁོ་ཡག་པོ་རེད། *kho yak-po re* or ཁོ་ཡག་པོ་འདུག། *kho yak-po-du*.

3. *Negative form.*

ང་མན་ (མིན་) *nga men* or མེད་ *me*, I am not.

ཁྱོད་མེད་ *khyö me* or མ་རེད་ *ma-re* or མི་འདུག་ *min-du*, thou art not.

ཁོ་མེད་ *kho-me* or མ་རེད་ *ma-re* or མི་འདུག་ *min-du*, he is not.

ང་ཚོ་མན་ (མིན་) *ngan-tsho men* or མེད་ *me*, we are not.

ཁྱོད་ཚོ་མེད་ *khyön-tsho me* or མ་རེད་ *ma-re* or མི་འདུག་ *min-du*, ye are not.

ཁོ་ཚོ་མེད་ *khon-tsho me* or མ་རེད་ *ma-re* or མི་འདུག་ *min-du*, they are not.

The distinction between མེད་ and མེན་ (མིན་) is the same as between ཡོད་ and ཡིན ||

e.g., ཡི་གེ་འདི་བྲིས་མཁན་ང་མེན་ (མིན་) ཁོ་ཡིན། *yi-ge di tri-khen nga men kho yin*, IT IS HE, NOT I, THAT WROTE THIS LETTER (lit. THE WRITER OF THIS LETTER, I AM NOT, HE IS).

The negative form is ཡོད་པ་མ་རེད། *yo-wa-ma-re*, e.g., ཁོ་ཡག་པོ་མི་འདུག། *kho-yak-po min-du*, HE IS (I KNOW) NOT GOOD, ཁོ་ཡག་པོ་ཡོད་པ་མ་རེད། *kho-yak-po yo-wa-ma-re*, HE IS (I UNDERSTAND) NOT GOOD.

4. IS, ARE, WAS, WERE, joined to other verbs, or in the sense of THERE IS,T HERE ARE, THERE WAS, THERE WERE, may be expressed by ཡོད། འདུག། or ཡོད་པ་རེད་ *yo-wa-re*. As a general rule it may be said that ཡོད་ means IT IS THERE ; I SAW IT THERE AND KNOW THAT IT IS STILL THERE. འདུག་ means I SAW IT THERE, BUT AM NOT SURE WHETHER IT IS STILL THERE OR NOT. ཡོད་པ་རེད་ means I DID NOT SEE IT, BUT UNDERSTAND THAT

IT IS THERE, e.g., THE DALAI LAMA IS RESIDING AT LHASA NOW A DAYS, སྐྱབས་མགོན་རིན་པོ་ཆེ་དེང་སང་ལྷ་ས་ལ་བཞུགས་གདན་འཛུགས་ཡོད། *kyam-gön rim-po-chhe teng-sang hla-sa la sku-den-ja yö.* This means "I saw the Dalai Lama at Lhasa and know that he is still residing there." If we substitute འདུག་ for ཡོད། it means "I saw the Dalai Lama at Lhasa, but am not sure whether he is still residing there." With ཡོད་པ་རེད་ instead of ཡོད་ it means "I understand that the Dalai Lama is residing at Lhasa."

5. To form the interrogative add པས་ or པ་ to ཡོད། ཡིན། རེད་ or མེད་ e.g., ཡོད་པས། *yö-pe,* ཡིན་པས། *yin-pe;* འདུག་ *du,* forms འདུག་གས་ (གམ་) *duk-ke,* according to the ordinary rule for reduplication. [Cap. I, para. 27 (*b*).] Thus, མི་འདི་ཡག་པོ་རེད་པས། *mi di yak-po re-pe?* IS THIS MAN GOOD? མི་དེ་ནང་ལ་ཡོད་པས་ *mi te nang-la yö-pe,* IS THE MAN AT HOME? (lit. IS THE MAN INSIDE?). The interrogative particle is often omitted where the existence of an interrogative pronoun, *who, what, where,* etc., shows that an interrogation is intended, e.g., མི་འདི་སུ་རེད།. *mi di su re,* WHO IS THIS MAN?

6. The *imperfect indicative, I was,* and the *perfect indicative, I have been,* are the same as the present indicative, the adverb སྔོན་ལ་ *ngen-la,* FORMERLY or other adverb of time being placed in front. Thus, མི་འདི་ཡག་པོ་རེ། *mi di yak-po re,* THIS MAN IS GOOD. སྔོན་ལ་མི་འདི་ཡག་པོ་རེད་ད་ལྟ་ཡག་པོ་མ་རེད། *ngen-la mi di yak-po re tan-da yak-po ma-re,* THIS MAN FORMERLY WAS GOOD; NOW HE IS NOT GOOD. ཁས་ས་ང་དང་མཉམ་དུ་ཁྱོད་མེད། *khe-sa nga tang nyam-tu khyö me,* YOU WERE NOT WITH ME YESTERDAY. If the sense is clear from the context the adverb of time may be omitted.

7. The *future* is ཡོང་ *yong*, which is the same for all persons, singular and plural, thus, ང་ཡག་པོ་ཡོང་ *nga yak-po yong*, I WILL BE GOOD; ཁོ་ཚོ་ཡག་པོ་ཡོང་ *khon-tsho yak-po yong*, THEY WILL BE GOOD. For the negative insert མི་ *mi* before ཡོང་ *yong*, thus, ཁྱོད་ཡག་པོ་མི་ཡོང་ *khyö yak-po mi-yong*, YOU WILL NOT BE GOOD. Interrogative ཡོང་ངས་ (ངམ) *yong-nge* or ཡོང་ང་ (ངམ་) *yong-nga.*

8. The *conditional* is ཡོད་ན་ *yö-na*, or འདུག་ན་ *du-na*, for all persons, singular and plural, past and present; thus, ང་ཡག་པོ་ཡོད་ན་ *nga yak-po yö-na*, IF I AM GOOD, or, IF I WERE GOOD; ཁྱོད་ཡག་པ་ཡོད་ན་ *khyö yak-po yö-na*, IF THOU ART GOOD, or, IF THOU WERT GOOD. The negative is མེད་ན་ *me-na*, e.g., ཁོ་ཡག་པོ་མེད་ན་ *kho yak-po me-na*, IF HE IS (OR WAS) NOT GOOD.

9. The infinitive and verbal noun are formed from the root with པ་ added; i.e., ཡོད་པ། *yö-pa*, ཡིན་པ། *yim-pa*, TO BE, THE BEING, TO HAVE BEEN, THE HAVING BEEN, TO BE ABOUT TO BE. The context tells whether they are present, past or future; e.g., མི་འདི་ཡག་པོ་ཡིན་པ་ངས་གོ་བྱུང་། *mi di yak-po yim-pa nge ko chung*, I HAVE HEARD THAT THIS MAN IS GOOD; སྔོན་ལ་མི་འདི་ཡག་པོ་ཡིན་པ་གོ་བྱུང་སྟེ་ད་མི་ངན་བྱས་ཤག། *ngen-la mi di yak-po yim-pa ko chung-te ta mi-ngen che sha*, I HEARD FORMERLY THAT THIS MAN WAS GOOD, BUT NOW HE HAS BEHAVED BADLY (lit. HAS ACTED THE BAD MAN).

10. The *present participle* is rendered by ཡོད་དུས་ *yö-tü*, negative མེད་དུས་ *me-tü*, lit. *at the time of being*, ང་ཡག་པོ་ཡོད་དུས་ *nga yak-po yö-tü*, WHEN I AM (OR WAS) GOOD; ཁོ་ཡག་པོ་མེད་དུས་ *kho yak-po me-tü* WHEN HE IS (OR WAS) NOT GOOD.

This participle is also rendered by ཡོད་པའི་དུས་ལ་ *yö-pe tü-la*, lit. AT THE TIME OF BEING or by ཡོད་པ་དང་ *yö-pa tang*. Past time to be distinguished by adding སྔོན་ལ་ *ngen-la*, as with the imperfect and perfect indicative.

11. The *past participle* is formed by ཡོད་ནས་ *yö-ne*, negative མེད་ནས་ *me-ne;* e.g., ཁྱོད་ཡག་པོ་ཡོད་ནས་ *khyö yak-po yö-ne*, THOU, HAVING BEEN GOOD; ཁོ་ཚོ་ཡག་པོ་མེད་ནས་ *khon-tsho yak-po-me-ne*, THEY, NOT HAVING BEEN GOOD.

12. ཡོད་མཁན་ *yö-khen*, or ཡོད་པ་ *yö-pa*, forms a participle used in an agentive sense. (See Cap. III, para. 3.) Thus, མི་འདི་ཡོན་ཏན་ཡོད་མཁན་ཅིག་རེད། *mi di yön-ten yö-khen chi-re*, THIS MAN IS A LEARNED ONE.

13. This verb has no imperative of its own. The sense of the imperative is often supplied by བྱས་ pronounced *chi* —negative མ་བྱེད་ *ma-che*, these being the imperative of the verb བྱེད་པ་ *che-pa*, TO DO; thus, ལྐུགས་པ་མ་བྱེད་ *kuk-pa ma-che*, DO NOT BE STUPID.

14. For denoting *vagueness* or *generality*, ཡོང་ *yong*, may be used, e.g., བོད་ལ་ལུག་མང་པོ་ཡོང་ *pö la lu mang-po yong*, THERE ARE MANY SHEEP IN TIBET.

15. ཡོད་ *yö*, is also used to denote *having, possessing*, with the subject in the dative. Thus, ཁྱོད་ལ་རྟ་ཡོད་པས། *khyö-la ta yö-pe?* HAVE YOU A HORSE? སྔོན་ལ་ཡོད་ད་མེད། *ngen-la yö ta me*, I HAD ONE, BUT I HAVE NOT GOT IT NOW. The ལ་ may also be omitted, thus: ཁྱོད་རྟ་ཡོད་པས། *khyö ta yö-pe?*

16. For, *potential, permissive, hortative* and *optative* forms of the auxiliary verb as well as for such expressions as "IN ORDER TO BE," IT IS PREPARED FOR, IT IS PROBABLE, IT IS SUITABLE FOR, see Chapter VII. For BECAUSE IT IS, see Chapter VI.

17. In conclusion, it should be noted that Tibetan sometimes employs another verb where the verb *to be* is employed in English; e.g., ཁྱོད་རེའི་ཨ་མ་ལྷ་ས་ལ་བསྡད་འདུག། *khyö-re a-ma hla-sa la de-du*, YOUR MOTHER IS (lit. IS REMAINING) AT LHASA.

WORDS.

He=ཁོ་རང་ *kho-rang.*

Is staying=བསྡད་འདུག་ *de-du.*

Pen=སྨྱུ་གུ་ *nyu-gu.*

When grown up, *lit.* when the years rise=ལོ་ལོང་ན་ *lo-long-na.*

Call, *lit.* make come=ཤོག་བྱེས་ (བྱེད་) *shochi.*

Monk=གྲྭ་པ་ *tra-pa.*

Where=ག་པ་ *ka-pa.*

Boy=བུ་གུ་ *pu-gu.*

Darjeeling=རྡོ་རྗེ་གླིང་ *Doo-je-ling.*

Will be a thief, *lit.* will steal =ཀུ་ (ཀུན་) མ་ཀུ་ཡོང་ *ku-ma ku-yong.*

Two= གཉིས་ *nyi.*

Tall, *lit.* long body=གཟུགས་པོ་རིང་པོ་ *suk-po ring-po.*

Many=མང་པོ་ *mang-po.*

Chinaman=རྒྱ་མི་ *gya-mi.*

The Chumbi Valley=གྲོ་མོ་ *tro-mo.*

At home, *lit.* within=ནང་ལ་ *nang-la.*

EXERCISE No. 9.

When he is (or was) at home. ཁོ་རང་ནང་ལ་ཡོད་དུས། *kho-rang nang-la yö-tü.*

He is (*lit.* is staying at Darjeeling) ཁོ་རྡོ་རྗེ་གླིང་ལ་བསྡད་འདུག། *kho-Dor-je-ling-la de du.*

This is not my pen; it is yours. འདི་ངའི་སྙུ་གུ་མ་རེད། ཁྱོད་རེའི་རེད། *di nge nyu-gu ma-re, khy-re re.*

He was a thief; now he is a good man. སྔོན་ལ་ཁོ་རྐུན་མ་རེད་ད་ཡག་པོ་རེད། *ngen-la kho ku-ma re, ta yak-po-re.*

If he is at home, call him here. ཁོ་ནང་ལ་འདུག་ན་མདངས་ (འདི་རུ་) ཤོག་བྱིས་ (བྱིད་)། *kho nang-la du na, de sho chi.*

He has been a monk, but is now a trader.* སྔོན་ལ་ཁོ་གྲྭ་པ་རེད་ད་ཚོང་པ་རེད *ngen-la kho tra-pa re, ta tshong-pa re.*

When the boy is grown up, he will be a thief. བུ་གུ་འདི་ལོ་ལོང་ན་རྐུན་མ་རྐུ་ཡོང་། *pu-gu di lo-long-na, ku-ma ku-yong.*

I have two ponies. ང་ལ་རྟ་གཉིས་ཡོད། *nga-la ta nyi yö.*

You are tall ཁྱོད་གཟུགས་པོ་རིང་པོ་རེད། *khyö śuk-po ring-po re.*

Are there many Chinamen in the Chumbi Valley? གྲོ་མོ་ལ་རྒྱ་མི་མང་པོ་ཡོང་ངས། *tro-mo la gya-mi mang-po yong-nge?*

Where is my mother? ངའི་ཨ་མ་ག་པ་བསྡད་འདུག། *nge a-ma ka-pa de du?*

EXERCISE No. 10.

A boy is here. This man is stupid. I am at home. If he has a good dog. He is not at home. Are all the men here? When I was in Darjeeling. The monk is cleverer than the trader. The trader's father is the cleverest.

* A common transition among Tibetans.

CHAPTER VI.

The Verb.

1. The Tibetan verb denotes *an impersonal action*, *a state of being, doing, happening*, etc., and is in effect a verbal noun. Thus: ཁོས་ལུག་ཤ་ཟ་གི་འདུག། *khö luk-sha śa-ki-du*, HE IS EATING MUTTON, *lit.*, BY HIM, AS REGARDS MUTTON, AN EATING IS; ཚོང་པ་དེ་སང་ཉིན་འབྱོར་ཡོང་། *tshong-pa te sang-nyi lep-yong*, THE TRADER WILL ARRIVE TO-MORROW, *lit.*, AS REGARDS THE TRADER, TO-MORROW, AN ARRIVING WILL BE.

2. There is no separate inflection in the verb itself, by which one can distingusih between the singular and plural numbers, or between the active and passive voices. Even the different tenses are often the same in the colloquial as used by ordinary, uneducated persons. By the accompanying noun or pronoun one can tell whether the singular or plural is meant. The accompanying auxiliary verb, and sometimes an alteration in the root, gives the tense. From the context and from the inflexion of the noun or pronoun, if any, one must judge whether the voice is active or passive. The infinitive, participles and some of the tenses are formed by adding monosyllabic particles, e.g., ཉི། ཉིས། དུས། etc., to the root.

3. The verbal root-inflections, i.e., the changes in the roots of the verbs for different tenses, are of less importance than they otherwise would be, since in the colloquial of uneducated

persons the great majority of verbs use the perfect root for all tenses. Thus, the verb *to put in* has in the literary language four roots, viz. :—

Present	root འཇུག་ *ju.*
Perfect	do. བཅུག་ *chu.*
Future	do. གཞུག་ *sh̄u.*
Imperative	do. ཆུག་ *chhu.*

But the ordinary colloquial employs the perfect root བཅུག་ for all the tenses.

4. The exceptions to the above rule are :—

(*a*) Verbs, the present root of which end in the inherent *a* ུ or ོ usually make this present root for the present indicative, future indicative formed by གི་ཡིན་ *k̄i-yin*, negative form of the imperative, present participle, agentive participle, present infinitive, and verbal noun, e.g., ཟ་གི་འདུག། *śa-k̄i-du*, HE IS EATING, from the present root ཟ་ not བཟས་ཀྱི་འདུག། *śe-k̄yi-du*; ཞུ་གི་རེད། *sh̄u k̄i-re*, HE WILL REQUEST, from the present root ཞུ་ not ཞུས་ཀྱི་རེད། *sh̄ü-k̄yi-re*, from the perfect root ཞུས། But བསྐོས་ཀྱི་འདུག་ *k̄ö-k̄yi-du*, HE APPOINTS, from the perfect root བསྐོས་ not སྐོ་གི་འདུག་ *k̄o-k̄i-du*, from the present root སྐོ །

Well-educated Tibetans use the present root of most verbs for those parts of the verb, which are detailed in (*a*) above. And, as the student improves, he will learn to do the same.

(*b*) In compound verbs, of which the second verb is གནང་བ་ *nang-wa* (such verbs are used in the honorific language), the first verb keeps the present root as a rule in all tenses ; e.g., གཏོང་ང་ (བ་) གནང་བ་ *tong-nga nang-wa*, TO SEND, *hon*.

(c) In the imperative the root is sometimes changed. This is dealt with below in the paragraph on the imperative (see para. 12).

(d) As regards those verbs whose present and perfect roots have the same pronounciation, it is immaterial whether we write the present or perfect root. The present root is therefore written for these, both in the grammar and dictionary, in order to avoid the necessity of adding the literary spelling in brackets in such cases.

5. The student is warned against using the different roots for the present, future, perfect and imperative given in general dictionaries. These hold good only for the literary language and would often lead him astray in the colloquial. For instance, the Lhasa man, educated or uneducated, will always say བཏབ་ཀྱི་འདུག། *taṗ-kyi-du*, HE SOWS (the field), never འདེབས་ཀྱི་འདུག། *deṗ-kyi-du* ; བཏབ་ being the perfect and འདེབས་ the present root.

So also always ཉོས་ཡོང་། *nyö-yong*, HE WILL BUY, from the perfect root ཉོས་ never ཉོ་ཡོང་། *nyo-yong*, from the future root ཉོ།

6. For simple conversation the perfect root is the most important. We will now consider each mood and tense in detail.

7. བླུག་པ་ *luk-pa*, TO POUR.

Present Indicative.

།ངས་ *nge* or ང་ཚོས་བླུག་གི་ཡོད་ *ngan-tshö luk-ki-yö*, I (*or* we) pour (*or* am pouring).

ཁྱོད་རེས་ (ཀྱིས་) *khyö-re* or ཁྱོད་ཚོས་བླུག་གི་འདུག་ *khyön-tshö luk-ki-du*, you (*or* ye) pour (*or* are pouring).

ཁོས *khö* or ཁོ་ཚོས་བླུག་གི་འདུག། *khon-tshö luk-ki-du*, he (*or* they) pours (*or* is pouring).

The ཡོད་ and འདུག་ are often omitted, e.g., ཁོས་བླུག་གི་ *khö luk-ki*, he is pouring.

Note that the agentive case of the pronoun is employed, this being a transitive verb. (Chapter III, para. 13.)

8. **Imperfect Indicative.**—This (*I was pouring*, etc.), like that of the auxiliary verb, is the same as the present with སྔོན་ལ་ *ngen-la* or other adverb of time added.

9. **Perfect Indicative.**— །ངས་ *nge or* ང་ཚོས་བླུགས་ཀ་ (པ་) ཡིན་ *ngan-tshö luk-ka-yin*, I (*or* we) poured (*or* have poured).
ཁྱོད་རེས་ (ཀྱིས་) *khyö re or* ཁྱོད་ཚོས་བླུགས་ཀ་ (པ་) རེད་ *khyön-tshö luk-ka-re.* You (*or* ye) poured (*or* have poured).
ཁོས་ *khö or* ཁོ་ཚོས་བླུགས་ཀ་ (པ་) རེད་ *khon-tshö luk-ka-re.*

He (*or* they) poured (*or* have poured).

Note the reduplication of the ཀ་ after བླུགས་; also that, as in the case of the auxiliary verb, where ཡོད་ is used for the 1st person, འདུག་ is ordinarily used for the 2nd and 3rd, and where ཡིན་ for the 1st person རེད་ for the 2nd and 3rd. The perfect is also rendered by བྱུང་ or སོང་ and sometimes by འདུག་ added to the root of the verb, and the same for all persons, thus, ངས་གོ་བྱུང་། *nge ko-chung*, I HEARD; ཁོ་ཤི་སོང་། *kho shi-song*, HE DIED.

Note also here the difference of root referred to in para. 4(*a*) of this chapter; ཁོས་ཞུ་གི་འདུག་ *khö shu ki-du*, HE IS PETITIONING, but ཁོས་ཞུས་པ་རེད་ *khö shü-pa re*, HE HAS PETITIONED.

10. **Pluperfect.**—This (I HAD POURED, etc.) is translated in the same way as the perfect, just as the imperfect is translated in the same way as the present. The context will sometimes include an adverb of time, and will in any case usually show whether the perfect or pluperfect is intended.

11. **Future Indicative.**—ངས་ *nge or* ང་ཚོས་ལྡུག་གི་ཡིན་ *ngan-tshö luk-ki-yin*, I (*or* we) will pour.

ཁྱོད་རེས་ (ཀྱིས་) *khyö-re or* ཁྱོད་ཚོས་ལྡུག་གི་རེད་ *khyön-tshö luk-ki-re*, you (*or* ye) will pour.

ཁོས་ *khö or* ཁོ་ཚོས་ལྡུག་གི་རེད་ *khon-tshö luk-ki-re*, he (*or* they) will pour.

ཡོང་ *yong* added to the perfect root of the verb may also be used for all persons, thus, ངས་ལྡུགས་ཡོང་ *nge luk-yong*, I WILL POUR; ཁོ་ཚོས་ལྡུགས་ཡོང་ *khon-tshö luk-yong*, THEY WILL POUR. Neither the present nor the future root is used with ཡོང་ in this sense, e.g., I WILL BUY ངས་ཉོས་ཡོང་། *nge nyö-yong*, not ངས་ཉོ་ཡོང་། *nge nyo-yong*. I WILL DO THIS WORK ངས་ལས་ཀ་འདི་བྱས་ཡོང་། *nge le-ka di che yong*; བྱས་ the perfect root is used, not བྱེད་ the present root, nor བྱ་ the future root. THE ICE WILL MELT RAPIDLY. ཁྱག་པ་མགྱོགས་པོ་བཞུས་ཡོང་། *khyak-pa gyok-po shü-yong*. Here again the perfect root བཞུས་ *shü* is used, not ཞུ་ *shu*, the present root, nor གཞུ་ *shu*, the future root.

12. **Imperative.**—In literary Tibetan many verbs have a separate root for the imperative as well as for the present, future and perfect tenses, and such roots are given in general dictionaries. But in the colloquial the imperative is usually the

present or perfect root of the verb. When the root contains an inherent *a* or ེ this is often changed to ོ; e.g., མིག་ལྟོས་ *mik-tö*, LOOK! from present root ལྟ་ *ta*.

SEND THIS MAN! མི་འདི་གཏོང་། *mi di tong.**

BUY THIS THING! སྤྱད་ལག་འདི་ཉོས། *cha-la di nyö.*†

TELL (YOUR) PETITION! སྙན་ཞུ་ཞུས། *nye-shu shü.*‡

SOW THIS FIELD! ཞིང་ཁ་འདི་བཏབ། *shing-kha di tap.*‡

In addressing servants, coolies and others of low rank ཤིག་ *shi* is often added, e.g., *Pour!* བླུགས་ཤིག་ *luk-shi.* In addressing persons of somewhat better position རོགས་གནང་ *ro-nang*, and རོགས་མཛད་ *ro-che*, the former being the slightly more polite of the two, are substituted for ཤིག། Thus, བླུགས་རོགས་གནང་། *luk-ro-nang*, PLEASE POUR. Other particles used after the *imperative* to soften it are དང་ pronounced *la* and ཨ་ *a*. These soften the order, but are not quite so polite as རོགས་གནང་ *ro-nang* or རོགས་མཛད་ *ro-che*, e.g., ལྟོས་དང་ *tö-la*, DO LOOK! འོ་ན་རྒྱུག་ཨ། *o-na gyu-a*, WELL, YOU MAY GO. མདས་ཤོག་ཨ། *de sho-a*, COME HERE, DO. ཁོ་ལ་དྲིས་རོགས་གནང་། *kho-la tri-ro-nang*, PLEASE ASK HIM.

13. The negative of the imperative is formed by putting མ་ *ma* before the imperative, e.g.—

DO NOT SEND THIS MAN, མི་འདི་མ་གཏང་། *mi-di ma-tong.*

DO NOT BUY THIS THING, སྤྱད་ལག་འདི་མ་ཉོ། *cha-la di ma-nyo.*

---

*Present root. †Perfect and imperative root.

‡Perfect root.

DO NOT TELL (YOUR) PETITION, སྙན་ཞུ་མ་ཞུ། *nye-shu ma-shu.*

DO NOT SOW THIS FIELD, ཞིང་ཁ་འདི་མ་བཏབ། *shing-kha di ma-tap.*

It will be noted from the above examples that verbs ending in ˇ or ˬ usually take the perfect root for the positive imperative and the present root for the negative imperative. Verbs ending in inherent *a* also take the present root for the negative imperative, e.g., མིག་མ་ལྟ་ *mik-ma-ta*, DO NOT LOOK. ཤ་མ་ཟ་ *sha-ma-sa*, DO NOT EAT MEAT. Those verbs, which form irregular imperatives, take the present root for the negative, e.g., ཤོག་ *sho*, COME! མ་ཡོང་ *ma-yong*, DO NOT COME! རྒྱུག་ *gyu*, GO! མ་འགྲོ་ *man-dro*, DO NOT GO!

14. It should be noted also that verbs of *telling*, *ordering* and the like govern the imperative, thus, ཁོ་ཕག་རི་ལ་སྡོད་ལབ་ཤིག། *kho pha-ri la dö lap shi*, TELL HIM TO STAY AT PHARI, lit. TELL HIM STAY AT PHARI.

15. **Conditional Tenses.**—They are formed thus: Present Conditional, IF HER SON IS ILL THE MOTHER WILL BE GRIEVED, བུ་འདི་ན་ན་ (if ill) ཨ་མས་སྡུག་བསྔལ་བྱེས་ཡོང་ *pu di na-na a-me duk-nge che-yong* (WILL BE GRIEVED, *lit.* WILL MAKE GRIEF). Past Conditional, IF I HAD KNOWN YESTERDAY, I WOULD HAVE GIVEN IT, ཁས་ས་ *she-sa* (YESTERDAY) ངས་ཧ་གོ་ན་ *nge ha-ko-na* (IF I HAD KNOWN) བཏེར་ར་(བ་)ཡོད། *te-ra-yö* (WOULD HAVE GIVEN). Note that both for the present and the past the clause beginning with *if* takes ན་ added to the root of the verb; that the second clause, as in English, takes the future, when joined to a present conditional clause; and that, when joined to a past conditional clause, the second clause takes the perfect indica-

tive changing ཡིན་ into ཡོད་ and རེད་ into འདུག་ Thus, IF HE HAD KNOWN YESTERDAY, HE WOULD HAVE GIVEN IT. ཁས་ས་ཁོས་ ཧ་གོ་ན་བསྟེར་ར་ (བ་) འདུག། *khe-sa khö ha-ko-na te-ra-du.*

16. AS, BECAUSE, SINCE is expressed by ཙང་, e.g., ཁྱོད་ཚོས་ བྱས་མ་ཐུབ་ཙང་ངས་བྱས་པ་ཡིན། *khyön-tshö che ma-thup-tsang nge che-pa-yin.* AS YOU COULD NOT DO IT, I DID IT. འདི་ཆེ་ དྲག་ཙང་སྤྱིག་གི་མ་རེད། *di chhe-tra-tsang drik-ki ma-re.* THIS WILL NOT DO AS IT IS TOO LARGE.

Note that the adjectival root ཆེ་ is here conjugated as a verb (see Chap. IV, para. 7).

17. **Present Participle.** This is formed by adding དུས་ *tü* to the root, e.g., ཁོས་དྲེ་བརྡུངས་དུས་མི་ཅིག་བསླེབས་སོང་། *khö tre dung-tü mi chi lep-song,* WHILE HE WAS BEATING THE MULE, A MAN ARRIVED. Or དུས་ལ་ may be added to the infinitive (see para. 23 below), the latter being put in the genitive; e.g., ཁོས་ དྲེ་བརྡུངས་པའི་དུས་ལ་ *khö tre dung-pe tü-la,* etc. This participle may also be formed by adding པ་དང་ or བ་དང་ to the root, e.g., ཁོས་དྲེ་བརྡུངས་པ་དང་མི་ཅིག་བསླེབས་སོང་།། *khö tre dung-pa-tang mi chi lep-song.*

18. **Past Participle.**—Formed by adding ནས་ *ne* to the perfect root, e.g., ཆུ་བླུགས་ནས་ *chhu luk-ne,* HAVING POURED OUT THE WATER. It takes also the place of a pluperfect and a gerund. Thus: HE HAS BECOME RICH BY TRADING, ཁོ་ཚོང་བརྒྱབ་ ནས་ཕྱུག་པོ་བྱུང་ང་ (བ་) རེད། *kho tshong gyap-ne chhuk-po chung-nga-re.* ཁོ་ (*he*) ཚོང་བརྒྱབ་ནས་ (*having traded*) ཕྱུག་པོ་

(*rich*) ཕྱུང་ང་ (བ་) རེད། (*has become*). AFTER HE HAD WRITTEN THE LETTER, HE DESPATCHED IT. ཁོས་ཡི་གེ་བྲིས་ནས་ (*having written*) བཏང་ང་ (བ་) རེད། *khö yi-ge tri-ne tang-nga-re.* This ནས། ན་ the conditional and དུས་ the present participle make up largely for the poverty of the Tibetan language in conjunctions.

19. **Agentive Participle.**—Formed by ངན། མཁན། པ་ or བ་ added to the root. These Agentive participles may have either a past, a present or a future signification. ངན་ and མཁན་ are used with animate objects and have an active signification. པ་ or བ་ when used with animate objects denote the passive. With inanimate objects པ་ or བ་ are used in preference to ངན་ or མཁན། བ་ is used after vowels and ང་ ར་ or འ་; པ་ after the other final consonants. EXAMPLES:—THE MESSENGER WHO WENT YESTERDAY. ཁས་ས་འགྲོ་ངན་ (མཁན་) བང་ཆེན་དེ། *khe-sa dro-ngen ṗang-chhen te.*

THE MESSENGER WHO WILL GO TO-MORROW. སང་ཉིན་འགྲོ་ངན་ (མཁན་) བང་ཆེན་དེ། *sang-nyi dro-ngen ṗang-chhen te.*

THE MAN WHO SENT THE LETTER YESTERDAY. ཁས་ས་ཡི་གེ་གཏོང་ངན་ (མཁན་) མི་དེ། *khe-sa yi-ge tong-ngen mi te.*

THE LETTER WHICH WAS SENT YESTERDAY. ཁས་ས་བཏང་ངའི་ (བའི་) ཡི་གེ་དེ། *khe-sa tang-nge yi-ge te.*

THE MAN WHO WAS SENT YESTERDAY. ཁས་ས་བཏང་ངའི་ (བའི་) མི་དེ། *khe-sa tang-nge mi te.*

It will be noticed from the above examples that ངན་ and མཁན་ do not usually take the genitive case.

20. **Verbal Noun.**—Either takes the infinitive form or is formed by adding ཡ་ *ya* to the root, e.g. བྲོས་ཡ་ *trö-ya*, THE RUNNING AWAY from བྲོས་པ་ *trö-pa*, TO RUN AWAY. དམག་རྒྱབ་དུས་བྲོས་ཡ་འདི་ཡག་པོ་མ་རེད། *mak gyap-tü trö-ya di yak-po ma-re*, THE RUNNING AWAY WHEN A BATTLE IS BEING FOUGHT (དམག་རྒྱབ་དུས་) IS WRONG. Again: NOW-A-DAYS IS THE TIME FOR GOING TO INDIA, ད་རིང་སང་རྒྱ་ལ་འགྲོ་བའི་ (or འགྲོ་ཡའི་) དུས་རེད་ *te-ring-sang gya-la dro-we tü re*, *lit.* ད་རིང་སང་ (NOW-A-DAYS) རྒྱ་ལ་ (TO INDIA) འགྲོ་བའི་ (OF GOING) དུས་ (THE TIME) རེད་ (IS). Infinitives and verbal nouns can also be formed from other parts of the verb. Thus, བྱེད་པ་ TO DO or THE DOING, བྱས་ཚར་ར་ (བ་) or བྱས་པ་ཡིན་པ་ THE HAVING FINISHED DOING, e.g., སྐད་ཆ་བྱས་ཚར་ར་ (བ་) ཡག་པོ་བྱུང་། *ke-chha che-tshar-ra yak-po chung*, *lit.* THE HAVING FINISHED THE DISCUSSION IS GOOD, i.e., IT IS GOOD THAT THE DISCUSSION HAS BEEN FINISHED. Similarly བྱེད་འགྲོ་ཡོད་པ་ THE BEING ON THE POINT OF DOING, བྱེད་རྒྱུ་ཡིན་པ་ THE BEING ABOUT TO DO, OR THAT WHICH IS TO BE DONE.

21. Verbs governed by verbs of SEEING, PERCEIVING, HEARING, THINKING, BELIEVING, KNOWING, SAYING, etc., take the form of the verbal noun; e.g. ཁོ་གླུགས་པ་ཡིན་པ་ངས་ཧ་གོ་སོང་། *kho kuk-pa yim-pa nge ha-ko song.* I PERCEIVED THAT HE WAS A SIMPLETON. ཁྱོད་ཁ་ལག་ཟས་ཚར་ར་ (བ་) ཡིན་ན་ (ནམ་) བསམས་བྱུང་། *khyö kha-la se-tshar-ra yin-na sam-chung.* I THOUGHT YOU HAD FINISHED EATING.

22. IN ORDER TO, FOR THE SAKE OF, FOR THE PURPOSE OF and the like are frequently rendered by the verbal noun in the genitive followed by དོན་ལ་ or དོན་དག་ལ་, e.g. ཁ་མཆུ་འདི་ཐོབ་པའི་དོན་ལ་ངས་དཀའ་ལས་མང་པོ་བརྒྱབ་པ་ཡིན། *kham-chhudithop-pe tön-la nge kap-le mang-po gyap-pa yin;* I HAVE ENDURED A GREAT DEAL OF TROUBLE IN ORDER TO SUCCEED IN THIS LAW-SUIT. ཞིང་ཁ་འདི་བཏབ་པའི་དོན་དག་ལ་ང་མདངས་ཡོང་ང་ (བ་) ཡིན། *shing-kha di tap-pe tön-ta-la nga de yong-nga-yin;* I HAVE COME HERE FOR THE PURPOSE OF SOWING THIS FIELD.

23. **Infinitive.**—This is the form of the verb found in dictionaries and vocabularies. It is the present root with པ་ *pa* added in the case of roots ending in ག་ད་ན་བ་མ་ས། *ka, ta, na, pa, ma, sa,* and with བ་ *wa* added in the case of roots ending in a vowel or ང་འ་ར་ལ། *nga, a, ra, la.* It is used in the sense of *in order to;* e.g., བཀའ་བློན་སྤུང་ལ་ཚོང་རྒྱག་ག་ (རྒྱབ་པ) ཕྱིན་པ་རེད། *ka lön-pung-la tshong gyak-ka chhim-pa-re,* HE HAS GONE TO KALIMPONG TO TRADE. རྒྱུ་ added to the present root also expresses the infinitive. Thus,ད་འགྲོ་རྒྱུ་གཚོད་ཡོད། *ta dro-gyu ka-tshö yö,* HOW FAR (HAVE WE) TO GO NOW?

Several verbs, e.g., དགོས་པ་ *gö-pa,* TO BE NECESSARY, ཐུབ་པ་ *thup-pa,* TO BE ABLE, ཆོག་པ་ *chhok-pa,* TO BE ALLOWED and འདོད་པ་ *dö-pa,* TO WISH, take the root and not the infinitive of the verb which they govern; e.g., ད་ཁྱོད་འགྲོ་ཆོག་གི་རེད། *ta khyö dro chho-ki-re,* YOU ARE PERMITTED TO GO NOW.

24. As a general rule, it may be said that when a verb can be turned into a verbal noun it should be translated as one. Thus "Now-a-days is the time to go to India" is translated into Tibetan as above "Now-a-days is the time *of going* to India." Similarly, "It is wrong *to run away* when a battle is being fought" is translated "*The running away* when a battle is being fought is wrong."

WORDS.

Official=དཔོན་པོ་ *pöm-po.*

Messenger=པང་ཆེན་ *pang-chhen.*

Muleman=དྲེ་པ་ *tre-pa.*

To, into the presence of=རྩ་ལ་ *tsa-la.*

To make effort, strive=སྙིང་རུས་བྱེད་པ་ *nying-rü che pa.*

Tibetan language=བོད་སྐད་ *pö-ke* (derived from བོད་ *pö* Tibet and སྐད་ཆ་ *ke-chha*, speech).

To know=ཤེས་པ་ *she-pa.*

Quickly, soon=མགྱོགས་པོ་ *gyok-po.*

Water=ཆུ་ *chhu.*

To learn= བསླབ་པ་ *lap-pa.*

Difficult=དཀའ་ལས་ཁག་པོ་ *ka-le khak-po.*

Letter=ཡི་གེ་ *yi-ge.*

To receive=འབྱོར་བ་ *jor-wa.*

Kalimpong=བཀའ་བློན་སྤུང་ *ka-lön-pung.*

To buy=ཉོ་བ་ *nyo-wa.*

EXERCISE NO. 11.

I see the house. ངས་ཁང་པ་མཐོང་གི་འདུག། *nge khang-pa thong-gi-du.*

I will see your house to-morrow. སང་ཉིན་ཁྱོད་རེའི་ཁང་པ་ངས་མིག་ལྟ་གི་ཡིན། *sang-nyi khyö-re khang-pa nge mik-ta-ki-yin.*

The official has sent a messenger to me. དཔོན་པོས་པང་ཆེན་ཅིག་ངའི་རྩ་ལ་གཏོང་ང་ (བ་) གནང་བྱུང་། *pöm-pö pang-chhen chi nge tsa-la tong nga nang-chung.*

You have sent your worst pony; please sell me a better one. ཁྱོད་རེས་ (ཀྱིས་) རྟ་སྡུག་ཤོས་ཅིག་བཏང་འདུག་ཡག་ག་ཅིག་ཚོང་རོགས་བྱེད། *khyö-re ta duk-shö chi tang-du yak-ka chi tshong-ro-chi.*

He is beating a mule. ཁོས་དྲེ་རྡུང་གི་འདུག། *khö tre dung-gi-du.*

He was beating the muleman yesterday. ཁས་ས་ཁོས་དྲེ་པ་རྡུང་གི་འདུག། *khe-sa khö tre-pa dung-gi-du.*

If you work hard (*lit.* make effort) you will soon know Tibetan. ཁྱོད་རེས་ (ཀྱིས་) སྙིང་རུས་བྱེད་ན་བོད་སྐད་མགྱོགས་པོ་ཤེས་ཡོང་། *khyö-re nying-rü che-na pö-ke gyok-po she-yong.*

Do not beat the pony. རྟ་མ་རྡུང་། *ta ma-dung.*

Tibetan is difficult (*lit.* the learning Tibetan is difficult). བོད་སྐད་བསླབ་ཡ་དཀའ་ལས་ཁག་པོ་རེད། *pö-ke lap-ya ka-le khak-po-re.*

I received the letter from Dawa Tshering (*lit.* sent by Dawa Tshering) yesterday. ཁས་ས་ཟླ་བ་ཚེ་རིང་གིས་བཏང་ངའི་ (བའི་) ཡི་གེ་དེ་ང་ལ་འབྱོར་བྱུང་། *khe-sa Da-wa Tshering-gi tang-nge yi-ge te nga-la jor-chung.*

After going to Darjeeling, go to Kalimpong. ཁྱོད་རྡོ་རྗེ་གླིང་ལ་ཕྱིན་ནས་བཀའ་བློན་སྤུང་ལ་རྒྱུག། *khyö Dor-je-ling-la chhin-ne ka-lön-pung-la gyu.*

When you are at Kalimpong, buy a pony. ཁྱོད་བཀའ་བློན་སྤུང་ལ་བསྡད་རྟ་ཅིག་ཉོས། *khyö ka-lön-pung-la de-tü ta-chi nyö.*

EXERCISE No. 12.

He is buying. The trader has bought these goods at (*lit.* from) Lhasa. Call my servant. Do not pour the water. I have sent a messenger to Darjeeling. If you had petitioned the official yesterday, he would have sent a good pony. I am going to the bazar to see whether there are any new arrivals (lit. *comers*, from ཡོང་བ་ to come) from Lhasa.

CHAPTER VII.

THE VERB—*continued.*

1. **Negatives.**—The negative used with the present and future indicative (except with རེད་) is མི་ *mi*. With all other tenses and with རེད་ *re* even though in the present or future མ་ *ma* is used. The negative with ཡིན་ *yin* is shortened into མན་ *men*, that with ཡོད་ *yö* into མེད་ *me*. Thus: ཁོ་ཡོང་གི་མི་འདུག་ *kho yong-gi min-du*, HE IS NOT COMING; ཁོ་ཡོང་གི་མ་རེད་ *kho yong-gi ma-re*, HE WILL NOT COME; སང་ཉིན་ཁོ་བསླེབས་མི་ཡོང་། *sang-nyi kho lep-mi-yong*, HE WILL NOT ARRIVE TO-MORROW; ང་འགྲོ་གི་མན། *nga dro-ki men*, I WILL NOT GO; ངས་ཤེས་ཀྱི་མེད། *nge shing-gi-me*, I DO NOT KNOW.

2. With the perfect indicative ending in རེད་ it is better to place the negative before the *root*; e.g., HE DID NOT GO YESTERDAY, ཁས་ས་ཁོ་མ་ཕྱིན་པ་རེད། *khe-sa kho ma-chhim-pa-re*, in preference to ཕྱིན་པ་མ་རེད། *chhim-pa ma-re*, though neither is incorrect.

3. NEVER is translated by མ་མྱོང་ *ma-nyong*, following the root of the verb, e.g., ང་རྡོ་རྗེ་གླིང་ལ་འགྲོ་མ་མྱོང་། *nga Dor-je-ling-la dro ma-nyong*, I HAVE NEVER BEEN TO DARJEELING.

4. **Interrogatives.**—These follow the rules given in Chapter V, para. 5. To these must be added the rule that བྱུང་ *chung*, སོང་ *song*, and མྱོང་ *nyong* (this latter without མ་ *ma*, meaning EVER) take ངས་ *nge*. Thus: HAS MY FATHER ARRIVED? ངའི་པ་པ་བསླེབས་བྱུང་ངས། *nge pa-pa lep chung-nge?* Again, HAVE YOU EVER BEEN TO DARJEELING? ཁྱོད་རྡོ་རྗེ་གླིང་ལ་འགྲོ་མྱོང་ངས། *khyö Dor-je-ling-la dro nyong-nge?* Sometimes ཡིན་ is used instead of རེད་ in interrogative sentences for the second person, singular and plural, e.g., ཁྱོད་ལྷ་ས་ལ་འགྲོ་གི་ཡིན་པས། *khyö hla-sa-la dro-ki yim-pe* ARE YOU GOING TO LHASA?

5. An interrogative is also formed by ཨ་ཡོད་ *a-yö* (present tense) ཨ་ཡོང་ *a-yong* (future tense). Thus, ལས་ཀ་འདི་བྱེད་ན་ཡག་པོ་ཨ་ཡོང་། *le-ka di che-na yak-po a-yong?* IF YOU DO THIS, WILL IT TURN OUT WELL? (lit. WILL IT BE GOOD?). བུ་གུ་འདི་བསླབ་གྲྭ་ལ་ཡག་པོ་བྱས་ནས་བརྡད་ཀྱི་ཨ་ཡོད། *pu-gu di lap-tra-la yak-po che-ne de-kyi a-yö?* IS THIS BOY DOING WELL AT SCHOOL?

6. Finally, an interrogative with a *future* meaning is formed by adding ག་ to the root. Thus, ང་ཚོ་ག་རེ་ལབ་ག། *ngan-tsho ka-re lap-ka?* WHAT ARE WE TO SAY? WHAT SHALL WE SAY?

7. **Passive Voice.**—As shown above (Chap. VI, para. 2) the Passive Voice is not distinguished from the Active in the same way as in English. Thus, *he is beating me*, is expressed

in Tibetan *by him to me a beating is.* So in the Passive Voice *I am being beaten* is expressed *to me a beating is.* The only difference therefore between the Active and Passive is that the Agent is omitted in the latter. Thus:—

Present ང་ (ཁྱོད་ཁོ་) རྡུང་གི་འདུག་ *nga* (*khyö, kho*) *dung-gi-du,* I (you, he) am being beaten.

Future ང་ (ཁྱོད་ཁོ་) བརྡུངས་ཡོང་ *nga* (*khyö, kho*) *dung-yong.* I (you, he) shall be beaten.

Perfect བརྡུངས་སོང་ *dung-song,* or བརྡུངས་འདུག་ *dung-du,* or བརྡུངས་བཞག་ *dung sha,* Have (has) been beaten.

Future Passive Participle རྡུང་རྒྱུ་ *dung-gyu,* To be beaten. So also གཡུ་འཚོང་རྒྱུ་ *yu tshong-gyu, Turquoises to be sold* or *turquoises for sale.*

The Passive should, as far as possible, be avoided in translating, the corresponding Active tense being used instead.

8. **Potential Verbs.**—When CAN, COULD mean IS ABLE TO, translate by ཐུབ་པ་ TO BE ABLE, added to the root of the verb; e.g., YOU CAN (i.e., ARE ABLE TO) GO TO DARJEELING, ཁྱོད་རྡོ་རྗེ་གླིང་ལ་འགྲོ་ཐུབ་ཀྱི་རེད། *khyö Dor-je-ling-la dro thup-kyi-re.* HE CAN DO THIS, ཁོས་འདི་བྱེད་ཐུབ་ཀྱི་རེད། *khö di che thup-kyi-re.* It will be seen from the above examples that the subject is put in the agentive case, when the main verb is transitive and in the nominative case, when the main verb is intransitive. A similar rule applies to the permissive verbs and to the hortative verbs dealt with in the two next paragraphs.

9. **Permissive Verbs.**—When CAN, COULD mean IS ALLOWED TO, translate by ཆོག་པ་ *chhok-pa*, added to the root of the verb; e.g., ཁྱོད་རྡོ་རྗེ་གླིང་ལ་འགྲོ་ཆོག་གི་རེད། *khyö Dor-je-ling-la dro chhok-ki-re*, YOU CAN (i.e., ARE ALLOWED TO) GO TO DARJEELING.

10. **Hortative Verbs.**—When SHOULD means OUGHT, NEED, WANT, WISH OR MUST, it is translated by དགོས་པ་ *gö-pa*, added to the root of the verb, e.g., YOU SHOULD (i.e., OUGHT TO, OR MUST) GO TO DARJEELING, ཁྱོད་རྡོ་རྗེ་གླིང་ལ་འགྲོ་དགོས་ཀྱི་རེད། *khyö Dor-je-ling-la dro go-kyi-re.*

11. **Optative Verbs.**—These, denoting WISH and REGRET, are rendered as follows:—

e.g., WOULD THAT MY BROTHER WERE HERE! ངའི་སྤུན་ཀྱག་མདས་ (འདི་དུ་) ཡོད་ན་ཨ། *nge pün-kya de yö-na-a.*

IF ONLY HE WOULD EAT HIS FOOD! ཁོས་ཁ་ལག་ཟ་རོགས་བྱས་ན་ཨ། *khö kha-la sa-ro che-na-a.*

IF ONLY HE WOULD BRING MY PONY! ཁོས་ངའི་རྟ་དེ་འཁྲིད་ཡོང་རོགས་བྱས་ན་ཨ། *khö nge ta-te thri yong-ro che-na-a.*

12. Another form, used in religious prayers or blessing, is as follows:—

MAY THE PROSPERITY OF THE (BUDDHIST) RELIGION LONG PREVAIL! བསྟན་པ་ཡུན་རིང་གནས་པའི་བཀྲ་ཤིས་ཤོག། *tem-pa yün-ring ne-pe tra-shi sho.*

This sentence is frequently used at the end of a prayer.

MAY YOU BE HAPPY! ཁྱོད་སྐྱིད་པོ་ཡོང་བར་ཤོག། *khyö kyi-po yong-nga sho.*

MAY YOU HAVE A LONG LIFE FREE FROM ILLNESS! ཁྱོད་ཚེ་རིང་ནད་མེད་ཡོང་བར་ཤོག། *khyö tshe-ring ne-me yong-nga sho.* These two latter examples might be used by an old man blessing a young one.

The language used is literary, rather than ordinary colloquial, but is used colloquially for the above purposes.

13. The *imminence* of an action is expressed by འགྲོ་ *tro*, added to the root; e.g., ཁོ་ཕག་རི་ལ་སླེབ་འགྲོ་འདུག། *kho pha-ri la-lep-tro-du*, HE HAS NEARLY REACHED PHARI.

14. *Probability, likelihood* are expressed by འགྲོ་ *tro* or པ་འདྲ་ *pa-dra*, e.g., ཁོ་ཕག་རི་ལ་བསྡད་ཀྱི་ཡིན་འགྲོ་ (or ཡིན་པ་འདྲ་) *kho pha-ri-la de-kyi yin-tro* or *yim-pa-dra*, HE WILL PROBABLY STAY AT PHARI. The negative forms are མན་འགྲོ་ (མིན་འགྲོ་) and མན་པ་འདྲ། (མིན་པ་འདྲ་) e.g., ཁོ་ཕག་རི་ལ་བསྡད་ཀྱི་མན་ (མིན་)པ་འདྲ། *kho pha-ri-la de-kyi mem-pa-dra*, HE WILL PROBABLY NOT STAY AT PHARI.

15. *Completion* is expressed by the verb ཚར་བ་ *tshar-wa*, TO FINISH, added to the root, e.g., ཁོས་ཏོ་ཟས་ཚར་སོང་། *khö to se-tshar-song*, HE HAS FINISHED EATING.

16. When an action is *habitual* or *general* the future form in རེད་ is used. Thus, ཉི་མ་རེ་རེ་ཆར་པ་བབ་ (འབབ་) ཀྱི་རེད། *nyi-ma re-re chha-pa pap-kyi-re*, RAIN FALLS EVERY DAY.

17. That an action is *continuing* is expressed by the root with གི་ once repeated and followed by the verb བྱེད་པ་ e.g., འགྲོ་གི་འགྲོ་གི་བྱེས་ (བྱེད་) ཨ། ང་ད་ལྟ་བསླེབས་ཡོང་། *dro-ki dro-ki chi-a, nga tan-da lep-yong*, KEEP MOVING ON; I WILL COME PRESENTLY.

18. Verbs of BECOMING CHANGING INTO, ALTERING INTO, GROWING, etc., are often expressed by འགྲོ་བ་ governing the dative, e.g., THIS YELLOW COLOUR IS BECOMING RED. ཚོས་སེར་པོ་འདི་དམར་པོ་ལ་འགྲོ་གི། *tshö ser-po di mar-po-la droki.* It is very common with the comparatives of adjectives; e.g., THIS HAS BECOME LESS འདི་ཉུང་དུ་ཕྱིན་ཤག། *di nyung-ru chhin-ska.*

Note the use of དུ་ here. It is used with some words in the place of ལ་

19. ས་ *sa*, PLACE, is joined to many verbal roots, e.g., སྡོད་ས་ *dö-sa*, RESIDENCE (lit. PLACE OF DWELLING, from སྡོད་པ་ TO REMAIN, DWELL) ལས་ཀ་བྱེད་ས་ *le-ka che-sa*, PLACE WHERE ONE DOES ONE'S WORK, from བྱེད་པ་ *che-pa*, TO DO.

20. To have *leisure to, time for* doing is expressed by ལོང་ *long*, joined to the root of the verb concerned, e.g., ང་མི་དེ་ཚོ་འཐུད་ལོང་མི་འདུག། *nga mi te-tsho thre-long min-du*, I HAVE NO TIME TO SEE THOSE MEN.

21. That the time for doing something has arrived is expressed by རན་ *ren*, e.g., ད་འགྲོ་རན་སོང་། *ta dro-ren-song*, IT IS TIME TO GO NOW; ད་ཟ་རན་འདུག། *ta sa-ren-du*, IT IS TIME TO EAT NOW (IT IS MEAL-TIME).

22. TO BE READY FOR, TO BE PREPARED FOR, is expressed by ཆོག་ *chho*, ཆོག་ཆོག་ *chhok-chho* joined to the root of the verb

TO BE FIT FOR, TO BE SUITABLE FOR is expressed by ཉེན་པ་ *nyem-pa* similarly joined (See Chap. IV, para. 6).

23. ཏ་ joined to the root of the verb, and followed later by ཏེ་ denotes

INDEED	...	...	... BUT
IT IS TRUE	...	...	... BUT
CERTAINLY	...	...	... BUT, etc.

e.g., HE CERTAINLY HEARS BUT HE DOES NOT HEED, ཀོ་ཏ་ཀོ་གི་འདུག་ཏེ་ཁོས་ཉན་གྱི་མ་རེད། *ko-ta ko-ki duk-te khö nyen-kyi ma-re*

I DID INDEED SEE HIM, BUT I DID NOT RECOGNISE HIM. མཐོང་ཏ་མཐོང་བྱུང་ཏེ་ངས་ངོ་ཤེས་མ་བྱུང་། *thong-ta thong-chung-te nge ngo-she ma-chung.*

In the literary language the spelling of this particle ཏེ་ varies according to the letter immediately preceding it, but in the colloquial the pronunciation is always *te.*

The meaning of ཏ་ . . . ཏེ་ corresponds to that of *to . . . lekin* in Hindustani.

24. Verbs of *receiving* follow the same rule as ཡོད་ in the sense of *possessing* (Cap. V, para. 15). Thus, ང་ལ་འབྱོར་བྱུང་། *nga-la jor-chung*, I HAVE RECEIVED.

25. A few common verbs which are irregular may be noted as follows :—

Infinitive.	Present.	Perfect.	Future.	Imperative.	Negative Imperative.
ཡོང་བ་ *yong-wa*, to come	ཡོང་གི་ཡོད་ *yong-gi-yö.*	ཡོང་ང་(བ་) ཡིན་ *yong-nga-yin.*	ཡོང་གི་ཡིན་ *yong-gi-yin.* not ཡོང་ *yong.*	ཤོག་ *sho.*	མ་ཡོང་ *ma-yong.*
འགྲོ་བ་ *dro-wa*, to go	འགྲོ་གི་ཡོད་ *dro-k̄i-yö.*	ཕྱིན་པ་ཡིན་ *chhim-pa-yin.*	འགྲོ་གི་ཡིན་ *dro-k̄i-yin* or ཕྱིན་ཡོང་ *chhin-yong.*	རྒྱུག་ *gyu.*	མ་འགྲོ་ *man-dro.*
བྱེད་པ་ *cħe-pa*, to do	བྱེད་ཀྱི་ཡོད་ *cħe-kyi-yö.*	བྱས་པ་ཡིན་ *cħe-pa-yin.*	བྱེད་ཀྱི་ཡིན་ *cħe-kyi yin.* or བྱེད་ཡོང་ *cħe-yong.*	བྱེས་ (བྱེད་) *cħi.*	མ་བྱེད་ *ma-cħe.*

Thus ང་ཡོང་གི་ཡོད་ *nga yong gi-yö*, I AM COMING (NOW). ཁོ་ཡོང་གི་རེད་ *khoyong-gi-re*, HE WILL COME. ཤོག་ *sho*, COME! མ་ཡོང་ *ma-yong*, DO NOT COME! ཁོ་འགྲོ་གི་འདུག་ *kho dro-k̄i-du*, HE IS GOING. ཁོ་ཕྱིན་པ་རེད། *kho chhim-pa-re*, HE HAS GONE.

26. As will have been noticed from the examples in this and the preceding chapters the verb is always placed at the end of the sentence. When there are two verbs in a sentence, one governing the other, the governing verb comes last; e.g., ཁྱོད་ཕྱིན་ཆོག་ག་ *khyö-chhin chhok-ka*, YOU MAY GO. ངས་ལས་ཀ་འདི་བྱེད་ཐུབ་ཀྱི་མ་རེད། *nge le-ka di che thup-kyi ma-re*, I CANNOT DO THIS WORK.

WORDS.

Mutton, (*lit.* sheep-flesh). ལུག་ཤ་ *luk-sha.*

Pork, (*lit.* pig-flesh). ཕག་ཤ་ *phak-sha.*

Darjeeling. རྡོ་རྗེ་གླིང་ *Dor-je-ling.*

Bazaar. ཁྲོམ་ *throm.*

Week. བདུན། བདུན་ཕྲག་ *dün; dün-thra.*

To assemble. འཚོགས་པ་ *tsho-pa.*

Sunday. གཟའ་ཉི་མ་ *sa-nyi-ma.*

Name. མིང་ *ming.*

To say, be called (of a name). ཟེར་བ་ *ser-wa.*

Before. སྔོན་ལ་ *ngen-la.*

Rinchengong. རིན་ཆེན་སྒང་ *rin-chen-gang.*

To make, build. བཟོ་བ་ *so-wa.*

To see. མཐོང་བ་ *thong-wa.*

At the time. སྐང་ལ་ *gang-la.*

Meaning, purpose. དོན་དག་ *tön-ta.*

Pleasant, comfortable. སྐྱིད་པོ་ *kyi-po.*

To look at, see. མིག་ལྟ་བ་ *mik-ta-wa.*

To arrive. སླེབ་པ་ *lep-pa.*

Village. གྲོང་གསེབ་ *trong-se.*

What. ག་རེ་ *ka-re.*

Lie. ཧམ་པ། *ham-pa.* ཀྱག་རྫུན་ *kyak-dzün.*

Whip. རྟའི་ལྕག་ *te-cha.*

New. གསར་པ་ *sa-pa.*

EXERCISE NO. 13.

The turnip has been eaten. ཉུང་མ་འདི་བཟས་སོང་། *nyung-ma di śe-song.*

The turnip will be eaten to-morrow. སང་ཉིན་ཉུང་མ་འདི་བཟས་ཡོང་། *sang-nyi nyung-ma di śe-ʒong.*

Eat this mutton, but do not eat this pork. ལུག་ཤ་འདི་ཟོ། ཕག་ཤ་འདི་མ་ཟ། *luk-sha di śo, phak-sha di ma-śa.*

Every week a large bazaar is held (*lit.* assembles) in Darjeeling. རྡོ་རྗེ་གླིང་ལ་བདུན་རེ་རེ་ལ་ཁྲོམ་ཆེན་པོ་རེ་འཚོགས་ཀྱི་ཡོད། *Dor-je-ling-la dün re-re-la throm chhem-po re tsho-kyi-yö.*

The large bazaar at (*lit.* of) Darjeeling will not be held to-morrow but will be held on Sunday. སང་ཉིན་རྡོ་རྗེ་གླིང་གི་ཁྲོམ་ཆེན་པོ་དེ་འཚོགས་ཀྱི་མ་རེད་གཟའ་ཉི་མ་འཚོགས་ཡོང་། *sang-nyi Dor-je-ling ki throm chhem-po te tsho-kyi ma-re śa-nyi-ma tsho-yong.*

He has almost finished building the house. ཁོས་ཁང་པ་འདི་བཟོས་ཚར་འགྲོ་འདུག། *khö khang-pa di śö tsha-tro-du.*

Did you see the man who came yesterday? ཁས་ས་ཡོང་མཁན་མི་དེ་ཁྱོད་རེས་ (ཀྱིས་) མཐོང་བྱུང་ངས། *khe-sa yong-khen mi te khyö-re thong chung-nge?*

I did not see (him). (He) came when I was out. ངས་མཐོང་མ་བྱུང་། ང་མེད་པའི་སྐང་ལ་ཡོང་ང་ (བ་) རེད། *nge thong-ma-chung, nga me-pe gang-la yong-nga-re.*

It is unnecessary for him to go Phari. (*Lit.* There is no reason of his having to go to Phari.) ཁོ་ཕག་རི་ལ་འགྲོ་དགོས་ཡའི་དོན་དག་ཡོད་པ་མ་རེད། *kho pha-ri-la dro go-ya tön-ta yo-wa ma-re.*

Have you ever been to Darjeeling? ཁྱོད་རྡོ་རྗེ་གླིང་ལ་འགྲོ་མྱོང་ངས། *khyö Dor-je-ling-la dro nyong-nge?*

No. (*lit.* not been). མ་མྱོང་ *ma-nyong.*

I am going to see whether Darjeeling is a pleasant place. རྡོ་རྗེ་གླིང་སྐྱིད་པོ་ཨ་ཡོད་ང་མིག་ལྟ་ག་ (བར་) འགྲོ་གི་ཡིན། *Dor-je-ling kyi-po a-yö nga mik ta-ka dro-ki-yin.*

EXERCISE NO. 14.

We have nearly reached the village. What is its name? (*Lit.* What is its name called)? Rinchengong. Have you ever been (*lit.* arrived) here before? Go on asking him about the road. Tell him that if he tells (any) lies he will be flogged. He is unable to come to Darjeeling. I am not allowed to buy pork. You ought to learn Tibetan.

CHAPTER VIII.

NUMERALS.

1. The numeral like the adjective follows the noun. If the noun is accompanied by an adjective the numeral follows the adjective. Thus, ང་ལ་རྟ་གསུམ་ (*three*) ཡོད། *nga-la ta sum yö*, I HAVE THREE PONIES. ང་ལ་རྟ་ཡག་པོ་གསུམ་ཡོད། *nga-la ta yak-po sum yö*, I HAVE THREE GOOD PONIES.

2. **The cardinal numerals** according to གྲངས་ཀྱི་ (or རྩིས་ཀྱི་) རྣམ་གྲངས་ *trang-kyi* (or *tsi-kyi*) *nam-trang*, i.e., arithmetical notation, are as follows :—

English figure.	Tibetan figure.	Tibetan word.	
		In Tibetan character.	In Roman character.
1	༡	གཅིག་	*chi.*
2	༢	གཉིས་	*nyi.*
3	༣	གསུམ་	*sum.*
4	༤	བཞི་	*shi.*
5	༥	ལྔ་	*nga.*
6	༦	དྲུག་	*truk.*
7	༧	བདུན་	*dün.*
8	༨	བརྒྱད་	*gye.*
9	༩	དགུ་	*gu.*

English figure.	Tibetan figure.	Tibetan word. In Tibetan character.	Tibetan word. In Roman character.
10	༡༠	བཅུ་ or བཅུ་ཐམ་པ་	*chu or chu-tham-pa.*
11	༡༡	བཅུ་གཅིག་	*chuk-chi.*
12	༡༢	བཅུ་གཉིས་	*chu-nyi.*
13	༡༣	བཅུ་གསུམ་	*chuk-sum.*
14	༡༤	བཅུ་བཞི་	*chup-shi.*
15	༡༥	བཅུ་ལྔ་	*chö-nga.*
16	༡༦	བཅུ་དྲུག་	*chu-truk.*
17	༡༧	བཅུ་བདུན་	*chup-dün.*
18	༡༨	བཅོ་བརྒྱད་	*chop-gye.*
19	༡༩	བཅུ་དགུ་	*chu-gu.*
20	༢༠	ཉི་ཤུ་ or ཉི་ཤུ་ ཐམ་པ་	*nyi-shu* or *nyi-shu tham-pa.*
21	༢༡	ཉི་ཤུ་རྩ་གཅིག་	*nyi shu tsak-chi.*
30	༣༠	སུམ་ཅུ་ or སུམ་ བཅུ་ཐམ་པ་	*sum-chu* or *sum-chu tham-pa.*
31	༣༡	སུམ་ཅུ་སོ་གཅིག་	*sum-chu so-chi.*
40	༤༠	བཞི་བཅུ་ or བཞི་ བཅུ་ཐམ་པ་	*ship-chu* or *ship-chu tham-pa.*
41	༤༡	བཞི་བཅུ་ཞེ་གཅིག་	*ship-chu she-chi.*
50	༥༠	ལྔ་བཅུ་ or ལྔ་བཅུ་ ཐམ་པ་	*ngap-chu* or *ngap-chu tham-pa.*
51	༥༡	ལྔ་བཅུ་ང་གཅིག་	*ngap-chu nga-chi.*
60	༦༠	དྲུག་ཅུ་ or དྲུག་ཅུ་ ཐམ་པ་	*truk-chu* or *truk-chu tham-pa.*

English figure.	Tibetan figure.	Tibetan word.	
		In Tibetan character.	In Roman character.
61	༦༡	དྲུག་ཅུ་རེ་གཅིག་	*truk-chu re-chi.*
70	༧༠	བདུན་ཅུ་ or བདུན་ཅུ་ཐམ་པ་	*dün-chu* or *dün-chu tham-pa.*
71	༧༡	བདུན་ཅུ་དོན་གཅིག་	*dün-chu tön-chi.*
80	༨༠	བརྒྱད་ཅུ་ or བརྒྱད་ཅུ་ཐམ་པ་	*gye-chu* or *gye-chu tham-pa.*
81	༨༡	བརྒྱད་ཅུ་གྱ་གཅིག་	*gye-chu gya-chi.*
90	༩༠	དགུ་བཅུ་ or དགུ་བཅུ་ཐམ་པ་	*gup-chu* or *gup-chu tham-pa.*
91	༩༡	དགུ་བཅུ་གོ་གཅིག་	*gup-chu ko-chi.*
100	༡༠༠	བརྒྱ་ or བརྒྱ་ཐམ་པ་	*gya* or *gya-tham-pa.*
101	༡༠༡	བརྒྱ་དང་གཅིག་	*gya-tang-chi.*
200	༢༠༠	ཉི་བརྒྱ་	*nyi-gya.*
300	༣༠༠	སུམ་བརྒྱ་	*sum-gya.*
400	༤༠༠	བཞི་བརྒྱ་	*ship-gya.*
500	༥༠༠	ལྔ་བརྒྱ་	*ngap-gya.*
1,000	༡༠༠༠	སྟོང་ཕྲག་ or སྟོང་	*tong-thra* or *tong.*
10,000	༡༠༠༠༠	ཁྲི་	*thri.*
100,000	༡༠༠༠༠༠	འབུམ་	*bum.*

English figure.	Tibetan figure.	Tibetan word.	
		In Tibetan character.	In Roman character.
1,000,000	༡༠༠༠༠༠༠	བྱེ་བ་	*c̄he-wa.**
10,000,000	༡༠༠༠༠༠༠༠	ས་ཡ་	*sa-ya.*
100,000,000	༡༠༠༠༠༠༠༠༠	དུང་འགྱུར་	*tung-gyur.*

Note *firstly*, that in the case of *tens* and *hundreds* when the smaller number follows the larger, addition is indicated, e.g., *fourteen=ten-four*; but when the larger number follows the smaller, multiplication is indicated, e.g., *forty=four-ten*. From the thousands upwards, when སྟོང་ཕྲག་ is used, the smaller number always follows the larger, e.g., སྟོང་ཕྲག་བཞི་ *tong-thra s̄hi*, FOUR THOUSAND. སྟོང་ཕྲག་གཅིག་དང་བཞི་ *tong-thra-chi tang s̄hi*, ONE THOUSAND AND FOUR. But with སྟོང་ the multiplying number precedes, e.g., བཞི་སྟོང་དང་བཞི་ *s̄hip-tonq tang s̄hi*, FOUR THOUSAND AND FOUR.

Note *secondly*, that in the case of multiplication གཉིས་ is spelt ཉི་, གསུམ་ is spelt སུམ་ and བཅུ་ as the second part of a compound, the first part of which ends in a consonant, is spelt ཅུ་

*It is curious that Jäschke and Sarat Chandra Das in their dictionaries give བྱེ་བ་ as ten millions and ས་ཡ་ as one million, but numerous Tibetans have been independently consulted and all agree that བྱེ་བ་ means one million and ས་ཡ་ ten millions.

Note *thirdly*, that the use of ཐམ་པ་ after full tens is optional. When used it implies completion, e.g., དྲུག་ཅུ་ཐམ་པ་ *truk-chu tham-pa=sixty and no more.* ཐམ་པ་ *tham-pa*, is also, but less commonly, used after complete hundreds, e.g., ཉི་བརྒྱ་ཐམ་པ་ *nyi-gya tham-pa*, and when so used has a similar sense of completion.

Note *fourthly*, the different conjunctions for each series between 20 and 100, i.e., for the 20 series, for the 30 series, for the 40 series and so on.

Note *fifthly*, that we can add the usual plural form ཚོ་ to ཁྲི། འབུམ། བྱེ་བ། and ས་ཡ་ and the higher numbers to make them plurals, but it is not necessary to do so. ཁྲི་ and འབུམ་ may take ཕྲག་ also as a plural form. ཚོ་ and ཕྲག་ seem to be used mainly in an indefinite sense, e.g., I HAVE SEVERAL TENS OF THOUSANDS OF SHEEP. ང་ལ་ལུག་ཁྲི་ཚོ་ཁ་ཤས་ཅིག་ཡོད། *nga-la luk thri-tsho kha-she chi yö.* THERE ARE TWO HUNDRED THOUSAND SOLDIERS IN THAT COUNTRY. ལུང་པ་དེ་ལ་དམག་མི་འབུམ་གཉིས་ཡོད། *lung-pa te-la ma-mi bum-nyi yö.*

The noun qualified by a numeral remains in the singular; e.g., four ponies=རྟ་བཞི་ not རྟ་ཚོ་བཞི་ (see also Chapter III, para. 12).

3. Alphabetical Notation ཀ་ཁའི་རྣམ་གྲངས་ *ka-khe nam-trang.*

This is used for paging books, for numbering the different volumes or parts in books, for Indices, etc. It is possible to count up to three hundred by it.

1 to 30	ཀ་	ཁ་	ག་	ང་	through	the	alphabet	to	ཨ་
31 „ 60	ཀི་	ཁི་	གི་	ངི་	„	„	„	„	ཨི་
61 „ 90	ཀུ་	ཁུ་	གུ་	ངུ་	„	„	„	„	ཨུ་
91 „ 120	ཀེ་	ཁེ་	གེ་	ངེ་	„	„	„	„	ཨེ་
121 „ 150	ཀོ་	ཁོ་	གོ་	ངོ་	„	„	„	„	ཨོ་
151 „ 180	ཀཱ་	ཁཱ་	གཱ་	ངཱ་	„	„	„	„	ཨཱ་
181 „ 210	ཀཱི་	ཁཱི་	གཱི་	ངཱི་	„	„	„	„	ཨཱི་
211 „ 240	ཀཱུ་	ཁཱུ་	གཱུ་	ངཱུ་	„	„	„	„	ཨཱུ་
241 „ 270	ཀཱེ་	ཁཱེ་	གཱེ་	ངཱེ་	„	„	„	„	ཨཱེ་
271 „ 300	ཀཱོ་	ཁཱོ་	གཱོ་	ངཱོ་	„	„	„	„	ཨཱོ་

4. In counting most weights or measures and some divisions of money གང་ *kang* is used instead of གཅིག་ *chi* and དོ་ *to* instead of གཉིས། *nyi.* Thus, སོར་གང་ *sor-kang,* ONE FINGER-BREADTH, སྲང་དོ་ *sang-to,* TWO SANG (i.e., three rupees five annas), but སྒོར་མོ་གཉིས་ *gor-mo nyi,* TWO RUPEES.

5. In some dialects ཁལ་ *khe* is used as *a score,* thus ཁལ་གཉིས་དང་ལྔ་ *khe-nyi tang nga* = forty-five (lit. *two score and five*). This method of counting is not used in Lhasa where ཁལ་ *khe* denotes a measure containing twenty བྲེ་ *tre* (a measure varying in different districts, but often equal to about one-fourteenth of a cubic foot).

6. **Ordinals.**—*The first* is translated by དང་པོ། *tang-po.* All subsequent numbers by adding པ་ *pa* to the cardinal; e.g., གཉིས་པ་ *nyi-pa*, THE SECOND, སུམ་ཅུ་སོ་གཅིག་པ་ *sum-chu so-chik-pa*, THE THIRTY-FIRST. In reckoning Tibetan dates the word ཚེས་པ་ *tshe-pa*, DATE is used and is followed by the *cardinal* number concerned, e.g., ཟླ་བ་གཉིས་པའི་ཚེས་པ་གསུམ་ *da-wa nyi-pe tshe-pa sum*, THE THIRD OF THE SECOND MONTH, lit. THE THREE-DATE OF THE SECOND MONTH. And ཚེས་པ་གཅིག་ *tshe-pa chi* is used for *the first*, not ཚེས་པ་དང་པོ་ *tshe-pa tang-po*. Also ཉེར་གཅིག་ *nyer-chi* or ཉི་ཤུ་གཅིག་ *nyi-shu chi* is used instead of ཉི་ཤུ་རྩ་གཅིག་ *nyi-shu tsa-chi* and ཉེར་གཉིས་ *nyer-nyi* or ཉི་ཤུ་གཉིས་ *nyi-shu nyi* instead of ཉི་ཤུ་རྩ་གཉིས་ *nyi-shu tsa-nyi*, and so on up to the twenty-ninth inclusive. The last day is གནམ་གང་ *nang-kang.* If the month contains less or more than thirty days, the omission or repetition of earlier dates is prescribed. The last day is always གནམ་གང་། For English dates the Hindustani word ཏ་རིཀ་ *tarikh* is used. A further difference is that ཉི་ཤུ་རྩག་ཅིག *nyi-shu tsa-chi*, ཉི་ཤུ་རྩ་གཉིས་ *nyi-shu tsa-nyi*, etc., are written for the 21st, 22nd, etc., instead of the forms noted above as used with ཚེས་པ ||

7. **Conjunctive Numerals.**—ཀ་ *ka* added to the cardinal up to ten inclusive denotes *conjunction.*, Thus, གཉིས་ཀ་ *nyi-ka*, BOTH, གསུམ་ཀ་ *sum-ka*, THE THREE TOGETHER, ALL THREE. In the colloquial ཅ་ *cha* often takes the place of ཀ་ *ka*, e.g., གཉིས་ཅ་ *nyi-cha*, གསུམ་ཅ་ *sum-cha*, etc. Thus, ངས་ཇག་པ་དྲུག་ཅ་ཟིན་ཡོད། *nye chak-pa truk-cha sim-yö*, I HAVE CAUGHT ALL SIX ROBBERS.

8. **Distributive Numerals.**—To express *distributive* numerals, i.e., *two at a time*, *five at a time*, etc., repeat the cardinal and add བྱས་ནས། *che-ne.* Thus, BRING THEM TO ME TWO AT A TIME ཁོང་ཚོ་ངའི་རྩ་ལ་གཉིས་གཉིས་བྱས་ནས་འཁྲིད་ཤོག། *khon-tsho nge-tsa-la nyi nyi che-ne thri-sho.* BRING THEM TO ME FOURTEEN AT A TIME. ཁོང་ཚོ་ངའི་རྩ་ལ་མི་བཅུ་བཞི་བཅུ་བཞི་བྱས་ནས་འཁྲིད་ཤོག། *khon-tsho nge-tsa-la mi chup-shi chup-shi che-ne thri-sho.*

To express *two each*, etc., omit the བྱས་ནས་ *che-ne*, e.g., GIVE EACH COOLY (LOAD-CARRIER) TWO TRANG-KAS (a trangka= four annas at present, 1917), དོས་པོ་འཁྱེར་མཁན་གྱི་མི་རེ་རེ་ལ་ཊཾ་ཀ་གཉིས་གཉིས་སྤྲོད། *to-po khe-khen-kyi mi re-re-la trang-ka nyi-nyi trö.* For *one at a time, each* or *one each* རེ་རེ་ *re-re* is used instead of གཅིག་གཅིག་, e.g., BRING THEM TO ME ONE AT A TIME, ཁོ་ཚོ་ངའི་རྩ་ལ་རེ་རེ་བྱས་ནས་འཁྲིད་ཤོག། *khon-tsho nge-tsa-la re-re che-ne thri-sho.* GIVE EACH COOLY ONE TRANG-KA དོས་པོ་འཁྱེར་མཁན་མི་ཧྲང་རེ་རེ་ལ་ཊཾ་ཀ་རེ་རེ་སྤྲོད། *to-po khe-khen mi-hrang re-re-la trang-ka re-re trö.* Where a cardinal numeral has more than two syllables the whole numeral is not repeated. The last two syllables may be repeated, e.g., GIVE EACH MAN THIRTY-FOUR RUPEES. མི་རེ་རེ་ལ་སྒོར་མོ་སུཾ་* ཅུ་སོ་བཞི་སོ་བཞི་སྤྲོད། *mi re-re-la gor-mo sum-chu sopshi sop-shi trö.* Or we may add རེ་ to the numeral instead of repeating, thus, མི་རེ་རེ་ལ་སྒོར་མོ་སུམ་ཅུ་སོ་བཞི་རེ་སྤྲོད། *mi re-re-la gor-mo sum-chu sop-shi re trö.*

---

*མ་ as a final consonant may always be written in this way.

9. **Fractions.**—HALF is ཕྱེད་ཀ། *chhe-ka*, ONE AND A HALF, is expressed by ཕྱེད་དང་གཉིས་ *chhe-tang nyi*, lit. *with a half (it is) two.* TWO AND A HALF=ཕྱེད་དང་གསུམ་ *chhe-tang sum*, and so on. གཅིག་དང་ཕྱེད་ཀ་ *chhik-tang chhe-ka* may be used instead of ཕྱེད་དང་གཉིས་ *chhe-tang nyi* and so on, but the latter forms are more common. ONE OF A PAIR is ཡ་གཅིག་ *ya-chi*, e.g., དཀར་ཡོལ་ཡ་གཅིག་ *ka-yö ya-chi*, ONE CUP OF A PAIR. གསུམ་ཆ་ *sum-chha*,=A THIRD and བཞི་ཆ་ *s̄hip-chha*=A FOURTH, and so on for other numbers; but fractions beyond one-fourth are not very much used in the colloquial language. Thus, མར་འདི་ང་ལ་གསུམ་ཆ་གཉིས་དགོས་པ་ཡོད། *ma-di nga-la sum-chha-nyi go-wa yö*, I WANT TWO-THIRDS OF THIS BUTTER. ཤ་འདི་ནས་བཞི་ཆ་གསུམ་ཁོ་ལ་འཁྱོད། *sha di-ne s̄hi- chha-sum kho-la trö.* GIVE HIM THREE QUARTERS OF THIS MEAT; རས་འདི་རིང་ཐུང་ལ་ཁྲུ་བཞི་དང་ཁྲུ་གཅིག་གི་བཞི་ཆ་གཅིག་ཡོད་པ་རེད། *re di ring-thung-la thru s̄hi tang thru chik-ki s̄hip-chha-chi yo-wa-re.* THIS COTTON CLOTH IS 4¼ CUBITS IN LENGTH.

10. **Alternative Numbers.**—*Two or three, seven or eight*, etc., are expressed by the two numbers being placed one directly after the other. They may also be followed by གཅིག་ *chi*; this is optional. Thus, སང་ཉིན་མི་ཡོང་མཁན་དྲུག་བདུན་གཅིག་ཡོད། མི་རེ་རེ་གིས་ཏ་གཉིས་གསུམ་འཁྲིད་སླེབ་ཡོང་། *sang-nyi mi yong-khen truk dün chi yö, mi re-re ki ta nyi sum thri lep-yong*, THERE ARE SIX OR

SEVEN MEN COMING TO-MORROW; EACH MAN WILL BRING (lit. WILL ARRIVE BRINGING)* TWO OR THREE PONIES.

11. ONCE, TWICE, THRICE, etc., are rendered by ཐེངས་ *theng* or ཚར་ *tshar*, both of which mean TIME, joined to the cardinal numeral. ONCE MORE is ད་རུང་ཐེངས་ (or ཚར་) གཅིག་ *ta-rung theng-chi* and so on, e.g., HE HAS COME HERE TWICE. ཁོ་མདས་ (འདི་རུ་) ཐེངས་གཉིས་བསླེབས་སོང་། *kho de theng-nyi lep-song.* I HAVE BEEN TO LHASA FIVE TIMES AND SHALL GO ONCE MORE, ང་ལྷ་ས་ལ་ཚར་ལྔ་བསླེབས་སྒྱོང་། ད་རུང་ཚར་གཅིག་འགྲོ་གི་ཡིན། *nga hla-sa-la tshar-nga lep-nyong; ta-rung tshar-chi dro-ki-yin.*

12. The methods of reckoning *addition*, *subtraction*, *multiplication* and *division* will clearly appear from the following examples. Thus, གཉིས་དང་བཞི་བྱས་ན་དྲུག། *nyi tang shi che-na tru*, IF TWO AND FOUR ARE MADE, SIX. བཅུ་ནས་གསུམ་བཏེན་ན་བདུན། *chu-ne sum then-na dün*, IF THREE BE DRAWN FROM TEN, SEVEN. གཉིས་ལྔ་ལ་བཅུ། *nyi nga-la chu*, TWO TO FIVE, TEN

---

*To bring in the sense of *to lead*= འཁྲིད་པ་ *thri-pa*; in the sense of *to carry*= འཁྱེར་བ *khyer-wa* or འཁུར་བ་ *khur-ua.*

བཅུ་གཉིས་དུམ་བུ་གསུམ་ལ་བཏང་ན་བཞི། *chu-nyi ṭum-p̍u sum-la tang-na sh̄i*, IF TWELVE BE SENT INTO THREE PIECES, FOUR.

WORDS.

Soldier=དམག་མི་ *ma-mi.*

Behind=རྒྱབ་ལ་ *gyap̍-la.*

Wall=རྩིག་པ་ *tsik̍-pa.*

That...over there (indicating a place in sight) = ཕ་གི་ *pha-gi.*

Jong-pen, i.e., Official in charge of a district=རྫོང་དཔོན་ *Jong-pen.* He lives in a fort called the Jong (རྫོང་), built strongly with thick walls on a hill or ridge rising a little above the surrounding plain or valley.

To come, arrive, *hon.* = ཕེབ་པ་ *phep̍-pa.*

Wages=གླ་ *la.*

Boot (of Tibetan manufacture) =ལྷམ་ཁོག་ *hlam-kho.*

Boot (of English or Indian manufacture)=འཇུ་ཏ་ *ju-ta, Hin.*

Is lost (*lit.* having been lost, is not) = བརླགས་ནས་མི་འདུག་ *la-ne min-du.*

Finger-breadth=སོར་ *sor.*

Span (from the tip of the thumb to the tip of the middle finger when extended) =མཐོ་ *tho.*

Cubit (from the point of the elbow to the tip of the middle finger)=ཁྲུ་ *thru.*

Day=ཉི་མ་ *nyi-ma.*

New=གསར་པ་ *sa-pa.*

New year=ལོ་གསར་ *losa.*

EXERCISE No. 13.

1383. ༡༣༨༣།

One thousand three hundred and eighty-three. སྟོང་ཕྲག་གཅིག་དང་སུམ་བརྒྱ་བརྒྱད་ཅུ་རྒྱ་གསུམ། *trong-thra chi tang sum-gya gye-chu gya-sum.*

There are thirty or forty Tibetan soldiers behind that wall over there. ཕ་གི་རྩིག་པའི་རྒྱབ་ལ་བོད་པའི་དམག་མི་སུམ་ཅུ་བཞི་བཅུ་ཡོད་པ་རེད། *pha-gi tsik-pe gyap-la pö-pe ma-mi sum-chu ship-chu yo-wa-re.*

The Jong-pen will arrive here on the twenty-fifth. ཉི་ཤུ་ལྔ་ (ཉེར་ལྔ་) ལ་མདངས་ (འདི་རུ་) རྫོང་དཔོན་ཕེབ་ཡོང་། *nyi-shu nga-la de Jong-pen phe-yong.*

The Jong-pen will arrive here on the twenty-fifth of the sixth month. ཟླ་བ་དྲུག་པའི་ཉི་ཤུ་ལྔ་ལ་རྫོང་དཔོན་མདངས་ཕེབ་ཡོང་། *da-wa truk-pe nyi-shu nga-la Jong-pen de phe-yong.*

The Jong-pen will arrive here on the twenty-fifth of June. དབྱིན་ཟླ་དྲུག་པའི་ཉི་ཤུ་ལྔ་ལ་རྫོང་དཔོན་མདངས་ཕེབ་ཡོང་། *in-da truk-pe nyi-shu nga-la Jong-pen de phe-yong.*

Both men are here. མི་གཉིས་ཀ་མདངས་ཡོད། *mi nyi-ka de yö.*

They ask (*lit.* request, "please give") one and a half rupees each as wages. གླ་སྒོར་མོ་ཕྱེད་དང་གཉིས་གཉིས་གནང་རོགས་གནང་ཞུ་གི་འདུག། *la gor-mo chhe-tang nyi-nyi nang-ro-nang shu-ki-du.*

Give them one rupee each (*lit.* give each man one rupee). མི་རེ་རེ་ལ་སྒོར་མོ་རེ་རེ་དེ་སྤྲོད། *mi re-re-la gor-mo re-re trö.*

One boot of this pair is lost. ལྷམ་ཁོག་འདིའི་ཡ་གཅིག་བརླགས་ནས་མི་འདུག། *hlam-kho di-iya-chi la-ne min-du.*

Three and five are eight. གསུམ་དང་ལྔ་བྱས་ན་བརྒྱད། *sum tang nga che-na gye.*

Seven from nine leaves two. དགུ་ནས་བདུན་འཐེན་ན་གཉིས། *gu-ne dün then-na nyi.*

Seven times two are fourteen. བདུན་གཉིས་ལ་བཅུ་བཞི། *dün nyi-la chup-shi.*

Five into fifteen is three. བཅོ་ལྔ་དུམ་བུ་ལྔ་ལ་བཏང་ན་གསུམ། *chö-nga tum-pu nga-la tang-na sum.*

Ten finger-breadths make one span. མཐོ་གང་ལ་སོར་བཅུ་ཡོད་པ་རེད། *tho kang-la sor chu yo-wa-re.*

Two spans make one cubit. ཁྲུ་གང་ལ་མཐོ་དོ་ཡོད་པ་རེད། *thru kang-la tho to yo-wa-re.*

Exercise No. 14.

Four into twenty-four is six. Five from thirteen leaves eight. 28,407. Twenty-eight thousand four hundred and seven. Bring an armful of wood. Five or six new traders are arriving daily (= each day) at Kalimpong. When the New Year is over larger numbers (= more) will come (= arrive).

CHAPTER IX.

PRONOUNS.

1. Pronouns are, generally speaking, declined in the same way as nouns. Exceptions to this general rule will be noted below under the pronouns concerned.

2. **Personal Pronouns.**—These are ང་ *nga* or ང་རང་ *nga-rang*, I; ཁྱོད་ *khyö* or ཁྱོད་རང *khyö-rang*, THOU, YOU; ཁོ་ *kho* or ཁོ་རང་ *kho-rang*, HE; མོ་ *mo*, SHE; e.g., WILL YOU STAY HERE TO-MORROW? ཁྱོད་སང་ཉིན་མདས་སྡོད་ཀྱི་ཡིན་པས། *khyö sang nyi 'de dö-kyi yim-pe?* The system of honorific language in Tibetan is dealt with below in Chapter XIII, but here it must be briefly noted that there is a separate class of words which must be used in reference to a person of good position, both when speaking to and when speaking of such person. Not to do so will lay the student open to the charge of speaking what is known in India as "Cooly language." Even if his rudeness is known to be merely the result of ignorance, every sentence he utters will jar upon the person he addresses.

3. As regards personal pronouns the ordinary honorific form for THOU, YOU is ཁྱེད་ *khye* or ཁྱེད་རང་ *khye-rang* and for HE or SHE ཁོང་ *khong*. Of course the first person has no honorific form; nor in the Lhasa colloquial language are any other forms used for it except ང་ *nga* or ང་རང་ *nga-rang;* though in the Tsang colloquail བདག་ *da* is used in the deprecatory sense of "your humble servant," and in letter-writing in Lhasa and elsewhere བདག་ *da* and ཕྲན་ *thren* and other terms are used in the same

sense. For Tibetan gentlemen of the higher ranks a higher form of honorific should be employed, namely སྐུ་གཞོགས་ *ku-sho*, or སྐུ་ངོས་ *ku-ngö*, the meaning of which corresponds somewhat to the English *sir*, e.g., WILL YOU STAY HERE TO-MORROW, SIR? སྐུ་གཞོགས་སང་ཉིན་མདས་བཞུགས་གདན་འཛག་གི་ཡིན་པས། *ku-sho sang-nyi de shu-den jaki yim-pe?* For Tibetan ladies ལྕམ་སྐུ་གཞོགས་ *cham-ku-sho* is used. These latter are used as honorifics for YOU, HE or SHE; i.e., both when speaking *to* or *of* a person. The secular heads of the Tibetan Government, i.e., Lon-chhens and Sha-pes should be addressed by their titles, i.e., བློན་ཆེན་ *lön-chhen* and ས་དབང་ཆེན་པོ་ *sa-wang chhem-po*, respectively, the latter being the Sha-pe's honorific designation The wives of these high ministers are addressed as ལྷ་ལྕམ་སྐུ་གཞོགས་ *hla-cham ku-sho.* Similarly, for a high Lama སྐུ་གཞོགས་རིན་པོ་ཆེ་ *ku-sho rim-po-chhe*, PRECIOUS SIR! and for a nun of high position རྗེ་བཙུན་སྐུ་གཞོགས་ *je-tsün ku-sho* should be employed, e.g., WILL YOU (addressing a nun of high rank) STAY HERE TO-MORROW? རྗེ་བཙུན་སྐུ་གཞོགས་སང་ཉིན་མདས་བཞུགས་གདན་འཛག་གི་ཡིན་པས། *je-tsün ku-sho sang-nyi de shu-den ja-ki yim-pe?* If the Lama be an *avatar*, i.e., an incarnation of Buddha, of whom there are several hundreds in Tibet, སྐུ་གཞོགས་སྤྲུལ་སྐུ་ *ku-sho trü-ku* should be used. སྤྲུལ་སྐུ་ *trü-ku* means *incarnation.*

4. As regards declension it should be noted that ཁྱོད། *khyö* ཁོ་ *kho* and མོ་ *mo* in addition to making their genitive and instrumental singular according to the rules of declension for nouns, also take རེའི་ *re* for the genitive and རེས་ *re* for the instrumental case, e.g., ཁྱོད་རེའི་ *khyö-re* or ཁྱོད་ཀྱི་ *khyö-kyi*;

ཁོས་ *khö* or ཁོ་རེས་ *kho-re*. Again when personal pronouns are used in a plural sense, their plural forms are as a rule, used even though the sense of plurality is clear from the context. On this point also they differ from nouns (see Cap. III, para. 12). Thus, ད་རིང་ཆུ་འབི་ལ་ཚོང་པ་མང་པོ་ཡོད་པ་རེད། སང་ཉིན་ཁོ་ཚོ་སྒང་ཁ་ཕག་རི་ལ་འགྲོ་གི་རེད། *te-ring chhum-bi la tshong-pa mang-po yo-wa-re sang-nyi khon-tsho gang-kha pha-ri-la dro-ki-re,* THERE IS A, LARGE NUMBER OF TRADERS AT CHUMBI TO-DAY; THEY WILL ALL GO TO PHARI TO-MORROW. When joined to numerals, however, the plural form is not used, e.g., ང་གཉིས་ *nga-nyi* WE TWO. The plural of སྐུ་གཞོགས་ *ku-sho* and of སྐུ་ངོས་ *ku-ngö* may either be formed with ཚོ་ *tsho* in the ordinary way or by adding ལྷན་རྒྱས་ *hlen-gye;* e.g., སྐུ་གཞོགས་ལྷན་རྒྱས་ *ku-sho hlen-gye.* The latter form gives a somewhat higher honorific than the former.

5. The pronoun *it*, when used in the nominative or accusative case, is not translated into Tibetan, e.g., དོམ་དེ་ག་པ་ཡོད། ངས་བསད་པ་ཡིན། *tom te ka-pa yö? nge se-pa yin,* WHERE IS THAT BEAR? I HAVE KILLED IT. But ཤིང་སྡོང་འདི་རེད། དེའི་ཡལ་ག་སྒང་ཁ་བཅད་ནས་མི་འདུག། *shing-dong di re, te-ï ye-ga gang-kha che-ne min-du,* THIS IS THE TREE; ITS BRANCHES HAVE ALL BEEN LOPPED OFF (lit. HAVING BEEN LOPPED, ARE NOT).

6. Any personal pronoun will usually be omitted, if its omission does not cause any ambiguity in the sentence, e.g., ད་རིང་ང་མདས་ (འདི་རུ) སྡོད་ཀྱི་ཡིན། སང་ཉིན་འགྲོ་གི་ཡིན། *te-ring nga de dö-kyi-yin sang-nyi dro-ki-yin.* I WILL STAY HERE TO-DAY; I SHALL GO TO-MORROW.

7. **Possessive Pronouns.**—The Possessive Pronoun is expressed by the genitive of the Personal Pronoun, e.g., ངའི་ *nge* MY, MINE; ཁྱོད་རེའི་ *khyö-re* ཁྱོད་ཀྱི་ *khyö-kyi*, YOUR, YOURS. ཁོའི་ *khö* ཁོ་རེའི *kho-re*, HIS. མོའི་ *mö* མོ་རེའི་ *mo-re*, HER, HERS. Thus, འདི་ངའི་རྟ་རེད། *di nge ta re*, THIS IS MY HORSE; རྟ་འདི་ངའི་རེད། *ta di nge re*, THIS HORSE IS MINE; ཁྱོད་རེའི་མེ་མདའ་འཁྱེར་ཤོག། *khyö-re men-da khe-sho*, BRING YOUR GUN.

8. **Reflective Pronouns.**—MYSELF, YOURSELF, etc., are expressed by རང་ *rang*, e.g., ཁྱོད་རེས་དེ་འདྲ་བྱས་ན་རང་ལ་སྐྱོན་ (*injury*) བྱས་ཡོང་། *khyö-re ten-dra che-na rang-la kyöṇ che-yong*. IF YOU ACT IN THAT WAY YOU WILL HURT YOURSELF. རང་གི་ *rang-gi* and སོ་སོའི་ *so-sö*, MY OWN, YOUR OWN, etc., have the meaning of *apna* in Hindustani. Thus, མི་སོ་སོས་རང་། གི་རྟ་ཡག་ཤོས་ཡིན་བསམས་པ་རེད། *mi so-sö rang-gi ta yak-shö yin sam-pa-re*. EACH MAN THOUGHT HIS OWN PONY THE BEST. This might also be rendered མི་རེ་རེས་སོ་སོའི་རྟ་ཡག་ཤོས་ཡིན་བསམས་པ་རེད། *mi re-re so-sö ta yak-shö yin sam-pa-re*.

9. Other meanings of རང་ connected with the above meaning of SELF are shown in the following examples:—

Yes. It is *quite* so. ལགས་དེ་ག་རང་རེད། *la ta-ka rang re*.

This is *really* difficult. འདི་དཀའ་ལས་ཁག་ཐག་ཆོད་རང་འདུག་ *di ka-le khak-thak-chhö rang du*.

Your *mere* coming here has done good (*lit.*) by your mere coming here good has resulted. ཁྱོད་རང་མདས་ (འདིར་) ཡོང་བ་རང་གིས་ཡག་པོ་བྱུང་། *khyö-rang de yong-nga rang-gi yak-po chung*.

རང་ is often also used with negatives in the sense of VERY, e.g.—

Do not drink *very* much beer. ཆང་མང་པོ་རང་མ་འཐུང་། *chhang mang-po rang ma-tḵung.*

10. **Reciprocal Pronouns.**—EACH OTHER, ONE ANOTHER, *are expressed* by གཅིག་གཅིག་ *chi-chi*, e.g., ཁོ་རང་ཚོ་གཅིག་གིས་གཅིག་བརྡུངས་ང་ (པ་) རེད། *kho-rang-tsho chiḵ-ḵi-cḵi dung-nga-re*, THEY BEAT EACH OTHER. (Lit. *by one to one, they beat*).

11. **Demonstrative Pronouns.**—THIS is rendered by འདི་ *di* and THAT by དེ་ *te*, but when either THIS or THAT refers to a noun previousy mentioned དེ་ *te* is used, e.g., དེ་ཡག་པོ་རེད། *te yaḵ-po re*, THIS ONE (previously mentioned) IS GOOD. Both འདི་ and དེ་ follow the noun or adjective which they qualify, and take the case-inflection instead of the noun or adjective. They are also used by themselves, apart from nouns, e.g., the example just given, and འདི་ངའི་ཡིན། *dinge yin*, THIS IS MINE.

12. Other demonstrative pronouns in common use are འདི་རང་ *di-rang*, THIS VERY, དེ་རང་ *te-rang*, THAT VERY, emphatic forms of *this* and *that* respectively, also ད་ག་ *ta-ḵa* and ད་ག་རང་ *ta-ḵa-rang*, with the same meaning; e.g., IS THIS THE VERY MAN THAT I SAW YESTERDAY? མི་འདི་ཁས་ས་ངས་མཐོང་ང་ (བ་) དེ་རང་རེད་པས། *mi di khe-sa nge thong-nga te-rang re-pe?* YES, IT IS THE VERY SAME. ལགས་ད་ག་རང་རེད། *la ta-ḵa-rang re.* Also, ཡ་གི་ *ya-gi*, THAT UP THERE, མ་གི་ *ma-gi*, THAT

DOWN THERE, and ཕ་གི་ *pha-gi*, THAT OVER THERE, THAT YONDER; these latter three forms being used with or without དེ་ as per the following examples. ཡ་གི་མི་དེ་ཚོ་མར་ཡོང་གི་འདུག། *ya-gi mi ten-tsho ma yong-gi-du*, THOSE MEN UP THERE ARE COMING DOWN. འདི་ངའི་ཞྭ་མོ་ཡིན། ཕ་གི་ཁོའི་རེད། *di nge sha-mo yin; pha-gi khö re*, THIS IS MY HAT; THAT ONE OVER THERE IS HIS.

Also འདི་འདྲ་ *din-dra*, OF THIS KIND, LIKE THIS and དེ་འདྲ་ *ten-dra*, OF THAT KIND, LIKE THAT. ཅ་ལག་ (ཆ་ལག) འདི་འདྲ་འཚོང་རྒྱུ་ཡོད་པས། *cha-la din-dra tshong-gyu yö-pe*, HAVE YOU GOT THINGS OF THIS KIND FOR SALE? འདི་འདྲ་ also has the sense of WHAT in interjections, e.g., WHAT A COLD DAY! འདི་འདྲའི་གནམ་གྲང་ང་ལ། *din-dre nam trang-nga-la!* The same sense may also be expressed without འདི་འདྲ་ e.g., WHAT A LARGE HORSE! རྟ་དེ་ཆེ་བ་ལ་ *ta te chhe-a-la!*

13. As with the personal pronouns, so also འདི་ *di* and དེ་ *te* usually take their plural forms, even when the sense is clear from the context, e.g., མི་དེ་ཚོ་སྒང་ཁ་ཤོག་བྱེས་ (བྱེད་)། *mi ten-tsho gang-kha sho chi*, CALL (lit. MAKE COME) ALL THOSE MEN. But not when joined to numerals, e.g., མི་དེ་གཉིས་ཤོག་བྱེས་ (བྱེད་)། *mi te-nyi sho chi*, CALL THOSE TWO MEN.

14. **Relative Pronouns.**—Except ག་རེ་ *ka-re* and གང་ *kang*, WHAT, WHICH relative pronouns are not used. ག་རེ་ is used more often than གང་ in the Lhasa colloquial language. The relative clauses must be expressed by participial clauses, in which ག་རེ་ or གང་ may be used, but more often are not used.

The participle is treated as an adjective, being put in the genitive, if it precedes the noun, and if it follows the noun, taking the case-inflection of the latter.

15. Thus, དྲེ་ངས་མཐོང་བ་དེ་བཙོང་ཚར་ར་ (བ་) རེད། *tre nge thong-nga te tsong tshar-ra re*, THE MULE, WHICH I SAW, HAS BEEN SOLD. Again, ཁྱོད་རེའི་ཁྱི་རྐུན་མ་རྐུ་མཁན་དེ་ངས་ཟིན་ཡོད། *khyö-re khyi ku-ma ku-khen te nge śun-yö.* I HAVE CAUGHT THE MAN WHO STOLE YOUR DOG. (Lit. *I have caught-the-your-dog-stealer*). Again, ལྷ་ས་ནས་ཡོང་མཁན་གྱི་དམག་མི་དེ་ཚོ་ཕར་ལོག་སོང་། *hla-sa ne yong-khen-kyi ma-mi ten-tsho pha lok-song.* THE SOLDIERS WHO CAME FROM LHASA HAVE GONE BACK THERE. (Lit. *the-from-Lhasa-coming soldiers have gone back there*). Once more, བོད་པའི་དམག་མིས་རྩིག་པ་བཟོས་པ་དེ་བཤིག་ནས་མི་འདུག། *pö-pe ma-mi tsik-pa śö-pa te shik-ne min-du.* THE WALL WHICH WAS BUILT BY TIBETAN SOLDIERS HAS BEEN DEMOLISHED. (Lit. *the-by-the-Tibetans-built wall having been demolished, is not*). The distinction between the participles in མཁན་ *khen* and པ་ *pa* respectively has been noted above in Cap. VI. para. 19.

16. **Correlative Pronouns.**—I WHO, YOU WHO, HE WHO, WHOEVER, THAT WHICH, WHAT, WHATEVER, etc., are rendered either by the Agentive Participles, or by the interrogative pronoun with the conditional tense (Cap. VI, para. 15) followed by ཡང་ or ཀྱང་ or by both methods combined, or finally by using a causative sentence with ཙང་ AS BECAUSE, e.g.—

I WHO HAVE BEEN THERE KNOW THIS. ང་ཕ་གི་སླེབས་མྱོང་ཙང་ངས་ཤེས་ཀྱི་ཡོད། *nga pha-gi leṕ nyong-tsang nge shing-gi yö-*

HE WHO BROUGHT THE LETTER YESTERDAY IS MY MAN. ཁས་ས་ཡི་གེ་འཁྱེར་ཡོང་ངན་ (མཁན་) དེ་ངའི་མི་ཡིན། *khe-sa yi-ge khe yong-ngen te nge mi yin.*

LISTEN TO WHAT (i.e., THAT WHICH) I SAY. ངས་ལབ་པ་དེ་ཉོན། *nge lap-pa te nyön.*

WHOEVER COMES, MUST COME TO-DAY. སུ་ཡོང་ན་ཡང་དེ་རིང་ཡོང་དགོས་པ་རེད། *su yong-na-yang te-ring yong go-wa-re.*

WHOEVER IS AFRAID, MAY STAY HERE. སུ་ཞེད་ངན་ (མཁན་) ཡོད་ན་ཡང་མདངས་ (འདི་དུ་) བསྡད་ཆོག་གི་རེད། *su she-ngen yö-na yang de de-chho ki-re.*

17. **Interrogative Pronouns.**—These are སུ་ *su*, WHO! ག་རེ་ *ka-re* (and less often གང་ *kang*), WHAT ? WHICH ? ག་གི་ *ka-ki* WHICH OF THEM ? WHICH OF THESE ? WHICH OF THOSE ? ག་འདྲས་ *kan-dre*, OF WHAT KIND ? Examples of their use are as follow: འདི་སུའི་རྟ་རེད། *di sü ta re ?* or རྟ་འདི་སུའི་རེད། *tadisü re ?* WHOSE PONY IS THIS ? ཁྱོད་རེའི་མིང་ལ་ག་རེ་ཟེར་གྱི་ཡོད། *khyö-re ming-la ka-re śi-kyi-yö ?* WHAT IS YOUR NAME ? (Lit. WHAT IS SAID TO YOUR NAME?) སྒང་ཏོག་གི་ལམ་ཀ་ག་གི་རེད། *Gang-tok-kilang-ka ka-ki re*, WHICH OF THESE ROADS IS THE ONE TO GANGTOK. ད་ལོ་སྟོན་ཐོག་ག་འདྲས་འདུག་ *ta lo tön-tho kan-dre du*, WHAT ARE THE CROPS LIKE THIS YEAR ? རྟ་འདི་ཚོ་ནས་ངའི་རྟ་ག་གི་རེད། *ta di-tsho ne nge ta ka-ki re*, WHICH OF THESE PONIES IS MINE ? The interrogative form of the verb may also be used, e.g., ཁྱོད་རེའི་མིང་ལ་ག་རེ་ཟེར་གྱི་ཡོད་པ། *khyö-reming la ka-re śi-ki yö-pa ?* Both སུ

and ཀ་རེ་ are declined in the singular, e.g., འདི་ཀ་རེས་བཟོས་པ་རེད། *di ḳa-re sö-pa re?* OF WHAT SUBSTANCE IS THIS MADE? (Lit. FROM WHAT HAS THIS BEEN MADE?) Their plurals are formed by repeating them once; e.g., ཅ་ (ཆ་) ལག་དེ་ཚོ་ཀ་རེ་ཀ་རེ་རེད། *cha-la ten-tsho ḳa-re ḳa-re re?* WHAT ARE THOSE THINGS AT མི་དེ་ཚོ་སུ་སུ་རེད། *mi ten-tsho su-su re?* WHO ARE THOSE MEN? འདི་ཀ་རེས་ཀ་རེས་བཟོས་པ་རེད། *di ḳa-re ḳa-re sö-pa re?* OF WHAT SUBSTANCES IS THIS MADE? It will be noticed from the above examples that the interrogative pronoun stands in the sentence immediately before the verb, except when in the genitive, in which latter case it may precede the noun which it qualifies. WHICH OF YOU WILL GO WITH ME? ང་དང་མཉམ་དུ་ཁྱོད་ཚོ་སུ་འགྲོ་གི་ཡིན། *nga tang nyam-tu khyön-tsho su dro-ḳi-yin.* WHO WILL SHOW ME THE ROAD? ང་ལ་ལམ་ཀ་སུས་སྟོན་གྱི་རེད། *nga-la lang-ka sü tön-ḳyi-re.*

18. **Indefinite Pronouns.**—Among these we find the following in frequent use.—

- རེ་རེ། *re-re*, རེ། *re*, སོ་སོ། *so-so*, EACH.
- ཚང་མ། *tshang-ma*, ཐམས་ཅད། *tham-che*, སྒང་ཁ། *gang-kha*, ALL, EVERY.
- ཁ་ཤས། *kha-she*, SOME.
- སུ་ཡང་། *su-yang*, WHOEVER.
- སུ་ཡང་། *su-yang*, with a negative=NOBODY.
- ཀ་རེ་......ཡང་། *ḳa-re....yang*, with the verb in the conditional tense intervening, ANYTHING THAT, WHATEVER.
- ཀ་རེ་ཞིག་......ཡང་ *ka-re-shiḳ....yang*, ANYTHING THAT, WHATEVER. The addition of the ཞིག་ makes the meaning more emphatic.

ག་གེ་ (གང་ཡང་) *ka-ke* (with a negative) NOTHING.

གཅིག་ཡང་ *chik-yang*, with a negative=*lit.* NOT EVEN ONE, i.e., NOBODY AT ALL, NOTHING AT ALL.

གཞན་པ། *shem-pa*, ཡན་པ། *yem-pa*, OTHER.

གཞན་པ་གཅིག་ *shem-pa chi*, ཡན་པ་གཅིག་ *yem-pa chi*, ANOTHER.

གཅིག་གཅིག་ *chi-chi*, ONE ANOTHER, EACH OTHER.

གཅིག་པོ། *chik-po*, THE ONLY, THE SOLE.

གཅིག་པ། *chik-pa*, THE SAME.

མི་གཅིག་པ། *mi-chik-pa*, DIFFERENT, VARIOUS.

གཅིག་ཡང་། *chik-yang*, with a negative NOT EVEN ONE, NOT A SINGLE ONE.

Others will be found in the Dictionary and, being used in an ordinary way, present no difficulty. Indefinite pronouns can be employed either with nouns or alone.

19. The following examples will show how the above are used :—

Some men have arrived. མི་ཁ་ཤས་བསླེབས་བྱུང་། *mikha-she lep-chung.*

Give each man one rupee. མི་རེ་རེ་ལ་སྒོར་མོ་རེ་རེ་སྤྲོད་ཤོག། *mi re-re-la gor-mo re-re trö-sho.*

Any body who goes will die. སུ་ཕྱིན་ན་ཡང་ (or སུ་ཕྱིན་ནས་) ཤི་གི་རེད། *su chhin-na-yang* (or *su chhin-ne*) *shi-ki-re.*

There is nobody at Kampa Jong now-a-days. ད་རིང་སང་གམ་པ་རྫོང་ལ་སུ་ཡང་མི་འདུག། *te-ring-sang kam-pa dzong-la su-yang min-du.*

Burn anything that is in this house. ཁང་པ་འདིའི་ནང་ལ་ག་རེ་འདུག་ན་ཡང་ (or ག་རེ་འདུག་ནས་) སྲག་ (tra, སྲེག་) ཤོག། *khang-pa di-ï nang-la ka-re duk-na-yang* (*ka-re duk-ne*) *tra-sho.*

There is nothing in it. དེའི་ནང་ལ་ག་གའི་ (གང་ཡང་) མི་འདུག། *le-i nang-la ka-ke min-du.*

There is not a single person in this house. ཁང་པ་འདིའི་ནང་ལ་མི་གཅིག་ཡང་ཡོད་པ་མ་རེད། *khang-pa di-i nang-la mi chik-yang yo-wa ma-re.*

Call another servant. གཡོག་པོ་གཞན་པ་གཅིག་ཤོག་ཁྲིས་ (ཁྲིད་)། *yok-po shem-pa-chi sho chi.*

The others are all absent. གཞན་པ་སྒང་ཁ་བསྡད་མི་འདུག། *shem-pa gang-kha de min-du.*

This servant does not know the work; call another one. གཡོག་པོ་འདིས་ལས་ཀ་ཤེས་ཀྱི་མི་འདུག། གཞན་པ་གཅིག་ཤོག་ཁྲིས་ (ཁྲིད་)། *yok-po di le-ka shing-gi min-du ; shem-pa-chi sho chi.*

Boys, do not beat each other! པུ་གུ་ཚོ་གཅིག་གིས་གཅིག་ལ་མ་རྡུང་ཞིག། *pu-gu tsho chik-ki chik-la ma-dung-shi.*

Out of ten men I am the only one left. མི་བཅུའི་དཀྱིལ་ནས་ང་གཅིག་པོ་ལས་ལྷུང་། *mi chü kyi-ne nga chik-po le-chung.*

The religions of China and Tibet are the same. རྒྱ་བོད་གཉིས་ཀྱི་ཆོས་ལུགས་གཅིག་པ་རེད། *gya-pö nyi-kyi-chhö-lu chik-pa re.*

Various kinds of people come together in this bazaar. ཁྲོམ་འདི་ལ་མི་སྣ་མི་གཅིག་པ་མང་པོ་འཛོམས་ཀྱི་འདུག། *throm di-la mi-na mi-chik-pa mang-po dzóm-kyi-du.*

There is not even one with whom I am acquainted. ངས་ངོ་ཤེས་པ་གཅིག་ཡང་མི་འདུག། *nge ngo-shem pa chik-yang min-du.*

WORDS.

To say, tell, *hon.* = གསུང་བ་ *sung-wa.*

Syce, groom = ཆིབས་དཔོན་ *chhik-pön.*

Ghoom, a village near Darjeeling = ཀུམ་པ་རི་ *kum-pa-ri.*

Horse, *hon.* = ཆིག་པ་ (ཆིབས་པ་) *chhik-pa.*

To ride = ཞོན་པ་ *shöm-pa.*

To ride, *hon.* = འཆིབ་པ་ *chhip-pa.*

Behind = གཤུག་ལ་ *shu-la.*

To have a fight with = བདུང་རེས་བྱེད་པ་ *dung-re che-pa.*

To be drunk = ར་བཟི་བ། ར་བཟི་བྱེད་པ *ra-si-wa, rap-si che-pa.*

EXERCISE NO. 15.

Whose pony is that down there? མ་གི་སུའི་རྟ་རེད། *ma-gi sü ta re?*

Please tell your syce to take both ponies to Ghoom. ཁྱེད་རང་གི་ཆིབས་དཔོན་ལ་ཆིག་པ་ (ཆིབས་པ་) གཉིས་ཀ་ཀུམ་པ་རི་ལ་འཁྲིད་སོང་གསུང་རོགས་གནང་། *khye-rang-ki chhik-pön la chhik-pa nyi-ka kum-pa-ri la thri-song sung-ro-nang.*

We (two) have each riden ponies to Darjeeling (*lit.* have gone riding, etc.). ང་གཉིས་ཆིག་ (ཆིབས་) པ་བཅིབས་ནས་རྡོ་རྗེ་གླིང་ལ་ཕེབས་པ་ཡིན། *nga-nyi chhik-pa chip-ne Dor-je-ling-la phe-pa-yin.*

[Note that the honorific forms are employed in deference to the person who has ridden with me.]

Those are the traders who have come from Lhasa. ལྷ་ས་ནས་ཡོང་མཁན་གྱི་ཚོང་པ་དེ་ཚོ་རེད། *hla-sa ne yong-khen-kyi tshong-pa ten-tsho re.*

The others are coming behind. གཞན་པ་ཚོ་གཞུག་ལ་ཡོང་གི་ཡོད་པ་རེད། *shem-pa-tsho shu-la yong-ki yo-wa-re.*

They have been fighting with each other on the way. ཁོ་ཚོས་ལམ་ཀ་ལ་གཅིག་གིས་གཅིག་བརྡུང་རེས་བྱས་པ་རེད། *khon-tshö lang-ka-la chik-ki-chi dung-re che-pa-re.*

Probably they were all drunk. ཁོ་ཚོ་སྒང་ཁས་ར་བཟི་བྱས་པ་ཡིན་འགྲོ། *khon-tsho gang-khe-rap-si che-pa yin-tro.*

EXERCISE NO. 16.

What is the name of the trader who came yesterday? What things has he got? This is the very man that stole my pony. Nobody has arrived to-day. Those who come to-morrow will stay some days.

CHAPTER X.

ADVERBS.

1. Adverbs are formed in three ways, namely :—

(*a*) PRIMITIVE, such as ད་ལྟ་ *tan-da*, NOW, ལམ་སང་ *lam-sang*, AT ONCE and ཡང་སྐྱར་ *yang-kyar*, AGAIN. Most adverbs of time belong to this form.

(*b*) THOSE FORMED FROM NOUNS OR PRONOUNS, such as འདི་ནས་ *di-ne*, FROM HERE (lit. FROM THIS) ; ཁ་ནས་ *kha-ne*, ORALLY (lit. FROM MOUTH) ; and རྒྱབ་ལ་ *gyap-la*, BEHIND (lit. AT THE BACK). Many adverbs of place are formed in this way.

(*c*) THOSE FORMED FROM ADJECTIVES, as in English *quick*, *quickly*, etc. These in colloquial Tibetan take the form either of the adjective itself or of the adjective with བྱས་ནས་ *che-ne* added. Thus : མགྱོགས་པོ་རྒྱུག། *gyok-po gyu*, GO QUICKLY ; དྲང་པོ་བྱས་ནས་ཁ་མཆུ་འདི་ཐག་གཅོད་པ་གནང་། *trang-po che-ne kham-chhu di tha-chö-pa-nang*, DECIDE THIS CASE (LAW-SUIT) FAIRLY.

2. Adverbs used in the ordinary way require no special mention here ; they will be found in the Dictionary. Those which are formed or used in peculiar ways will now be noticed. Adverbs always precede the verb in a sentence. Those used interrogatively stand immediately before the verb in most cases, e.g., མི་ག་ཚོད་འདུག། *mi ka-tshö du?* HOW MANY MEN ARE HERE ?

3. (*a*) ABOUT, SOME = ཙ་ (ཙམ་) *tsa*, but གཅིག་ is sometimes added. Thus, མི་བཅུ་ཙ་ (ཙམ་) གཅིག། *mi chu-tsa chi*, ABOUT TEN MEN.

(*b*) EVEN, NOT EVEN. ཡང་ *yang* = EVEN, ALSO, and when accompanied by a negative means NOT EVEN and is used as in the following examples: ཁོ་ཚོས་མི་མདའ་རྒྱབ་ཡང་ཤེས་ཀྱི་མི་འདུག། *khon-tshö men-da gya-yang shing-gi min-du.* THEY DO NOT EVEN KNOW HOW TO FIRE A GUN. The emphasis is on the word *fire* རྒྱབ་ (gya) which is immediately followed by ཡང་ *yang* in the Tibetan sentence.

(*c*) HERE = མདས་ (འདི་རུ་) *de*; THERE = དད་ (དེ་རུ་) *te*. But instead of དད་ (དེ་རུ་) *te* ཕ་གི་ *pha-gi*, OVER THERE is frequently used. And if the HERE or the THERE is higher up or lower down than the person speaking ཡ་གི་ *ya-gi*, UP HERE, UP THERE, or མ་གི་ *ma-gi*, DOWN HERE, DOWN THERE should be employed. Thus, མི་གཅིག་ཡ་གི་ཡོད། *mi-chi ya-gi yö*, THERE IS A MAN THERE (i.e., *higher up*). Similarly with verbs of coming or going to or from Tibet, we should say "he is coming *down from* Tibet"; "he is going *up to* Tibet." Thus: ཚོང་པ་ཚོ་བོད་ལ་ཡར་ལོག་ག་ (པ་) རེད། *tshong-pa-tsho pö-la ya lok-ka-re.* THE TRADERS HAVE GONE BACK (UP) TO TIBET.

(*d*) HOW FAR. This is rendered by ཐག་རིང་ཐུང་ག་ཚོད། *lit.* HOW MUCH DISTANCE, e.g., ཁྱོད་རེའི་ལུང་པ་ལྷ་ས་ནས་ཐག་རིང་ཐུང་ག་ཚོད་ཡོད། *khyö-re lung-pa hla-sa-ne tha-ring-thung ka-tshö-yö?* HOW FAR IS YOUR COUNTRY FROM LHASA?

(*e*) How long, i.e., how many days, months, years, etc., is rendered thus: HOW MANY MONTHS IS IT SINCE YOU CAME? ཁྱོད་རང་ཡོང་ནས་ཟླ་བ་ག་ཚོད་སོང་། *khyö-rang yong-ne da-wa ka-tshö song?* YOU HAVING COME HOW MANY MONTHS HAVE GONE?

(*f*) HOW MUCH? HOW MANY?=ག་ཚོད་, e.g., HOW MANY MEN ARE THERE? མི་ག་ཚོད་འདུག། *mi ka-tshö-du?* But is referring to the time of day ག་ཚོད་ corresponds to WHAT, e.g., WHAT O'CLOCK IS IT? ཆུ་ཚོད་ག་ཚོད་རེད། *chhu-tshö ka-tshö re.*

(*g*) MUCH, MANY ཞེ་པོ་རང་། *she-po-rang* མང་པོ་རང་ *mang-po-rang.* Used only with a negative in the sense of NOT MUCH, NOT MANY. Thus, ལུང་པ་མདས་ (འདི་ལ་) ཁང་པ་མང་པོ་རང་མི་འདུག། *lung-pa de khang-pa mang-po-rang min-du,* THERE ARE NOT MANY HOUSES IN THIS TRACT OF COUNTRY.

(*h*) NOT AT ALL, NEVER is translated by a negative accompanied by ཙ་ནས་ *tsa-ne* or མ་ནས། *ma-ne.* Thus, འདི་ཙ་ནས་ (or མ་ནས་) ཡག་པོ་མི་འདུག། *di tsa-ne yak-po min-du,* THIS IS NOT AT ALL GOOD. ངས་ཤ་ཙ་ནས་ཟ་མ་མྱོང་། *nge sha tsa-ne sa ma nyong.* I HAVE NEVER EATEN MEAT. Also by བེད་ or བེད་དེ་ followed by a negative, e.g., བེད་དེ་ཡོད་པ་མ་རེད། *be-ts yo-wa-ma-re,* THERE ARE NONE AT ALL. བེད་དེ་ is more emphatic than བེད།

(*i*) OF COURSE—BUT, INDEED—BUT. These have been dealt with under the verb (Cap. VII, para. 23).

(*j*) ONLY, ENTIRELY, ALL, are often translated by ཤ་སྟག་ which immediately precedes the verb, e.g., མི་ཤ་སྟག་རེད། *mi sha-ta re*, THERE ARE MEN ONLY; (i.e., there are no animals, etc.) ཅ་ (ཆ་) ལག་འདི་ཚོ་ཡག་པོ་ཤ་སྟག་འདུག། *cha-la di-tsho yak-po sha-ta du*, THESE THINGS ARE ALL GOOD; (i.e., *there are no bad things among them*).

(*k*) SO, SO MUCH is often rendered by འདི་འདྲ་ *lit.* THIS KIND or by དེ་འདྲ་ *lit.* OF THAT KIND, e.g., སྐད་ཆེན་པོ་འདི་འདྲ་མ་རྒྱག། *ke chhem-po din-dra ma-gya*. DO NOT TALK LOUDLY, DO NOT MAKE SUCH A NOISE TALKING.

(*l*) TOO is expressed by དྲག་པ་ *trak-pa*, joined as a verb to the root of the adjective concerned, e.g., འཁར་རྒྱུག་ འདི་རིང་དྲག་ག་ (པ་) རེད། *khar-gyu di ring trak-ka re*, THIS STICK IS TOO LONG. འཁར་རྒྱུག་=*stick*; རིང་པོ་=*long*.

(*m*) VERY may be expressed by ཧ་ཅང་ *ha-chang* or by ཐག་ཆོད་ *thak-chho* added to the root of the adjective, or in some cases by repeating the adjective once in a raised tone of voice. Thus, VERY GREAT may be expressed by ཧ་ཅང་ཆེན་པོ་ *ha-chang chhem-po* or by ཆེ་ཐག་ཆོད་ *chhe-thak-chhö* or by ཆེན་པོ་ཆེན་པོ། *chhem-po chhem-po*. Here, however, it should be noticed that ཆུང་ཆུང་ *chhung-chhung* means simply SMALL; ཐུང་ཐུང་ *thung-thung*, SHORT; ཉུང་ཉུང་ *nyung-nyung*, FEW and so with a few others. In these latter VERY is not implied. The method of expressing VERY by raising the tone of the voice is found also in Nepalese (Khas-kura), with which Tibetan has a few grammatical affinities.

(*n*) WHY. This is frequently rendered by གང་ལ་ *lit.* FOR WHAT, e.g., ཁྱོད་ཁས་ས་གང་ལ་མ་ཡོང་ང་ *khyö-khe-sa kang-la ma yong nga?* WHY DID YOU NOT COME YESTERDAY? or by turning the sentence; thus, ཁྱོད་ཁས་ས་མ་ཡོང་བའི་དོན་དག་ག་རེ་རེད། *khyö khe-sa ma yong-nge tön-ta ka-re re?* (*Lit.* WHAT IS THE MEANING OF YOUR NOT COMING YESTERDAY?)

4. The treatment of negatives has been explained when dealing with verbs (see Cap. V, para. 3, Cap. VI, para. 13, and Cap. VII, paras. 1 and 2), and need not be repeated here.

WORDS.

Far off = ཐག་རིང་པོ་ *tha ring-po.*

Animal = སེམས་ཅན་ *sem-chen.*

Field glasses; (*lit.* distance glass) = རྒྱང་ཤེལ་ *gyang-she.*

To recognise = ངོ་ཤེས་པ་ *ngo-she-pa.*

Cold, *adj.* = གྲང་མོ་ *trang-mo.*

Indian = རྒྱ་གར་ *gya-ka.*

To fit (of clothes) = འགྲིག་པ་ *drik-pa.*

EXERCISE No. 17.

What are those animals up there? །ཡ་གི་སེམས་ཅན་དེ་ཚོག་རེ་ག་རེ་རེད། *ya-gi sem-chen te-tsho ka-re ka-re re.*

They are a very long way off. ཐག་རིང་ཐག་ཆོད་འདུག། *tha-ring thak-chhö du.*

I cannot make them out even with field-glasses. རྒྱང་ཤེལ་ལ་བལྟས་ན་ཡང་ངས་ངོ་ཤེས་ཀྱི་མི་འདུག། *gyang-she-la te-na-yang nge ngo-shing-gi min-du.*

There are no Indians at all here, as it is too cold for them. མདས་ (འདི་རུ་) གྲང་དྲག་ཚང་རྒྱ་གར་ཚ་ནས་མི་འདུག། *de trang tra-tsang gya-ka tsa-ne min-du.*

Exercise No. 18.

These boots are too large. They do not fit me at all. One of them is bigger than the other.

CHAPTER XI.

POSTPOSITIONS, CONJUNCTIONS AND INTERJECTIONS.

1. **Postpositions.**—These are of two kinds, namely, *simple* and *compound*. The former are monosyllabic, and govern the accusative. They include those used in the declension of the noun (Chapter III) and a few others. The latter are of two or more syllables, being formed from nouns, adjectives or verbs, and mostly govern the genitive. Postpositions may govern not only nouns, but also adjectives, verbs, articles, etc. The use of most postpositions is simple: only those, the uses of which require special explanations, in addition to those already given concerning them in the declension of nouns and other chapters, will be dealt with here. For other postpositions reference may be made to the Dictionary.

2. **Simple Postpositions.**—(*a*) ལ་ *lă* besides its datival sense dealt with in the Chapter on the Noun (Cap. III), is sometimes used where in English we should use *at*, *on* or *in*, though སྒང་ལ་ *gang-la* is more commonly used for *on*, and ནང་ལ་ *nang-la* for *in*. Thus, རིའི་སྒང་ལ་གཡག་འདུག། *ri-i gang-la ya du*, THERE ARE YAKS ON THE HILL; ཆུ་ཚོད་བཞི་ལ་ཤོག། *chhu-tshö shi-la sho*, COME AT FOUR O'CLOCK. ལ་ should always be used as above in telling the time of day. ལ་ is also used where in English *for* is used in the quotation of prices, e.g., གཡུ་འདི་སྒོར་མོ་གཉིས་ལ་ཉོས་པ་ཡིན། *yu di gor-mo nyi-la nyö-pa-yin*, I HAVE BOUGHT THIS TURQUOISE FOR TWO

RUPEES. And the following verbs may take ལ་ namely, verbs of *giving*, *showing*, *teaching* and *telling;* also the following common verbs, namely, དད་པ་བྱེད་པ་ *te-pa che-pa* to have faith *in* (a lama, etc.), ཞེད་པ་ *she-pa* to be afraid *of*, འཕོག་པ་ *phok-pa* to hit *against*, ཞུ་བ་ *shu-wa* to offer *to*, to petition, to beg *of*, རོགས་བྱེད་པ་ *ro-che-pa* to assist, འཁྱེར་ཡོང་བ་ *khe yong-wa* to bring *to*, and many others. But with all the above verbs and classes of verbs the ལ་ may be omitted and the simple accusative form used.

(*b*) ནས་ *ne* besides meaning OUT OF, FROM, expresses also *through*, *viâ*, e.g., ང་ཕག་རི་ནས་ཡོང་ནས་མཛེས་ལེབ་ལ་ནས་ཡོང་ང་ (བ་) ཡིན། *nga Pha-ri-ne yong-ne Je-lep-la-ne yong-nga-yin.* I HAVE COME FROM PHARI VIÂ THE JELEP PASS. བྱས་ནས་ *che-ne* may also be used in this sense. ནས་ also expresses *by*, in such sentences as CATCH THE DOG BY THE NECK ཁྱི་འདི་སྐེ་ནས་འཛུམ། *khyi di ke-ne jü.*

(*c*) ལས་ *le* besides its use in the sense of THAN, MORE THAN already dealt with in the comparison of adjectives (Cap. IV, para. 7), means also RATHER THAN, or EXCEPT, e.g., མདས་འདི་དུ) བསྡད་པ་ལས་ཕག་རི་ལ་ཕྱིན་པ་དགའ་གི་རེད། *de de-pa le Pha-ri la chhim-pa ga-ki-re,* I WOULD RATHER GO TO PHARI THAN STAY HERE. (Lit., *rather than the staying here, the going to Phari pleases.*) Again, ཕ་མའི་བ། ང་ལ་མ་ཉན་ཚང་འདི་ལས་མ་བྱུང་ང་ (བ་) རེད། *pha-me ka-la ma-nyen-tsang di-le ma-chung-nga-re.*

SINCE YOU HAVE NOT HEEDED THE ORDERS OF YOUR PARENTS, YOU HAVE FALLEN INTO TROUBLE. (Lit., *since you have not heeded the orders of your father and mother, except this it has not happened.*)

(*d*) དང་ *tang*, WITH is used with a few verbs such as those of MEETING, VISITING, FIGHTING, and with adjectives denoting *similarity*, e.g., ཁས་ས་ང་མི་འདི་དང་ཐུག་བྱུང་། *khe-sa nga mi di-tang thuk-chung* I MET THIS MAN YESTERDAY ; or ཁས་ས་ང་དང་མི་འདི་ཐུག་བྱུང་། *khe-sa nga-tang mi-di thuk-chung.* Again, ལུང་པ་འདི་དབྱིན་ཇི་ལུང་པ་དང་འདྲ་པོ་རེད། *lung-pa di in-ji lung-pa-tang dra-po re,* THIS COUNTRY IS LIKE ENGLAND. Except in such cases *with* should be translated by དང་མཉམ་དུ་ *tang-nyam-tu*, e.g., ཁོ་དང་མཉམ་དུ་རྡོར་རྗེ་གླིང་ལ་ཕྱིན་པ་ཡིན། *kho-tang nyam-tu Dor-je-ling-la chhim-pa-yin.* I WENT WITH HIM TO DARJEELING.

(*e*) Other postpositions governing the accusative are ཐུག་ *thu*, AS FAR AS, UP TO, and one or two others.

3. **Compound Postpositions.**—These, as stated above, mostly govern the genitive, e.g., རིའི་སྒང་ལ་ *ri-i gang-la*, ON THE HILL; ངའི་རྒྱབ་ལ་ *nge gyap-la*, BEHIND ME, etc. A few govern the accusative, for instance, མ་གཏོགས། *ma-to* མེན་པ་ (མིན་པ་) *mem-pa*, EXCEPT ; e.g., འདི་མ་གཏོགས་གཞན་པ་ཡོད་པ་མ་རེད། *di ma-to shem-pa yo-wa ma-re*, THIS IS THE ONLY ONE. (Lit., *except this there is not another.*) And one or two like ཐག་ཉེ་པོ་ *tha-nye-po*, NEAR, CLOSE TO, govern the ablative ; e.g., འདི་ནས་ཟམ་པ་ཐག་ཉེ་པོ་རེད། *di-ne sam-pa tha-nye-po-re*, THE BRIDGE IS CLOSE TO HERE.

4. **Conjunctions.**—Conjunctions are used in Tibetan much less frequently than in English, the sentences in which they occur being turned into participial and other verbal clauses, as has been already explained in the Chapter on the Verb. Thus, མདང་དགོང་ཡོང་ནས་དེ་རིང་ཕྱིན་པ་རེད། *dang-gong yong-ne ṭe-ring chhim-pa re*, HE CAME YESTERDAY EVENING AND LEFT TO-DAY.

5. Those conjunctions which are commonly employed in the colloquial language, and whose use requires special mention, are as follow. For the others reference may be made to the Dictionary.

(*a*) དང་། *ṭang*. This corresponds frequently to AND in English, though, as we have seen above, its literal meaning is WITH. Thus, ཕག་རི་ལ་གཡག་དང་ལུག་མང་པོ་ཡོད་པ་རེད། *Pha-ri la yak-ṭang lu mang-po yo-wa-re*, THERE ARE LOTS OF YAKS AND SHEEP AT PHARI. But when more than two nouns are thus joined, དང་ is used after the first one only or not at all, e.g., ཕག་རི་ལ་གཡག་ (དང་) ར་ལུག་མང་པོ་ཡོད་པ་རེད། *Pha-ri la yak* (*ṭang*) *ra-lu mang-po yo-wa-re*, THERE ARE LOTS OF YAKS, GOATS AND SHEEP AT PHARI. དང་ should always be spoken quickly after, and almost as a part of the word which precedes it, and this preceding word takes the accent.

(*b*) ད་རུང་། *ṭa-rung* ད་རུང་ཡང་ *ṭa-rung yang*, ད་འདོ། *ṭan-do* or ཡང་། *yang*, means BESIDES, MORE YET and precedes the word which it qualifies, e.g., ངས་སྒོ་ང་སྒང་ཁ་མ་ཉོས་ད་རུང་ཏོག་ཙ་ཡོད། *nge go-nga gang-kha ma-nyö ṭa-rung tok-tsa yö*, I HAVE NOT BOUGHT ALL THE EGGS; THERE ARE A FEW MORE YET.

(*c*) EITHER—OR is expressed by ཡང་མིན་ན་—ཡང་མིན་ན་ *yang-men-na—yang-men-na*, or by ཡང་ན་—ཡང་ན། *yang-na—yang-na.* The first ཡང་མིན་ན་ (or ཡང་ན་) is omitted often in Tibetan as well as in English, e.g., དཔོན་པོ་ལ་སྙན་ཞུ་ཞུས་པ་ལས་ཡང་མིན་ན་མ་ཞུས་པ་ (ཞུ་བ་) དགའ་འདུག་གས། *pöm-po la nyen-shu shü-pa le yang-men-na ma-shü-pa ga duk-ke?* DO YOU PREFER THAT I SHOULD REPRESENT THE MATTER TO THE OFFICIAL, OR THAT I SHOULD NOT. (*Lit.*, RATHER THAN REPRESENTING THE CASE TO THE OFFICIAL, OR DOES NOT REPRESENTING PLEASE). Often the OR in Tibetan is omitted altogether, e.g., ས་ཧེབ་བཞུགས་འདུག་ག་མི་འདུག། *sa-hep shu duk-ka min-du ?* IS THE SAHIB AT HOME (lit. *seated*) OR NOT ?

(*d*) The translation of ALTHOUGH and of IF has already been explained in the Chapter on the Verb (Cap. V, para. 8, and Cap. VI, para. 15).

Occasionally ཀལ་སྲིད་ *ke-si* is used for IF ; e.g., ཉོ་ཐུབ་ན་ཉོས་རོགས་གྲིས་ (གྲིད་)། ཀལ་སྲིད་ཉོ་མ་ཐུབ་ན་ཐབས་ཡོད་པ་མ་རེད། *nyo thup-na nyö-ro-chi, ke-si nyo ma-thup-na thapyo-wa ma-re.* PLEASE BUY ONE IF YOU CAN ; IF YOU CANNOT BUY ONE, IT CAN'T BE HELPED.

(*e*) BUT is usually expressed by turning the sentence and using ཡིན་ནས་ (ཡིན་ན་ཡང་) *yin-ne* or some other word meaning ALTHOUGH, IN SPITE OF, e.g., དེ་རིང་ང་འགྲོ་ཐུབ་མ་བྱུང་ཡིན་ནས་སང་ཉིན་ང་འགྲོ་གི་ཡིན། *te-ring nga dro thup ma-chung, yin-ne sang-nyi nga dro-kyi-yin.* I COULD NOT GO TO-DAY, BUT I WILL GO TO-MORROW. (*Lit.*, IN SPITE OF MY NOT BEING ABLE TO GO TO-DAY, I WILL GO TO-MORROW).

(*f*) SINCE, SINCE THE TIME THAT, AGO. The translation of these is best shown by examples. Thus, IT IS SIX MONTHS SINCE

I LEFT LHASA. ང་ལྷ་ས་ནས་ཐོན་ནས་ཟླ་བ་དྲུག་སོང་། *nga hla-sa-ne thön-ne da-wa tru song.* I HAVE NOT BEEN TO DARJEELING FOR TWO YEARS. ང་རྡོ་རྗེ་གླིང་ལ་མ་ཕྱིན་པ་ལོ་གཉིས་སོང་། *nga Dor-je-ling-la ma-chhim-pa lo nyi song.*

(*g*) WHETHER—OR is expressed thus:—IT IS UNCERTAIN WHETHER HE WILL ARRIVE TO-DAY OR NOT. ཁོ་དེ་རིང་སླེབ་ཡོང་ང་མི་ཡོང་ཧྟེན་ཟྟན་མེད། *kho te-ring lep-yong-nga mi-yong ten-den me.* WHETHER YOU GO OR STAY, I SHALL REMAIN HERE. ཁྱོད་རང་ཕྱིན་ན་མ་ཕྱིན་ན་ང་མདས་(འདི་རུ་) སྡོད་ཀྱི་ཡིན། *khyö-rang chhin-na ma-chhin-na nga de dö-kyi-yin.*

6. **Interjections.**—Those commonly used are, ཀྱེ། *kye* ཝེ། *we,* OH! HULLO! HI! ཨ་ཁ་ཁ་ཁ་ *a-kha-kha kha,* ALAS! Exclamation of sorrow. ཨ་ཙི་ *a-tsi,* Exclamation of surprise. Thus, ཝེ་ཚེ་རིང་མགྱོགས་པོ་ཤོག་ཨ། *We! Tshe-ring gyok-po sho-a,* HI! TSHERING, PLEASE COME QUICKLY. ཀྱེ་ and ཝེ་ are used also by masters to call their servants in the same way as *Koï hai* is used in India.

WORDS.

Shi-ga-tse (capital of the Province of Tsang)=གཞི་ག་རྩེ་

Gang-tok (capital of Sikkim) =སྒང་ཏོག་

To put in, insert = བཙུག་པ་ (འཛུག་པ་) *chuk-pa.*

Small-pox (a very common disease in Tibet) = ལྷ་ འབྲུམ་ *hlan-drum.*

Country-house = གཞི་ཀ་ *shi-ka.*

Do. *hon.* = མགོན་གཞི་ *gön-shi.*

To stay, dwell, *hon.*= བཞུགས་པ་ *shu-pa.*

Yak's meat = གཡག་ཤ་ *yak-sha.*

Pork=ཕག་ཤ་ *phak-sha.*

Beef=གླང་ཤ་ *lang-sha.*

To obtain, procure= འབྱོར་བ་ *jor-wa.*

Expensive (*lit.* great price)= གོང་ཆེན་པོ་ *kong-chhem-po.*

Behind=རྒྱབ་ལ་ *gyap-la.*

Mountain, hill=རི་ *ri.*

To snow=གངས་རྒྱབ་པ་ *kang gyap-pa.*

Telegraph (*lit.* iron-thread)= ལྕགས་སྐུད་ *cha-kü.*

Wonder, wonderful thing= ཡ་མཚན་ *yam-tshen.*

EXERCISE No. 19.

He went from Shi-ga-tse to Gang-tok *vid* Phari. ཁོ་གཞི་ག་རྩེ་ནས་ཕག་རི་བྱུས་ནས་སྒང་ཏོག་ལ་ཕྱིན་པ་རེད། *kho shi-ga-tse ne Pha-ri, che ne Gang-tok la chhim-pa-re.*

He had only one servant with him then. དེ་སྐང་ལ་ཁོ་དང་མཉམ་དུ་གཡོག་པོ་གཅིག་ལས་མི་འདུག། *te gang-la kho wang nyam-tu yok-po chi-le min-du.*

Put some more wood on the fire. ད་རུང་མེ་ལ་ཤིང་བཙུག། *ta-rung me-la shing chu.*

On account of the small-pox at Lhasa, he (*hon.*) is staying at his country-house. ལྷ་ས་ལྷ་འབྲུམ་ཡོད་ཙང་སྐུ་གཞོགས་མགོན་གཞི་ལ་བཞུགས་ཡོད་པ་རེད། *hla-sa hlen-drum yö-tsang ku-sho gön-shi la shu yo-wa-re.*

Yak's meat, mutton, pork and beef are procurable here, but the pork and beef are expensive. གཡག་ཤ་ལུག་ཤ་ཕག་ཤ་གླང་ཤ་མདངས་ (འདི་རུ་) འབྱོར་ཡོང་དེ་ཡིན་ནས་ཕག་ཤ་དང་གླང་ཤ་གོང་ཆེན་པོ་རེད། *yak-sha luk-sha phak-sha lang-sha de jor-yong te yin-ne phak-sha tang lang-sha kong-chhem-po re.*

Moreover, many of the people are sending their yaks away to-day to the other side of the hills. ད་རུང་མི་མང་པོས་དེ་རིང་གཡག་རིའི་རྒྱབ་ལ་གཏོང་གི་འདུག། *ta-rung mi mang-pö te-ring yak ri-i gyap-la tong-gi-du.*

Ah! what a wonderful thing this telegraph is! ཨ་ཙི་ཕྲུགས་སྐུད་ཡ་མཚན་འདི་འདྲ་འདུག། *a-tsi cha-kü yam-tshen din-dra du.*

EXERCISE No. 20.

He has two servants with him. He has come *viâ* Gang-tok If it does not snow he will go to Phari to-morrow, but, if it snows, he will stay here. It is three years since he came to (=he arrived at) Darjeeling. Alas! will not the boy die?

CHAPTER XII.

THE ORDER OF WORDS IN A SENTENCE.

1. The order in which different parts of speech in a sentence follow each other has been in the main shown for each Part of Speech in the chapter which deals with it, but it may be convenient to the student that the principal rules should be grouped together here. The order is first the subject, then the object, and the verb last, e.g., ངས་ཁྱོད་རྡུང་གི་ཡིན། *nge khyö dung-gi-yin.* I WILL BEAT YOU.

2. The component parts of the subject or object are usually arranged among themselves as follows:—

(*a*) The genitive.

(*b*) The governing noun or pronoun.

(*c*) The adjective, unless in the genitive, in which case it precedes the noun.

(*d*) The numeral.

(*e*) The article or demonstrative pronoun.

3. Any relative or other clause dependent on the noun may either be put in the genitive and precede the noun, or take the case-inflection of the noun and follow it; but usually the former. Thus: THE MERCHANTS WHO CAME TO-DAY should be translated དེ་རིང་ཡོང་མཁན་གྱི་ཚོང་པ་དེ་ཚོ། *te-ring yong-khen kyi tshong-pa te-tsho* in preference to དེ་རིང་ཚོང་པ་ཡོང་མཁན་དེ་ཚོ། *te-ring tshong-pa yong-khen te-tsho.*

4. In correlative sentences the relative pronoun precedes the demonstrative pronoun, e.g., ལུག་གང་ཡོད་དེ་རྒྱས་ཉོས། *lu kang-yö te-gye nyö*, BUY ALL THE SHEEP THAT THERE ARE (*lit.*, WHAT SHEEP THERE ARE BUY THEM ALL).

5. The interrogative pronoun immediately precedes the verb, e.g., དུག་ལོག་ནག་པོ་གོན་མཁན་དེ་སུ་རེད། *tuk-lo nak-po kön-khen te su-re*, WHO IS THE PERSON THAT IS WEARING BLACK CLOTHES?

6. Participial and other dependent verbal clauses precede the main verb, e.g., ང་ལུང་པ་མདས་ (འདི་དུ་) མིག་ལྟ་ག་ (ལ་) ཡོང་ང་ (བ་) ཡིན། *nga lung-pa de mik-ta-ka yong-nga-yin*, I HAVE COME TO SEE THIS COUNTRY (*lit.*, TO SEE THE COUNTRY HERE). So also when one verb governs another, the former having a sense of CAUSING, PERMITING, COMPLETTING, BEING ABLE this governing verb comes last, e.g., ཁྱོད་ཕྱིན་ཆོག་ག་ *khyö chhin chhok-ka*, YOU MAY GO, i.e., YOU ARE PEMITTED TO GO (an ordinary form of dismissal).

CHAPTER XIII.

THE HONORIFIC LANGUAGE.

1. In the chapter on the Pronouns (Cap. IX, para. 2) reference has been made to the necessity of using the prescribed honorific forms when speaking to or of persons of good position. The difference between the honorific forms in Tibetan and Hindustani is that in the latter these are usually expressed by mere changes of termination, which are few in number and quickly learnt, e.g., *ao*, *aiye* (*come!*) whereas in the former the honorific is usually expressed by a partially or wholly different word.

2. In order therefore that he may converse with the higher classes of Tibetan society, it is necessary for the student in respect of a large number of words to master two Tibetan equivalents for each word, one for the common and one for the higher classes. The ordinary language should be used when speaking to cultivators, coolies, common monks and ordinary traders; the honorific language when speaking to persons of higher rank than the above. When conversing with the very highest classes, i.e., with members of the nobility, of whom there are about thirty families in the Ü (Lhasa) and Tsang (Shi-ga-tse) provinces, or with officials from the rank of De-pön, Tsi-pön or Pho-pön upwards, or with the highest Lamas, a still higher form of honorific should be employed, if such exists. The student need not, however, trouble to learn more than a very few words at first in the higher honorific since persons of the above high rank are not often met with and the ordinary honorific will therefore almost always carry him through.

3. The Dictionary at the end of this book is fairly complete in honorific terms, the ordinary honorific words being marked as *hon.* and the high honorific as *h. hon.* It only remains therefore to notice here such general principles as exist in the formation of honorifics, so that the student may be able in many cases to form them for himself.

4. Firstly, as regards verbs those only need be mentioned which occur frequently in compounds and otherwise :—

Meaning.	Ordinary Form.	Honorific Form.	High Honorific Form.
To put, attach, apply.	རྒྱབ་པ་ *gyap-pa.*	སྐྱོན་པ་ *kyöm-pa.*	སྐྱོན་པ་གནང་བ་ *kyöm-pa nang-wa.*
To sit, dwell, remain.	བསྡད་པ་ (སྡོད་པ་) *de-pa.*	བཞུགས་པ་ *shu-pa.*	བཞུགས་གདན་ འཇག་པ་ *shu-den-ja-pa.*
To stand up	ལང་བ་ *lang-wa.*	བཞང་བ་ (བཞེང་བ་) *shang-wa.*	སྐུ་བཞང་ (བཞེང་) གནང་བ་ *ku-shang nang-wa.*
To say, tell	ལབ་པ་ *lap-pa.* ཟེར་བ་ *ser-wa.*	གསུང་བ་ *sung-wa.*	བཀའ་གནང་བ་ *ka-nang-wa.*

Meaning.	Ordinary Form.	Honorific Form.	High Honorific Form.
To eat	ཟ་བ་ *śa-wa*	བཞེས་པ་ *sh̄e-pa*	བཞེས་པ་གནང་བ་ *sh̄e-pa nang-wa.*
To take	ལེན་པ་ *lem-pa*		
To wear, put on (clothes).	གོན་པ་ *köm-pa*		
To go, come.	འགྲོ་བ་ *to go =dro-wa.* ཡོང་བ་ *to come =yong-wa.*	ཕེབ་པ་ *phep-pa*	འཆིབ་རྒྱུ་གནང་བ་ *chhip-gyu nang-wa.*
To do	བྱེད་པ་ *ch̄e-pa*	གནང་བ་ *nang-wa.*	
To give	སྟེར་པ་ *ter-wa*		

5. By far the commonest of the above forms is གནང་བ། *nang-wa.* In addition to its meanings given above, it can be added for the formation of an honorific to most verbs that have not got special honorific forms of their own, e.g., ཚོང་པས་བཏང་ང་ (བ་) རེད། *tshong-pe tang-nga re,* THE TRADER SENT; དཔོན་པོས་གཏོང་ང་ (བ་) གནང་ང་ (བ་) རེད། *pöm-pö tong-nga nang-nga re,* THE OFFICIAL SENT. And here it should be noticed that verbs which use the past or perfect root in their ordinary forms take, as a rule, the present root in their honorific forms, e.g., the example just given.

6. The above honorific forms are, as already stated, applied to persons of position higher than the ordinary. There are also a few verbs applied to persons, both of high or of low position, when such persons are dealing with persons above them. These

verbs are in the Dictionary labelled *inf.* to *sup.* (i.e., inferior to superior). Two of the commonest are ཞུ་བ་ *shu-wa*, for ལབ་པ་ *lap-pa*, TO SAY; and ཕུལ་བ་ (འབུལ་བ་) *phü-wa*, for སྟེར་བ་ *ter-wa*, TO GIVE. Thus མདའ་དཔོན་སྐུ་གཞོགས་ལ་ཞུས། *De-pön ku-sho-la shü*, REPRESENT (THE MATTER) TO THE DE-PON.

When the inferior is himself a person of good position, the verb implying inferiority takes itself an honorific form, e.g., སྐུ་གཞོགས་རྫོང་ དཔོན་ གྱིས་ མདའ་ དཔོན་སྐུ་གཞོགས་ལ་ཆིག་པ་ (ཆིབས་པ་ horse, *hon.*) གཅིག་འབུལ་ར་ (བ་) གནང་སོང་། *ku-sho Jong-pen kyi De-pön ku-sho-la chhik-pa chi bü-ra nang-song*, THE JONG-PEN HAS GIVEN A PONY TO THE DE-PON. Note the honorific form འབུལ་ར་ (བ་) གནང་སོང་ *bü-ra nang-song*, and ཆིག་པ་ (ཆིབས་པ་) *chhik-pa*, the honorific of རྟ་ *la*, HORSE.

7. A great many words, mostly nouns, are formed from the honorific terms applied to different parts of the body. Thus—

(*a*) སྐུ་ *ku* gives honorific for many parts of the body, e.g., གཟུགས་པོ་ *suk-po*, BODY, སྐུ་གཟུགས་ *ku-su*, BODY, *hon.*; བྲང་ཁོག་ *pang-kho*, CHEST (of BODY), སྐུ་བྲང་ *ku-pang*, CHEST, *hon.*

(*b*) ཕྱག་ *chha*, the honorific form of ལག་པ་ *lak-pa*, HAND is used for many things connected with or manipulated by the hand, e.g., ཕྱག་ལྡེ་ *chhan-di*, *hon.* of ལྡེ་མིག་ *di-mi*, KEY. ཕྱག་སྒམ་ *chha-gam*, *hon.* of སྒམ་ *gam* BOX.

(*c*) ཞབས་ *shap*, the honorific form of རྐང་པ་ *kang-pa*, FOOT is used for things connected with the foot, e.g., ཞབས་ཆགས་ *shap-chha* (or ཞབས་ལྷམ་) *hon.* of ལྷམ་ *hlam*, BOOT.

(*d*) ཞལ་ *she*, the honorific form of ཁ་ *kha*, MOUTH, e.g., ཞལ་སྐྱེམས་པ་ *she-kyem-pa*, *hon.* of ཁ་སྐོམ་པ་ *kha-kom-pa*, TO BE THIRSTY.

(*e*) དབུ་ *wu*, the honorific form of མགོ་ *go*, HEAD; e.g., དབུ་ཞྭ་ *wu-sha*, *hon.* of ཞྭ་མོ་ *sha-mo*, HAT.

(*f*) ཤངས་ *shang*, the honorific form of སྣ་ཁུག་ (སྣ་) *na-khu*, NOSE; e.g., ཤངས་འཕྱིད་ *shang-chhi*, *hon.* of སྣ་འཕྱིད་ *nap-chhi* HANDKERCHIEF.

(*g*) སྙན་མཆོག་ *nyen-chho*, the honorific form of ཨམ་མཆོག་ (ཨ་མཆོག་) *am-chho*, EAR; སྙན་མཆོག་གི་ཨི་ཁུང་ *nyen-chho-ki i-khung*, *hon.* of ཨམ་མཆོག་ (ཨ་མཆོག་) གི་ཨི་ཁུང་ *am chho-ki i-khung*, EAR-HOLE.

(*h*) སྤྱན་ *chen*, the honorific form of མིག་ *mi*, EYE, e.g., སྤྱན་ལྤགས་ *chhem-pa*, *hon.* of མིག་ལྤགས་ *mik-pa*, EYE-LID; and སྤྱན་ཕེབ་ཞུ་བ་ *chem-phe shu-wa* (lit. *to request the coming of the eye*) the *inf.* to *sup.* form of བསྟན་པ་ (སྟོན་པ་) *tem-pa*, TO SHOW.

(*i*) The other parts, e.g., ཚེམས་ *tshem*, *hon.* of སོ་ *so*, TOOTH; ལྗགས་ *ja*, *hon.* of ལྕེ་ *che*, TONGUE; མགུལ་ *gü*, *hon.* of སྐེ་ *ke*, NECK have also their compounds formed on lines similar to those above.

8. Other honorific forms from which compounds are often constructed are as follows :—

(*a*) ཐུགས་ *thu*, the honorific form of སེམས་ *sem*, MIND. Frequently used in mental and moral attributes, e.g., ཐུགས་འདོད་ *thung-dö*, *hon.* of འདོད་པ་ *dö-pa*, WISH.

(*b*) བཀའ་ *ka*, ORDER gives the honorific in many words connected with *speaking* and the like, e.g., བཀའ་ལན་ *ka-len*, *hon.* of ལན་ *len*, ANSWER.

(*c*) བཞེས་ *shé*, give the honorific in words connected with food and drink, e.g., བཞེས་ཤ་ *shé-sha*, *hon.* of ཤ་ *sha*, MEAT.

(*d*) གསོལ་ *sö*, also gives the honorific in many words connected with food and drink, and especially in connection with their preparation, e.g., གསོལ་ཐབ་ *sö-thap*, *hon.* of ཐབ་ཚང་ *thap-tshang*, KITCHEN.

9. As the honorific of verbs is often formed by གནང་བ་ *nang wa* so the high honorific is frequently formed by adding བཀའ་ *ka*, ཐུགས་ *thu*, or other of the honorific forms specified above, to the beginning of the words;

e.g., ཞིབ་དཔྱོད་བྱེད་པ་ *shíp-chö ché-pa*, to investigate.
ཞིབ་དཔྱོད་གནང་བ་ *shíp-chö nang-wa*, to investigate, *hon.*
བཀའ་ཞིབ་གནང་བ་ *ka-shíp nang-wa*, to investigate, *h. hon*

and རྩོམ་པ་ *tsom-pa*, to compose (writing, etc.).

རྩོམ་པ་གནང་བ་ *tsom-pa nang-wa*, to compose (writing, etc.) *h. hon.*
བཀའ་རྩོམ་གནང་བ་ *ka-tsom nang-wa*, to compose (writing, etc.) *h. hon.*

10. When a word has no separate honorific of its own, ལགས་ *lā* is often added to express respect, e.g., སྲུ་མོ་ལགས་ *su-mo-lā*, *hon.* of སྲུ་མོ་ *su-mo*, MATERNAL AUNT. And ལགས་ *lā*, ལགས་སི་ *le-si* (*h. hon.* ལགས་ལགས་སི་ *lā-les* or ལང་ཕྱོང་ *la-wong*) introduced into a sentence always signify respect.

11. The lower trades, such as *blacksmith*, *carpenter*, *mason*, etc., take དབུ་མཛད་ *um-dze*, as their honorific, though དབུ་མཛད་ is, strictly speaking, the honorific of ཚེམ་བུ་ *tshem-pu*, TAILOR.

12. རྣམ་པ་ཚོ་ *nam-pa-tsho* and རྣམ་པ་ *nam-pa* are used instead of ཚོ་ *tsho* to form the plurals of *hon.* nouns and pronouns, e.g., དཔོན་པོ་རྣམ་པ་ཚོ་ *pöm-po nam-pa-tsho*, THE OFFICIALS, *hon.*, ཁྱེད་རང་རྣམ་པ་ཚོ་ *khye-rang nam-pa-tsho*, YOU (plural) *hon.*

13. Lamas have a few honorifics which are not shared by laymen in addition to those specified in the chapter on the Pronouns (Cap. IX, para. 3). Such as སྐུ་ཞིང་ལ་ཕེབ་པ་ *ku-shing-la phep-pa* or higher still སྐུ་ཞིང་ལ་འཆིབ་རྒྱུ་གནང་བ་ *ku-shing-la chhip-gyu nang-wa* which mean TO DIE, lit. *to go to heaven.*

WORDS.

Road, journey=ལམ་ཀ་ *lang-ka.*

Do. *hon.*=ཕེབ་ལམ་ *phep-lam.*

Distance=ཐག་རིང་ཐུང་ *tha-ring-thung.*

Do. *hon.*=ཕེབ་ཐག་ *phep-tha.*

Near=ཐག་ཉེ་པོ། ཉེ་པོ་ *tha-nye-po, nye-po.*

Difficult=ཁག་པོ་ *khak-po.*

Do. *hon.*=སྐུ་མཉེལ་པོ་ *ku-nye-po.*

Far=ཐག་རིང་པོ་ *tha-ring-po.*

Do. *hon.* = ཕེབ་ཐག་རིང་པོ་ *phep-tha ring-po.*

To ride=ཞོན་པ་ *shöm-pa.*

Do. *hon.*=འཆིབ་པ་ *chhip-pa.*

Rideable (*lit.* riding place)=ཞོན་ས་ *shön-sa.*

Do. *hon.*=ཆིབས་ས་ *chhip-sa.*

On foot=རྐང་ཐང་ *kang-thang.*

On foot, *hon.* = ཞབས་ཐང་ *shap-thang.*

Country = ལུང་པ་ *lung-pa.*

Extensive = རྒྱ་ཆེན་པོ་ *gya-chhem-po.*

Moderate, middling = འཚམས་པོ་གཅིག་ *tsham-po-chi.*

To be seated, to dwell, *h. hon.* = བཞུགས་གདན་འཇག་པ་ *shu-den-ja-pa.*

To go for a walk = ཆམ་ཆམ་ (འཁྱམ་འཁྱམ) ལ་འགྲོ་བ་ *chham-chham-la dro-wa.*

To go for a walk, *hon.* = སྐུ་ཆམ་ (འཁྱམ་) ལ་ཕེབ་པ་ *kun-chham la phep-pa.*

For *h. hon.* substitute འཆིབ་རྒྱུ་ གནང་བ་ *chhip-gyu nang-wa* for ཕེབ་པ་ *phep-pa.*

Very well = འོ་ན་ *o-na.*

Slowly = ཀ་ལེ་ཀ་ལེ་ *ka-le ka-le.*

Tea = ཇ་ *cha.*

Do. *hon.* = གསོལ་ཇ་ *sö cha.*

Exercise No. 21.

On a Journey.

Ordinary Language.

What is the distance of our journey to-day ? ། དེ་རིང་ལམ་ཀ་ཐག་རིང་ཐུང་ག་ཚོད་ཡོད་པ། *te-ring lang-ka tha-ring-thung ka-tshö yö-pa ?*

Only a short way; it is not difficult. ད་རང་ལམ་ཀ་ཐག་ཉེ་པོ་ཡོད་ཁག་པོ་མེད། *te-ring lang-ka tha-nye-po yö khak-po-me.*

How far have we to go to-morrow ? སང་ཉིན་འགྲོ་རྒྱུ་ག་ཚོད་ཡོད་པ། *sang-nyi dro-gyu ka-tshö yö-pa ?*

A long way, and the road is bad. སང་ཉིན་ཐག་རིང་པོ་ཡོད་ལམ་ཀ་སྡུག་རྡུལ་ཡིན། *sang-nyi tha-ring-po yö lang-ka duk-rü yin.*

Can we ride to-morrow ? སང་ཉིན་རྟ་ཞོན་ནས་འགྲོ་ས་ཡོད་པས། *sang-nyi ta shön-ne dro-sa yö-pe ?*

It is rideable for a bit of the way, and for a bit of the way we shall have to walk. ཏོག་ཙ་ཏོག་ཙ་ལ་ཞོན་ས་ཡོད་ཏོག་ཙ་ཏོག་ཙ་ཀང་ཐང་ལ་འགྲོ་དགོས་ཀྱི་ཡོད། *tok̄-tsa tok̄-tsa-la s̄hön-sa-yö tok̄-tsa tok̄-tsa kang-thang-la dro go-kyi-yö.*

Is the district an extensive one? ལུང་པ་དེ་རྒྱ་ཆེན་པོ་འདུག་གས། *lung-pa te gya-chhem-po duk̄-k̄e?*

It is of moderate size. ཆེ་ཆུང་འཚམས་པོ་གཅིག་འདུག། *chhe-chhung tsham-po chi du.*

Honorific Language.

།དེ་རིང་ཕེབ་ལམ་ཐག་རིང་ཐུང་ག་ཚོད་ཡོད་པ་གནང་ངང་། *te-ring phep̄-lam tha-ring-thung k̄a-tshö yö-pa nang-nga ?*

དེ་རིང་ཕེབ་ཐག་ཉེ་པོ་ཡིན་སྐུ་མཉེལ་པོ་མེད། *te-ring phep̄-tha nye-po yin ku-nye-po me.*

སང་ཉིན་ཕེབ་རྒྱུ་ག་ཚོད་ཡོད་པ། *sang-nyi phep̄-gyu k̄a-tshö yö-pa.*

སང་ཉིན་ཕེབ་ཐག་རིང་པོ་ཡོད་ཕེབ་ལམ་ཡང་ཡག་པོ་མེད། *sang-nyi phep̄-tha ring-po yö phep̄-lam yang yak̄-po me.*

སང་ཉིན་ཆིག་ (ཆིབས་) པ་འཆིབས་ནས་ཕེབ་ས་ཡོད་པས། *sang-nyi chhik̄-pa chhip̄-ne phep̄-sa yö-pe ?*

ཏོག་ཙ་ཏོག་ཙ་ལ་འཆིབ་ས་ཡོད་ཏོག་ཙ་ཏོག་ཙ་ཞབས་ཐང་ལ་ཕེབ་དགོས་ཀྱི་ཡོད། *tok̄-tsa tok̄-tsa-la chip̄-sa yö tok̄-tsa tok̄-tsa s̄hap̄-thang-la phep̄ go-kyi-yö.*

ལུང་པ་དེ་རྒྱ་ཆེན་པོ་འདུག་གས། *lung-pa te gya-chhem-po duk̄-k̄e ?*

ལགས་ཆེ་ཆུང་འཚམས་པོ་གཅིག་འདུག། *lā chhe-chhung tsham-po-chi du.*

Exercise No. 22.

(To be translated into honorific language).

Is the Sahib at home (=Is the Sahib seated)? No Sir, he has gone for a walk. Very well, I will call again (=come) to-morrow. I cannot understand what you say; please speak slowly. Give the Sahib some tea.

CHAPTER XIV.

MISCELLANEOUS.

1. **I. Monetary System.**—This is as follows:—

2 *kha*	make 1	*kar-ma-nga*	སྐར་མ་ལྔ།
3 *kha*	„ 1	*chhe-gye*	ཕྱེད་བརྒྱད།
4 *kha*	„ 1	*sho-kang*	ཞོ་ཀང་།
5 *kha*	„ 1	*kha-chha*	ཁ་ཆག།
6 *kha*	„ 1	*trang-ka*	ཊཾ་ཀ།

One *trang-ka* at present (1918) is equal to four annas.

5 *sho* (or 3 *trang-kas* and 1 *kar-ma-nga*) make *sho-nga* (ཞོ་ལྔ་) =thirteen annas and four pies.

10 *sho* (or 6 *trang-kas* and 1 *sho*) make 1 *ngü-sang* (དངུལ་སྲང་) =one rupee eleven annas approximately.

50 *ngü-sang* make 1 *do-tshe* (རྡོ་ཚད་)=eighty-three rupees seven annas approximately.

In addition to the above there are lumps of silver in the shape of a pony's hoof, which are of different sizes and consequently of different values. Such a lump is known as a *ta-mi-ma* (རྟ་རྨིག་མ།)

2. The above values are not all coined. The silver coins are: *trang-ka, sho-nga, ngü-sang.* The copper coins are:— *kha-kang, kar-ma-nga, chhe-gye.*

In addition to these coins and the *ta-mi mas* already mentioned, Indian rupees, Chinese rupees and Indian currency notes are used in Tibet.

There are no gold coins.

3. **II. Weights and Measures.**—For weighing gold, silver, corals, pearls, etc., the abovementioned coins and money values up to and including a *ngü-sang* are used as weights. In weighing gold, a *ngü-sang* (*silver sang*) is known as a *ser-sang* (གསེར་སྲང་) (*gold sang*), and in weighing corals, pearls, etc., is known simply as a *sang*. For weighing gold of large amount we have—

5 *ser-sang* make 1 *tum-pu* (ཏུམ་བུ།)

Similarly for silver of large amount, 75 *ngü-sang* make 1 *ta-mi-ma*, 1 *kha*, 1 *sho*, 1 *sang*, 1 *ngü-sang* or 1 *ser-sang* is expressed by ཁ་ཀང་ *kha-kang* and not ཁ་གཅིག་ etc. Two of the above (except ཁ་ which is not much used in the plural) by ཞོ་དོ་ *sho-to*, etc. The divisions of money and the weights for gold, silver, etc., are constant throughout Tibet. The weights and measures for meat, grain, etc., vary in different parts of the country; those for the Ü (Lhasa) province will be given here.

4. *Meat, butter*, etc., are weighed by *por* (སྦོར་), *nya-ka* (ཉ་ག་) and *khe* (ཁལ་). 4 *por* = 1 *nya-ka* and 20 *nya-ka* = 1 *khe*, a *por* being equal to about an ounce.

5. *Grain* is not weighed but measured. Of the *tre* (བྲེ་) there are two sizes, viz., the large *tre*, known as *tre-chhe* * (བྲེ་ཆེ་), of which 16 make 1 *ten-dzin kha-ru* (བསྟན་འཛིན་ཁལ་རུ་) and the small *tre*, known as *kha-tre* (ཁལ་བྲེ་) of which 20 make one *ten-dzin kha-ru*. Sixteen of the *kha-tre* make 1 *sang-bo* (ཟངས་འབོ་). A *ten-dzin kha-ru* contains 33 lbs. of barley or peas and 17 lbs. of barley flour.

---

* Or *se-tre* (སེར་བྲེ)།

6. *Tea* is always carried in compressed packets, shaped like bricks and known as *pa-ka* (པ་ཀག). The weight of each brick varies with the different kinds; a brick of *dru-tang* (འབྲུ་དང་) tea which is the best kind of tea, weighing about 6 lbs., while a brick of the worst kind, known as *gye-pa* (བརྒྱད་པ་) weighs about 3 lbs.

4 *brick* = 1 *khu-tru* (ཁུ་དྲུག་)

3 *khu-tru* = 1 *gam* (སྒམ་)

7. **Lineal Measurements.**—Those commonly used are as follows:—

Sor (སོར་): the breadth of one finger.

Tho (མཐོ་): the span from the tip of the thumb to the tip of the middle finger.

Thru (ཁྲུ་): the distance from the elbow to the tip of the middle finger.

Dom (འདོམ་): the distance from the middle finger tip of one hand to that of the other with both arms outstretched.

Ke ko-sa-tsa (སྐད་གོ་ས་ཙ་): the distance the voice carries, e.g., མི་དེ་སྐད་གོ་ས་ཙ་ (ཙམ་) ལ་འདུག། *mi te ke ko-sa tsa-la du*, THAT MAN IS JUST WITHIN EARSHOT.

Tsha-pho (ཚ་འཕོག་): or *Tsha-sa* (ཚ་ས་); about 3 hours, march or 7 to 10 miles in easy country.

Sa-tshi (ས་ཚིག་): a full day's march or about 15 to 20 miles in easy country.

8. **III. Divisions of Time.**—Time is reckoned by cycles, the commonest of which is that of twelve years, known as the *lo-khor* (ལོ་འཁོར་) and is as follows:—

1. བྱི་བ་ *chi-wa*, MOUSE.
2. གླང་ *lang*, BULL.
3. སྟག་ *tak*, TIGER.
4. ཡོས་ *yö*, HARE.
5. འབྲུག་ *druk*, DRAGON.
6. སྦྲུལ་ *drü*, SNAKE.
7. རྟ་ *ta*, HORSE.
8. ལུག་ *lu*, SHEEP.
9. སྤྲེ་ *tre*, MONKEY.
10. བྱ་ *cha*, BIRD.
11. ཁྱི་ *khyi*, DOG.
12. ཕག་ *pha*, PIG.

It should be noted that the ordinary word for HARE is *ri-kong* རི་བོང་ (རི་ཝོང་), and the Lhasa word for *monkey* is *peu* སྤྲེའུ་ (སྤྲེའུ་). But in the *lo-khor* ཡོས་ *yö* and སྤྲེ་ *tre* are always used.

9. A cycle of sixty years, known as *long kham* (ལོ་ཁམས་) is formed by joining the five elements, namely, ཤིང་ *shing*, WOOD, མེ་ *me*, FIRE, ས་ *sa*, EARTH, ལྕགས་ *cha*, IRON, and ཆུ་ *chhu*, WATER to the twelve creatures of the *lo-khor* in the following manner:—

1. ཤིང་བྱི་ལོ་ *shing-chi lo*=WOOD-MOUSE YEAR.
2. ཤིང་གླང་ལོ་ *shing-lang lo*=WOOD BULL YEAR.
3. མེ་སྟག་ལོ་ *me-tak lo*=FIRE-TIGER YEAR.
4. མེ་ཡོས་ལོ་ *me-yö lo*=FIRE-HARE YEAR.

And so on. The first round of elements ends at the 10th year WATER-BIRD YEAR (ཆུ་བྱ་ལོ་), *chhu-cha lo*, and is at once recommenced, so that the 11th year is the WOOD-DOG YEAR (ཤིང་ཁྱི་ལོ་) *shing-khyi lo*, the 12th year is the WOOD-PIG

YEAR (ཤིང་ཕག་ལོ་) *shing-phak lo*, and so on. At sixty years the two series end together, the *lo-khor* having run five times and the elements six times. We then get the WOOD-MOUSE YEAR again, and the cycle runs through as before. The present years are as follow :—

1917—FIRE-SNAKE YEAR མེ་སྦྲུལ་ལོ་ *me-drü lo.*

1918—EARTH-HORSE YEAR ས་རྟ་ལོ་ *sa-ta lo.*

1919—EARTH-SHEEP YEAR ས་ལུག་ལོ *sa-luk lo.*

1920—IRON-MONKEY YEAR ལྕགས་སྤྲེ་ལོ་ *chak-tre lo.*

1921—IRON-BIRD YEAR ལྕགས་བྱ་ལོ་ *chak-cha lo.*

1922—WATER-DOG YEAR ཆུ་ཁྱི་ལོ་ *chhu-khyi lo.*

1923—WATER-PIG YEAR ཆུ་ཕག་ལོ་ *chhu-phak lo.*

1924—WOOD-MOUSE YEAR ཤིང་བྱི་ལོ་ *shing-chi lo.*

1925—WOOD-BULL YEAR ཤིང་གླང་ལོ་ *shing-lang lo.*

1926—FIRE-TIGER YEAR མེསྟག་ལོ་ *me-tak lo.*

1927—FIRE-HARE YEAR མེ་ཡོས་ལོ་ *me-yö lo.*

1928—EARTH-DRAGON YEAR སའབྲུག་ལོ་ *sa-druk lo.*

10. Practically every Tibetan can tell the date of his birth and otherwise reckon in the *lo-khor*, but comparatively few can do so in the sixty years' cycle. The latter is, however, used in Government papers, in books and in correspondence. Thus, ང་རྟ་ལོ་པ་ཡིན། *nga ta-lo-pa yin* means I WAS BORN IN THE HORSE YEAR (*lit.* I AM A HORSE YEAR PERSON).

11. The *four seasons* are as follows :—

SPRING—དཔྱིད་ཀ་ *chi ka.*

SUMMER—དབྱར་ཀ་ *yar-ka.*

AUTUMN—སྟོན་ཀ་ *tön-ka.*

WINTER—དགུན་ཀ་ *gün-ka.*

12. **Dates.**—Months have no names, but are numbered 1, 2, 3, etc. The 1st month commences in February, but the actual date varies as the Tibetan year is shorter than ours and therefore every third year an extra month named ཟླ་ཤོལ་ *da-shö* is added. Each month has about thirty days. The manner in which the different days of a month are expressed has been dealt with in the chapter on the Numerals (Cap. VIII, para. 6).

13. **The Days of the Week** are as follows :—

SUNDAY—གཟའ་ཉི་མ་ *śa-nyi-ma.*

MONDAY—གཟའ་ཟླ་བ་ *śa-dawa.*

TUESDAY—གཟའ་མིག་དམར་ *śa-ming-ma.*

WEDNESDAY—གཟའ་ལྷག་པ་ *śa-hlak̄-pa.*

THURSDAY—གཟའ་ཕུར་བུ་ *ïa-phur-p̄u.*

FRIDAY—གཟའ་པ་སངས་ *śa-pa-sang.*

SATURDAY—གཟའ་སྤེན་པ་ *śa-pem-pa.*

14. **The Time of Day.**—This is reckoned as follows :—

བྱ་སྐད་དང་པོ་ *cha-ke tang-po*, first cock crow.

བྱ་སྐད་གཉིས་པ་ *cha-ke nyi-pa*, second cock crow, 10 or 15 minutes after the first.

ཐོ་རངས་ *tho-rang*, the time shortly before dawn.

ནམ་ལངས་ *nam-lang*, dawn.

ཉི་ཤར་ *nyi-shar*, or རྩེ་ཤར་ *tse-shar*, sunrise.

The latter means, lit. *shining on the peaks.*

ཞོགས་ཀས་ *shok-ke* or སྔ་དྲོ་ *nga-tro* the time from sunrise to about 8 A.M.

ཚ་ཏིང་ *tsha-ting*, from 8 A.M. till 10 or 11 A.M.

ཉིན་དགུང་ *nyin-kung*, midday.

དགོང་དག་ *gong-ta*, the afternoon from four o'clock till sunset.

ཉི་གས་ *nyi-ge*, sunset.

ས་རིབ་ (སྲོད་དུབ་) *sa-rip*, dusk.

ནམ་ཕྱེད་ *nam chhe*, midnight.

ཉི་མ་ *nyi-ma*, day-time.

དགོང་མོ་ *gong-mo* or མཚན་མོ་ *tshem-mo*, night-time.

ཞག་པོ་ *shak-po*, day of 24 hours.

AT WHAT TIME, AT WHAT O'CLOCK may be rendered by སྔ་ཕྱི་ག་ག་ཙ་ (ཙམ་) ལ་ *ngam-chhi ka-ka-tsa-la* (lit. *at how much early-late*); e.g., ང་སང་ཉིན་སྔ་ཕྱི་ག་ག་ཙ་ (ཙམ་) ལ་བཅར་དགོས་ཡིན་ན། *nga sang-nyi ngam-chhi ka-ka-tsa la chu go yin-na.* AT ABOUT WHAT TIME TO-MORROW SHOULD I COME? ཉིན་དགུང་ལ་ཤོག། *nyin-kung-la sho*, COME AT MIDDAY. But usually ཆུ་ཚོད་ *chhu-tshö* (lit. *water-measure*) corresponding to the English *o'clock* is used. Thus: ABOUT WHAT TIME TO-MORROW SHOULD I COME? སང་ཉིན་ཆུ་ཚོད་ག་ཚོད་ཙ་ལ་ང་བཅར་དགོས་པ་ཡིན་ན་ (ནམ།) *sang-nyi chhu-tshö ka-tshö tsa-la nga cha go-wa yin-na?* COME AT FOUR O'CLOCK. ཆུ་ཚོད་བཞི་ལ་ཤོག། *chhu-tshö shi-la sho.*

COME AT HALF PAST FIVE. ཆུ་ཚོད་ལྔ་དང་ཕྱེད་ཀ་ཤོག། *chhu-tshö nga-tang chhe-ka sho.*

WORDS.

Ornament=རྒྱན་ཆ་ *gyen-chha.*

Price=རིན་ *ring.*

Weight (*lit.* light heavy)= ཡང་ལྗི། ལྗིད་ *yang-ji ; ji.*

Woollen cloth=སྣམ་བུ་ *nam-bu.*

Festival (*lit.* great time)= དུས་ཆེན་ *tü-chhen.*

EXERCISE NO. 23.

This ornament is made of silver. །རྒྱན་ཆ་འདི་དངུལ་གྱི་བཟོས་པ་རེད། *gyen-chha di ngü-kyi sö-pa-re.*

Its price is thirty-two *trang-kas* and one *sho.* དེའི་རིན་ཏྲཾ་ཀ་སུམ་ཅུ་སོ་གཉིས་དང་ཞོ་གང་རེད། *te-i ring trang-ka sum-chu so-nyi tang sho-kang re.*

It weighs (*lit.* is the weight of) twelve and half rupees. སྒོར་མོ་ཕྱེད་དང་བཅུ་གསུམ་གྱི་ལྗིད་ཡོད་པ་རེད། *gor-mo chhe-tang chuk-sum kyi ji yo-wa-re.*

Please sell me two *dom* of woollen cloth. ང་ལ་སྣམ་བུ་འདོམ་དོ་འཚོང་རོགས་གྱིས་ (བྱེད་)། *nga-la nam-bu dom to tshong-ro-chi.*

It is rather farther than a *tsha-pho* from here. འདི་ནས་ཚ་འཕོག་ས་ལས་ཐག་རིང་ཙ་ (ཙམ) ཡོད། *di-ne tsha-pho sa-le tha-ring-tsa yö.*

How old are you? ཁྱོད་ལོ་ག་ཚོད་ཡིན་པ། *khyö lo ka-tshö yim-pa?*

I was born in the *hare year.* ང་ཡོས་ལོ་པ་ཡིན། *nga yö-lo-pa yin.*

There will be a festival on the twenty-fourth of the first month. ཟླ་བ་དང་པོའི་ཉི་ཤུ་བཞི་ལ་དུས་ཆེན་གཅིག་ཡོང་། *da-wa ťang-pö nyi-shu sh̓i-la ťü-chhen-chi yong.*

Come on Wednesday morning. གཟའ་ལྷག་པའི་ཞོགས་ཀས་ཤོག། *śa hlak̓-pe sh̓ok-k̓e sho.*

Exercise No. 24.

I will sell it for five *ṅyü-sang* and a *kar-ma.* It weighs twenty-three *trang-kas.* I will leave (= go out from) here on the morning of the eighteenth, and will reach Gangtok on the afternoon of the twentieth. The price of this woollen cloth is two *trang-kas* and a *kha-chha* per *thru.*

CHAPTER XV.

A CONVERSATION TRANSLITERATED, TRANSLATED AND PARAPHRASED.

1. It has often been stated with regard to grammars of Oriental languages that they are rendered more useful by the inclusion in them of a passage of the language translated literally into English, transliterated as exactly as possible into the Roman character, and accompanied by a grammatical analysis of every word. This plan enables the student to ascertain the true pronunciation and also to understand the working of rules that he knows only by rote. And although in this grammar the rules of pronunciation and of grammar have not merely been enunciated but have also at the time of enunciation been separately and fully explained by examples, yet a final example giving effect to the above suggestion may prove helpful to the student before we pass on to the conversational series in the next chapter.

On a journey. Asking the way.

Which is the road ...	*Dor-je-ling*	*ki*	*lam-ka*	
	རྡོ་རྗེ་གླིང	གི་	ལམ་ཀ་	
	Darjeeling	of	road	
to Darjeeling? ...	*K'a-pa*	*re.*		
	ག་པ་	རེད་		
	where	is?		
Straight on, Sir, as your are going.	*La*	*kha-thu*	*tak-ka*	*re.*
	ལགས་	ཁ་ཐུག་	དག་ག་	རེད།
	Sir!	Straight	like that	is;

You cannot mistake it — *nor-sa tsa-ne me.*
ནོར་ས་ ཙ་ནས་ མེད།
mistaking-place at all is not.

Is the road good? ... — *Lam-ka de-po yö-pe.*
ལམ་ཀ་ བདེ་པོ་ ཡོད་པས།
Road good is it?

Yes, Sir, it is very good. — *La de-thak-chhö yö.*
ལགས་ བདེ་ཐག་ཆོད་ ཡོད།
Sir! very good is.

How far is it from here? — *T'a dro-ghu ka-tshö yö-pa.*
ད་ འགྲོ་རྒྱུ་ ག་ཚོད་ ཡོད་པ།
Now to go how much is there?

It is not very far from here, just a short distance. — *T'a phe-gyu she-po rang me.*
ད་ ཕེབ་རྒྱུ་ ཞེ་པོ་ རང་ མེད།
Now to go very much is not?
Tok-tsa chi yö.
ཏོག་ཙ་ གཅིག་ ཡོད།
A little is.

Thank you, Good-day — *Wong ya chung ka-le*
ཝོང་ ཡག་ བྱུང་ ག་ལེ་
Well! good happened. Gently
gyu-a.
རྒྱུག་ ཨ།
go.

Good-day, Sir ... — *la-si ka-le the-a.*
ལགས་སི་ ག་ལེ་ ཐས་ཨ།
Sir! Gently go.

GRAMMATICAL ANALYSIS.

རྡོ་རྗེ་གླིང་གི Genitive Singular. གི་ and not ཀྱི་ or གྱི་ because the preceding word ends in ང་ (Cap. III, para. 9).

ལམ་ཀ་ Nominative Singular. *The* is omitted because it does not represent *this* or *that* (Cap. II, para. 7).

ག་པ་ Interrogative Pronoun. It immediately precedes the verb (Cap. IX, para. 17).

རེད་ 3rd person singular, present indicative.

ལགས་ Honorific term.

ཁ་སྣུག་ Adverb.

དག་ག་ Adverb.

ནོར་ས་ Nominative Singular. Derived from ནོར་བ་ *to mistake* and ས་ place (Cap. VII, para. 19).

ཙ་ནས་ Adverb. Used with negatives only [Cap. X, para. 3 (*h*)].

མེད་ Negative form of 3rd person singular, present indicative.

ལམ་ཀ་ Nominative Singular. *The* is omitted because it does not represent *this* or *that*.

བདེ་པོ་ Nominative Singular.

ཡོད་པས་ Interrogative form of the 3rd person singular present indicative (Cap. V, para. 5).

བདེ་ཤག་ཚོད་ Nominative Singular. *Very* expressed by adding ཤག་ཚོད་ to the root of the adjective [Cap. X, para. 3 (*m*)].

ཡོད་ 3rd person singular, present indicative.

ད་ Adverb.

འགྲོ་རྒྱུ་ Gerund of འགྲོ་བ་

ག་ཚོད་ Adverb. Being used interrogatively immediately precedes the verb [Cap. X, para. 3 (*f*)].

ཡོད་པ་ Interrogative form of the 3rd person, singular present indicative (Cap. V, para. 5).

ཕེབ་རྒྱུ་ Infinitive of ཕེབ་པ་ *hon.* of འགྲོ་བ་ (Cap. VI, para. 23).

ཞེ་པོ་རང་ Adverb. Used with negatives only [Cap. X, para. 3 (*g*)].

རྟག་ཙོ་གཅིག་ Adverb.

ལྷོང་ Adverb.

ཡག་ Abbreviation of ཡག་པོ་

བྱུང་ Past Participle of ཡོང་བ་ *to become, to happen.*

ག་ལེ་ Adverb.

རྒྱུག་ཨ་ Imperative of འགྲོ་བ་ polite form used to inferior.

ལགས་སི་ Honorific term.

ཕས་ཨ་ Polite Imperative of ཕས་པ་ which is an *hon.* form of འགྲོ་བ ॥ ॥

CHAPTER XVI.

CONVERSATIONAL EXERCISES.

1. *General Conversation.*

Who are you? ཁྱོད་སུ་ཡིན་པ། *khyö su yim-pa ?*

What is your name? ཁྱོད་མིང་ལ་ག་རེ་ཟེར་གྱི་ཡོད། *khyö ming-la ka-re śi ki-yö ?*

Sir, what is your name? *hon.* སྐུ་གཞོགས་ཀྱི་མཚན་ལ་ག་རེ་ཞུ་གི་ཡོད་ད། *ku-sho-kyi tshen-la ka-re shu-ki-yö ta ?*

My name is Dorje. ངའི་མིང་ལ་རྡོ་རྗེ་ཟེར་གྱི་ཡོད། *nge-ming-la Dorje śi-kyi yo.*

Do you know this? *hon.* འདི་མཁྱེན་པ་གནང་གི་ཡོད་པས། *di khyem-pa nang-gi yö-pe ?*

I don't know. ངས་ཤེས་ཀྱི་མེད། *nge shing-gi me.*

Do you know this man? *hon.* མི་འདི་ངོ་མཁྱེན་པ་གནང་གི་ཡོད་པས། *mi di ngo-khyem-pa nang-gi yö-pe ?*

I don't know him. ངས་ཁོ་ངོ་ཤེས་ཀྱི་མེད། *nge kho ngo-shing-gi me.*

What country have you come from? ཁྱོད་ལུང་པ་ག་ནས་ཡིན་པ། *khyö lung-pa ka-ne yim-pa ?*

Sir, where were you born? *hon.* སྐུ་གཞོགས་འཁྲུང་ས་ག་ནས་ཡིན་པ་གནང་ང་། *ku-sho thrung-sa ka-ne yim-pa nang-nga ?*

I was born in Kongbu. ང་སྐྱེ་ས་ཀོང་པོ་ནས་ཡིན། *nga kye-sa kong-po-ne yin.*

A man has come. མི་གཅིག་བསླེབས་བྱུང་། *mi chi lep-chung.*

Who is that boy? བུ་གུ་དེ་སུ་རེད། *pu-gu te su-re?*

I want to be off to-morrow (*lit.* I am counting on starting to-morrow). ང་སང་ཉིན་འཐོན་པའི་རྩིས་ཡོད། *nga sang-nyin thöm-pe tsi yö.*

Will he come now? ཁོ་ད་ལྟ་སླེབ་ཡོང་ངས། *kho tan-da lep yong-nge?*

Open the window a little please. སྒེ་ཁུང་ཏོག་ཙ་ཕྱེ་རོགས་གནང་། *gi-khung tok-tsa chhe-ro-nang.*

Shut the door. སྒོ་རྒྱབ། *go-gyap.*

When did he go? ཁོ་ག་དུས་ལངས་སོང་། *kho ka-tü lang-song?*

How do you like this place? (*lit.* Sir, is this place pleasant?) *hon.* སྐུ་གཞོགས་ས་ཆ་འདི་སྤྲོ་པོ་འདུག་གས། *ku-sho sa-chha di tro-po duk-ke?*

It is very quiet. ས་ཆ་འདི་ཁ་གུ་སིམ་པོ་འདུག་ *sa-cha di kha-ku-sim-po du.*

I am very pleased to have come (*lit.* it is very good that I have come here). ང་མདས་བཙར་ནས་ཡག་ཐག་ཆོད་བྱུང་།། *nga de char-ne yak-thak-chhö chung.*

---

2. *The same continued.*

Please give me a cup of water. ང་ལ་ཆུ་དཀར་ཡོལ་གང་སྟེར་ད། *nga-la chhu ka-yö kang te-da.*

Tell the man to come to me. མི་དེ་ཚུར་ཤོག་ཁྱིས། *mi te tshu sho chi.*

Please give this bundle to the woman. དོག་ཁྲེད་འདི་སྐྱེ་དམན་དེ་ལ་སྐུར་རོགས་གནང་། *dok-thre di kyi-men te-la kur-ro-nang.*

Can I go there? ང་ཕ་གེ་ཕྱིན་ཆོག་གི་རེད་པས། *nga pha-ke chhin chhok-ki-re-pe?*

Are you coming with me? ཁྱོད་ང་མཉམ་པོ་ཡོང་གི་ཡིན་པས། *khyö nga nyam-po yong-gi yim-pe?*

He can come. ཁོ་ཡོང་ཆོག་གི་རེད། *kho yong chhok-ki-re.*

Where have you come from? ཁྱོད་ག་ནས་ཡོང་ང་། *khyö ka-ne yong-nga?*

I came from Phari this morning. ང་ད་རང་གཞོག་གས་ཕག་རི་ནས་ཡོང་ང་ཡིན། *nga ta-rang shok-ke pha-ri ne yong-nga yin.*

Are you quite well? *hon.* སྐུ་གཞོགས་སྐུ་གཟུགས་བདེ་པོ་ཡོད་པས། *kü-sho ku-su de-po yo-pe?*

Fairly well, thanks. ལགས་ཨའུ་ཙེ་ཡོད། *lā au-tse yo.*

When will the man come to see me? མི་དེ་ངའི་རྩ་ལ་ག་དུས་ཡོང་གི་རེད། *mi-te nge tsa-la ka-tü yong-gi-re?*

I don't know whether he will come for some months. ཟླ་ཤས་སླེབ་ཨེ་ཡོང་ངས་ཡག་པོ་རང་ཤེས་ཀྱི་མེད། *da-she lep-e-yong nge yak-po-rang shing-gi-me.*

How long are you staying on here? *hon.* མདས་ག་ཚོད་བཞུགས་གདན་འཛག་གི་ཡིན་པ། *de ka-tshö shu-den-ja-ki yim-pa?*

How do you know he is a Bhutanese? ཁོ་འབྲུག་པ་ཡིན་པ་ཁྱོད་རས་ག་འདྲས་བྱས་ནས་ཤེས་ཀྱི་ཡོད། *kho druk-pa yim-pa khyö-re kan-dre che-ne shing-gi-yö?*

Is this story true? ཁོའི་སྐད་ཆ་འདི་དངོས་ནས་རེད་པས། *khö ke chha di ngo-ne re-pe?*

It is a good deal exaggerated (*lit.* he has tied on many feathers). སྐད་ཆ་དེ་སྒྲོ་མང་པོ་བཏགས་ནས་བཤད་པ་རེད། *ke-chha te dro mang-po tak-ne she-pa re.*

You had better not do that (*lit.* your not doing like that is preferable). ཁྱོད་དེ་འདྲ་མ་བྱས་པ་དགའ་གི་རེད། *khyö-ten-dra ma che-pa ga-ki-re.*

It does not matter. ཁྱད་མི་འདུག *khye min-du.*

There is no help for it (*lit.* there is no means of doing for this). འདི་བྱེད་ཐབས་ཡོད་པ་མ་རེད། *di-che-thap yo-wa ma re.*

That would not be quite right. དེ་ཏོག་ཙ་ཡོང་བ་མི་འདུག། *te tok-tsa yong-nga min-du.*

---

3. *Talk with Servants.*

Come here ! མདས་ཤོག *de sho.*

Go away ! ཕར་རྒྱུག *pha gyu.*

Come quickly ! མགྱོགས་པོ་ཤོག *gyok-po sho.*

Don't delay ! འགོར་པོ་མ་བྱེད། *gor-po ma-che.*

Throw this away ! འདི་ཕར་དབྱུག་ཤོག *di pha yuk-sho.*

Be careful ! ཏན་པོ་བྱིས། *tem-po chi.*

Take this away ! འདི་ཕར་འཁྱེར། *di pha khye.*

Wait a moment ! ཏོག་ཙ་སྒུག་ཤིག *tok-tsa gu-shi.*

I will come presently. ང་ལམ་སང་སླེབ་ཡོང་། *nga lam-sang lep-yong.*

Don't do that ! དེ་འདྲ་མ་བྱེད། *ten-dra ma-che.*

Don't make such a noise ! སྐད་དེ་འདྲ་མ་རྒྱག *ke ten-dra ma-gyak.*

Do this first and do that afterwards ! འདི་སྔན་ (སྔོན་) ལ་བྱིས། དེ་གཤུག་ལ་བྱིས། *di ngen-la chi ; te shuk-la chi.*

What is this ? འདི་ག་རེ་རེད། *di ka-re re?*

Is everything ready ? ཚང་མ་གྲལ་སྒྲིག་སོང་ངས། *tshang-ma tra-dri song-nge ?*

Where have you put my umbrella ? I cannot find it. ངའི་ཉི་གདུགས་ག་པ་བཞག་ཡོད། དེ་ང་བརྙེད་མ་བྱུང་། *nge nyi-du ka-pa sha yö ? te nga nye-ma-chung.*

---

4. *The same continued.*

Fetch some hot water ! ཆུ་ཚ་པོ་ཏོག་ཙ་འཁྱེར་ཤོག *chhu tsha-po tok-tsa khye sho.*

Please bring dinner (*hon.*) at half past seven. དགོང་མོའི་ཞལ་ལག་ཆུ་ཚོད་བདུན་དང་ཕྱེད་ཀ་ལ་ཕྱུལ། *gong-mö she-la chhu-tshö dün tang chhe-ka lā phü.*

Call me at a quarter past six to-morrow morning ! སང་ཞོགས་སྔ་པོ་ཆུ་ཚོད་དྲུག་དང་མི་ལི་བཅོ་ལྔ་ལ་ང་སྐད་གཏོང་། *sang-sho nga-po chhu-tshö truk tang mi-li che-nga la nga ke-tong.*

I want breakfast at a quarter to nine. ངའི་ཞོགས་གེའི་ཁ་ལག་ཆུ་ཚོད་དགུ་ཏུང་ང་ལ་མི་ལི་བཅོ་ལྔའི་སྔན་ལ་འཁྱེར་ཤོག *nge shok-kei kha-la chhu-tshö gu dung-nga lā mi-li che-nge ngen-la khye-sho.*

Call my servant ! ངའི་གཡོག་གོ་ (པོ་) སྐད་གཏོང་། *nge yok-ko ke-tong.*

The cook is ill to-day. དེ་རིང་མ་ཆེན་ན་གི་འདུག *te-ring ma-chhen na-ki-du.*

Have you swept this room? ཁང་པ་མདས་གེ་རྒྱབ་པས། *khang-pa de ke gyap-pe?*

Clean all the brass ornaments (*lit.* articles)! རག་གི་ཅ་ལག་སྒང་ཁ་འཕྱིད་དར་གཏོང་། *rak-ki cha-la gang kha chhi-dar tong.*

Put those there and throw these away! དེ་ཚོ་ཕ་གས་ཤོག། འདི་ཚོ་ཕར་དབྱུག *te-tsho pha-ke sho, di-tsho pha yu.*

Do you understand? ཁྱོད་ཧ་གོ་ཕྱུང་ངས། *khyö ha-ko chung-nge?*

What had we better do now? (*lit.* the doing what now is preferable). ད་ག་རེ་བྱས་པ་དགའ་གི་རེད། *ta ka-re che-pa ga-ki-re?*

Please take this letter to the post. ཡི་གེ་འདི་ཡིག་ཁང་ལ་འཁྱེར་རོགང་གྱིས། *yi-ge di yik-khang la khye-ro-chi.*

Come in! ནང་ལ་ཤོག *nang la-sho.*

Take this letter to the doctor, *hon.* ཨམ་ཆི་ལགས་ལ་ཡི་གེ་འདི་སྐྱེལ་ཤོག *am-chhi lā lă yi-ge di kye-sho.*

Let me know when the doctor *hon.* comes. ཨམ་ཆི་ལགས་ཕེབ་ཕྱུང་ན་ང་ལན་འཁྱེར་ཤོག *am-chhi la phe-chung-na, nga len khye-sho.*

5. *Food.*

I want a little drinking water. ང་འཐུང་ཡ་གི་ཆུ་ཏོག་ཙ་དགོས་ཡོད། *nga thung-ya-ki chhu tok-tsa go yö.*

Have you boiled it? ཆུ་དེ་སྐོལ་ར་ (བ་) ཡིན་པས། *chhu te kö-ra yim-pe?*

Is it from a spring or from a stream? ཆུ་མིག་གི་ཆུ་རེད་པ། རྒྱུག་ཆུའི་ཆུ་ཡིན་པ། *chhu-mi-ki chhu re-pa, gyuk-chhü-chhu yim-pa?*

Is milk obtainable here? མདས་འོ་མ་འབྱོར་ཡོང་ངས། *de o-ma jor-yong-nge?*

No, Sir, there are no cows. ལགས་སྐུ་གཞོགས་མདས་འབྱོར་མི་ཡོང་། མདས་བ་ཕྱུགས་ཡོད་པ་མ་རེད། *lā ku-sho de jor mi-yong; de pa-chhu yo-wa-ma-re.*

Bring tea at five o'clock. ཆུ་ཚོད་ལྔ་ལ་ཇ་འཁྱེར་ཤོག *chhu-tshö nga-la cha khye sho.*

Do you take milk and sugar in your tea? *hon.* འོ་མ་དང་ཅེ་མ་ཀ་ར་ཡོད་པའི་གསོལ་ཇ་ངར་མོ་བཞེས་ཀྱི་ཡོད་པས། *o-ma tang che-ma-ka-ra yö-pe sö-ja nga-mo she-kyi yök-pe?*

A little of each please. ལགས་ཏོག་ཙ་ཏོག་ཙ་འཐུང་གི་ཡོད། *lā tok-tsa tok-tsa thung-gi-yö.*

A Tibetan gentleman is coming to lunch with me to-morrow, *hon.* སང་ཉིན་བོད་པའི་སྐུ་དྲག་གཅིག་ངའི་རྩ་ལ་ཉིན་དགུང་ཞལ་ལག་བཞེས་ག་ཕེབ་པ་ཡོད། *sang-nyin pö-pe ku-tra chi nge tsa-la nyin-gung she-lu she-ga phe-pa-yö.*

What is there to eat? ཟ་ཡ་ག་རེ་ཡོད་པ། *śa-ya ka-re yö-pa?*

Mutton, fowls, eggs, Sir, and various kinds of vegetables. སྐུ་གཞོགས་གསོལ་སྐྲུམ་ལུག་ཤ་བྱ་ཏེའི་ཤ་བཞེས་སྒོང་དང་བཞེས་ཚས་སྣ་ཚོགས་ཡོད། *ku-sho sö-trum luk-sha cha-tei-sha she-gong tang she-tshe na-tsho yö.*

Will the Tibetan gentleman eat English food? *hon.* བོད་པའི་སྐུ་དྲག་གིས་དབྱིན་ཇིའི་ཞལ་ལག་བཞེས་ཡོང་ངས། *pö-pe ku-tra ki in-ji she-la she-yong-nge?*

Keep the kitchen thoroughly clean! གསོལ་ཐབ་གཙང་ཐག་ཆོད་བྱས་ནས་ཞོག *sö-thap tsang thak-chhö che-ne sho.*

I want two bottles of milk a day as long as I stay here. ང་མདངས་སྡོད་པའི་སྐང་ལ་ཉི་མ་རེ་ལ་འོ་མ་ཤེལ་དམ་གཉིས་གཉིས་དགོས་ཡོད། *nga de dö-pe gang-la nyi-ma re-la o-ma she-tam nyi-nyi go-yö.*

---

6. *Time of the Day, Days of the Week, Dates, Seasons, etc.*

What o'clock is it? ད་ལྟ་ཆུ་ཚོད་ག་ཚོད་རེད། *tan-da chhu-tshö ka-tshö re?*

It is three o'clock. ཆུ་ཚོད་གསུམ་རེད། *chhu-tshö sum re.*

It is half past ten. ཆུ་ཚོད་བཅུ་དང་ཕྱེད་ཀ་རེད། *chhu-tshö chu tang chhe-ka re.*

It is a quarter past three. ཆུ་ཚོད་གསུམ་དང་མི་ལི་བཅོ་ལྔ་སོང་། *chhu-tshö sum tang mi-li chö-nga song.*

It is a quarter to five. ཆུ་ཚོད་ལྔ་སླེབ་པ་ལ་མི་ལི་བཅོ་ལྔ་འདུག *chhu-tshö nga lep-pa la mi-li chö-nga du.*

What is the English date to-day? དེ་རིང་ཏ་རིག་ག་ཚོད་ཡིན་པ། *te-ring ta-rik ka-tshö yim-pa?*

It is the twenty-fifth! དེ་རིང་ཏ་རིག་ཉི་ཤུ་ཙ་ལྔ་*ཡིན། *te-ring ta-rik nyi-shu-tse-nga yin.*

What is the Tibetan date to-day? དེ་རིང་ཚེས་པ་ག་ཚོད་རེད། *te ring tshe-pa ka-tshö re?*

It is the twenty-second! དེ་རིང་ཉི་ཤུ་གཉིས་*རེད། *te-ring nyi-shu-nyi re.*

What day of the week is it? དེ་རིང་གཟའ་ག་རེ་རེད། *te-ring sa ka-re re?*

It is Thursday. དེ་རིང་གཟའ་ཕུར་བུ་རེད། *te-ring sa phur-pu re.*

Where did you go to yesterday? ཁྱོད་ཁས་ས་ག་པ་ཕྱིན་པ། *khyö khe-sa ka-pa chhim-pa?*

Don't come to-morrow, but come the day after to-morrow. སང་ཉིན་མ་ཡོང་། གནངས་ཉིན་ཀ་ཤོག *sang-nyin ma-yong; nang-nyin-ka sho.*

When it rains in the morning, it always clears up in the afternoon. ཞོགས་གས་ཆར་པ་རྒྱབ་ན། དགོང་མདག་ཏག་པར་གནམ་དྭངས་པོ་ཡོང་གི་འདུག *shok-ke chhar-pa gyap-na gong-da tak-pa nam tang-po yong-gi-du.*

---

* Note the difference between ཉི་ཤུ་ཙ་ལྔ་ and ཉི་ཤུ་གཉིས་ (Cap. VIII, para. 6).

It freezes hard at Phari during the whole winter and some times snows even in summer. ཕག་རིས་དགུན་ཀ་ཁྱགས་པ་རྒྱག་གི་འདུག་མཚམས་མཚམས་དབྱར་ཀ་ཡང་གངས་རྒྱག་གི *pha-re gün-ka khyak-pa gyak-ki du ; tsham-tsham yar-ka yang kang gyak-ki.*

To-day is the last day of the 2nd fourth month of the Wood-Dragon year. དེ་རིང་ཤིང་འབྲུག་ཟླ་བ་བཞི་པའི་ཉིས་བརྩེགས་ཀྱི་ནམ་གང་རེད། *te-ring shing-druk da-wa shi-pe nyi-tsak-kyi nam kang-re.*

---

7. *The same continued.*

Last month and this month the rain has been heavy, but it will probably not rain very much next month. ཟླ་བ་རྙིན་མ་དང་ཟླ་བ་འདི་ལ་ཆར་པ་ཞེ་སྐྲག་རྒྱབ་བྱུང་། ཕྱས་ཚང་ཟླ་བ་གཞུག་མ་དེ་ལ་ཆར་པ་མང་པོ་རང་འབབ་ཀྱི་མིན་འདུག *da-wa ngen-ma tang da-wa di-la chhar-pa she-tra gyap chung ; che-tsang da-wa shuk-ma te-la chhar-pa mang-po-rang bap-kyi min-dra.*

There is a lot of mist during the summer. དབྱར་ཀ་སྨུགས་པ་མང་པོ་འདུག *yar-ka muk-pa mang-po du.*

Will you meet him this evening? ཁྱོད་ར་དོ་དགོང་ཁོ་ཐུག་ཡོང་ངས། *khyö-ra to-gong kho thuk yong-nge?*

I cannot this evening, but perhaps to-morrow morning. དོ་དགོང་ཐུག་མི་ཡོང་། གཅིག་ཕྱས་ན་སང་ཞོགས་སྔ་པོ་ཐུག་ཡོང་། *to-gong thuk mi yong ; chik-che-na sang-sho nga-po thuk yong.*

The crops were bad last year and this year. Unless they are good next year, there will be great distress. ཟླ་སྙིང་དང་ད་ལོ་སྟོན་ཐོག་ཡག་པོ་མ་བྱུང་། ཕྱི་ལོ་ཡང་ཡག་པོ་མ་བྱུང་ན། གང་མན་ཚད་བྱེད་ཀྱི་རེད། *da-nying tang tu-lo tön-tho yak-po ma-chung; chhi-lo yang yak-po ma-chung na kang men-tshe che-kyi-re.*

Is my watch right? ངའི་ཆུ་ཚོད་འཁོར་ལོ་རྟེན་ལྡན་འདུག་གས། *nge chhu tshö khor-lo ten-den duk-ke?*

No, it is ten minutes fast. མི་འདུག། མི་ལི་བཅུས་མགྱོགས་ཀ། *min-du; mi-li chü gyok-ka.*

When did he leave here? ཁོ་འདི་ནས་ག་དུས་ཕྱིན་སོང་། *kho di-ne ka-tü chhin-song?*

From Lhasa to the Chumbi Valley is a fortnight's journey. ལྷ་ས་ནས་གྲོ་མོ་བར་ལ་བདུན་གཉིས་ཀྱི་ལམ་རེད། *hla-sa ne tro-mo par-la dün nyi-kyi lam-re.*

---

8. *The weather.*

What a strong wind! འདི་འདྲེའི་ལྷགས་པ་ཚ་ལ། *din-dre hlak-pa tsha la.*

What a cold day! འདི་འདྲེའི་གནམ་གྲང་ང་ལ། *din-dre nam trang-nga-la.*

I feel qnite warm. ང་དྲོ་ཐག་ཆོད་འདུག *nga tro thak-chhö du.*

There was a heavy dew last night. མདང་དགོང་མཚན་ལ་ཟིལ་པ་མང་པོ་བབ་འདུག *dang-gong tshen-la sil-pa mang-po pap-du.*

It is misty ; we cannot see the snow mountains. རྨུགས་པ་འཐིབ་བཞག། ང་ཚོས་གངས་རི་མཐོང་གི་མི་འདུག *muk-pa thip-sha ; ngan-tshö kang-ri thong-gi min-du.*

Do you think it will rain ? ཁྱོད་ཆར་པ་རྒྱབ་ཡོང་བསམ་གྱི་འདུག་གས། *khyö chhar-pa gyap-yong sam-kyi duk-ke ?*

It will probably be fine till midday. ཉིན་དགུང་བར་གནམ་ཡག་པོ་ཡོང་གི་ཡིན་པ་འདྲ། *nyin-gung par nam yak-po yong-gi yim-pa-dra.*

Will there be moonlight to-night ? དོ་དགོང་མཚན་ལ་ཟླ་དཀར་ཤར་གྱི་རེད་པས། *to-gong tshen-la da-kar sha-kyi re-pe ?*

There was heavy rain yesterday and a rainbow was visible. ཁས་ས་ཆར་པ་མང་པོ་བབ་སོང་། དེའི་འཇུག་ལ་འཇའ་གཅིག་ཟུག་སོང་། *khe-sa chhar-pa mang-po pap-song ; te-ï-juk-la ja chi suk-song.*

It is raining a little. ཆར་པ་ཏོག་ཙ་བབ་ཀྱི་འདུག *chhar-pa tok-tsa pap-kyi du.*

The rain has stopped. ཆར་པ་ཆད་སོང་། *chhar-pa chhe-song.*

A storm is coming up. རླུང་ཚུབ་གཅིག་ལང་གི་འདུག *lung-tshup chi lang-gi-du.*

Did you see the lightning ? ཁྱོད་གློག་རྒྱབ་པ་མཐོང་བྱུང་ངས། *khyö lo-gyap-pa thong-chung-nge ?*

I heard thunder. ངས་འབྲུག་སྐད་རྒྱབ་པ་གོ་བྱུང་། *nge druk-ke gyap-pa ko-chung.*

It won't freeze to-night, because it is cloudy. གནམ་འཐིབས་འདུག། བྱས་ཙང་དོ་དགོང་མཚན་ལ་ཁྱགས་པ་ཆགས་ཀྱི་མ་རེད། *nam thip du ; che-tsang to-gong tshen-la khyak-pa chha-kyi ma-re.*

9. *Conversation with the teacher*, hon.

Please speak slowly. ག་ལེ་བྱས་ནས་གསུང་རོགས་གནང་། *ka-le che-ne sung-ro nang.*

Please speak louder. གསུང་སྐད་ཆེ་ཙ་གསུང་རོགས་གནང་། *sung-ke chhe-tsa sung-ro-nang.*

What is he saying? ཁོང་གིས་ག་རེ་གསུང་གི་འདུག *khong-gi ka-re-sung-gi-du?*

I do not know. ངས་ཤེས་ཀྱི་མེད། *nge shing-gi me.*

Did I say that correctly? ངས་དེ་སྒྲ་དག་པོ་ལབ་སོང་ངས། *nge te dra-tak-po lap song-nge?*

We will read this letter. ང་རང་གཉིས་ཕྱག་བྲིས་འདི་ཀློག་ག་གནང་འདོ། *nga-rang-nyi chha-ri di lok-ka nang-do.*

This is easy. འདི་ལས་སླ་པོ་རེད། *di le-la-po re.*

I made a lot of mistakes. ངས་མང་པོ་ནོར་སོང་། *nge mang-po nor-song.*

I could not understand him; he spoke the Sikkimese dialect. ཁོས་འབྲས་ལྗོངས་སྐད་ལབ་ཙང་། ངས་ཁོའི་སྐད་ཆ་ཧ་གོ་མ་བྱུང་། *khö dren-jong ke lap tsang, nge khö ke-chha ha-ko ma-chung.*

Please arrange for a dandywala to come to me for an hour every day. ཕེབ་དཔྱང་ང་གཅིག་ཆུ་ཚོད་རེ་རེ་ཉི་མ་རེ་བཞིན་ངའི་རྩ་ལ་ཡོང་དགོས་རེད་ཟེར་བཀའ་གནང་རོགས་གནང་། *phep-chang-nga chi chhu-tshö re-re nyi-ma-re shin nge tsa-la yong go re se ka nang-ro-nang.*

It is essential that he should be a Lhasa man. ལྷ་ས་རང་གི་མི་ཅིག་དགོས་པ་ཡོད། *hle-sa rang-gi mi chi go-wa-yö.*

Please ask him to tell me stories. ང་ཁོས་སྒྲུང་ཤོད་གསུང་རོགས་གནང་། *nga khö drung shö sung-ro-nang.*

It is of no use trying to read this; it is too difficult. བརྩོན་འགྲུས་བྱས་ནས་འདི་ཀློག་ནས་ཕན་གང་ཡང་ཐོབ་ཀྱི་མི་འདུག། འདི་དཀའ་ལས་ཁག་པོ་རེད། *tsön-drü-che-ne di lok-ne phen kang-yang thok-ki min-du; di ka-le-khak-po re.*

I am sorry I am late; I met an acquaintance on the way (*lit.* I met an acquaintance on the way; therefore I am late. Please do not be angry). ང་དང་ལམ་འགག་ལ་ངོ་ཤེས་གཅིག་ཐུག་བྱུང་། བྱས་ཙང་ཕྱི་པོ་བྱས་སོང་དགོངས་པ་མ་མཚུངས། *nga-tang lang-ga la ngo-she chi thuk-chung; che-tsang chhi-po che-song gong-pa ma-tshung.*

That is enough for to-day. དེ་རིང་ད་གས་ཡོང་ང་། *te-ring ta-ke yong-nga.*

10. *Relatives*

She is my niece. མོ་ངའི་ཚ་མོ་* ཡིན། *mo nge tsha-mo yin.*

I have two younger brothers. ངའི་སྤུན་ཆུང་ང་ (བ་) གཉིས་ཡོད། *nge pün-chhung-nga nyi yö.*

These two are brother and sister. འདི་གཉིས་སྤུན་ཀྱག་རེད། *di nyi pün-kya re.*

How many nephews have you? ཁྱོད་ལ་ཚ་བོ† ག་ཚོད་ཡོད། *khyö-la tsha-wo ka-tshö yö?*

---

* and † Usually however སྤུན་ཀྱག་ though meaning also *brother*, *sister*, *cousin* is used for nephew and niece also.

My younger sister died three years ago. ངའི་སྤུན་ཀྱ་བུ་མོ་ཆུང་ང་ (བ་) གྲོངས་ནས་ལོ་གསུམ་སོང་། *nge pün-kya pu-mo chhung-nga trong-ne lo sum song.*

His elder sister is my maternal aunt. ཁོའི་ཨ་ཆེ་ངའི་སྲུ་མོ་ཡིན། *khö a-chhe nge su-mo yin.*

Their daughter was married to Tshering's adopted son. ཁོ་གཉིས་ཀྱི་བུ་མོ་ཚེ་རིང་གི་གསོས་ཕྲུག་ལ་མནའ་མ་སྟེར་སོང་། *kho-nyi kyi pu-mo tshe-ring-gi sö-thruk la na-ma te song.*

My son married his daughter. ངའི་བུས་ཁོའི་བུ་མོ་མནའ་མ་ལེན་སོང་། *nge pü-khö pu-mo na-ma len-song.*

Her grandfather is my paternal uncle. མོའི་པོའོ་ངའི་ཨ་ཁུ་ཡིན། *mö po nge a-khu yin.*

Only a few of my relatives live in Darjeeling, but I have a large number of acquaintances there. ངའི་ཉེ་བ་ཁ་ཤས་ཅིག་རྡོ་རྗེ་གླིང་ལ་སྡོད་ཀྱི་ཡོད། ཡིན་ན་ཡང་ངོ་ཤེས་མང་པོ་ཡོད། *nge nye-wa kha-she-chi Dor-je-ling-la dö-kyi-yö ; yin-na-yang ngo-she mang-po yö.*

---

11. *On the March.*

Let us start now; it is getting late. ད་ང་ཚོ་འགྲོ་གི་ཡིན། ཕྱི་པོ་ཁྱིས་ཀྱི་རེད། *ta ngan-tsho dro-kyi-yin ; chhi-po chi-kyi re.*

That box is very heavy; will the cooly be able to carry it? སྒམ་དེ་ལྗིད་ཐག་ཆོད་འདུག། མི་ཧྲང་གིས་འཁྱེར་ཐུབ་ཨ་ཡོང་། *gam-te ji thak-chhö-du ; mi-hrang-gi khye-thup a-yong?*

Tell the syces to saddle the ponies and bring them round at once. ཆིབས་དཔོན་ལ་ རྟའི་སྒ་བརྒྱབ་ནས་རྟ་ ཚོ་ལམ་སང་ཚུར་འཁྲིད་ཤོག་ལབ། *chhik-pön-la te-ga gyap-ne ta-tsho lam-sang tshu-thri-sho lap.*

It rained heavily last night; the road will be very muddy. མདང་དགོང་མཚན་ལ་ཆར་པ་ཤེ་སྟག་རྒྱབ་བྱུང་། ཇུས་ཚང་ལམ་འགག་ལ་རྫབ་ཤེ་སྟག་ཡོང་གི་རེད། *dang-gong tshen-la chha-pa she-tra gyap-chung; che-tsang lang-ga la dzap she-tra yong-gi-re.*

There is no wind; so it will not be cold. ད་ལྟ་ལྷགས་པ་རྒྱག་གི་མི་འདུག། ཇུས་ཚང་གནམ་གྲང་མོ་ཡོང་ང་མི་འདུག *tan-da hlak-pa gyak-ki min-du; che-tsang nam trang-mo yong-nga min-du.*

What is the road like? ལམ་འགག་བདེ་ལོས་ག་འདྲས་འདུག *lang-ga de-lö kan-dre du?*

Which is the best road? ལམ་འགག་ཡག་ཤོས་ཏེ་ག་གི་འདུག *lang-ga yak-shö te ka-ki du?*

To-day's march is down hill. དེ་རིང་གི་འགྲོ་ས་ཐུར་རེད། *te-ring-gi dro-sa thur re.*

It is steep up hill. གྱེན་གཟར་པོ་འདུག *kyen sar-po du.*

The servants and coolies have gone on ahead. ཞབས་ཕྱི་དང་མི་ཧྲང་ཚོ་སྔོན་ལ་ཕྱིན་སོང་། *shap-chhi tang mi-hrang-tsho ngen-la chhin song.*

They will reach Kalimpong before you do, Sir. བཀའ་བློན་སྤུང་ལ་སྐུ་གཤོགས་མ་ཕེབ་གོང་ལ་ཁོ་ཚོ་བསླེབ་ཡོང་། *ka-lön-pung-la ku-sho ma phep kong-la khon-tsho lep-yong.*

We have nearly arrived. ང་ཚོ་སླེབ་འ་གྲོ་ཡོད། *ngan-tsho-lep tro yö.*

The bedding is wet. ཉལ་ཆས་སྦངས་བཞག *nge-chhe bang sha.*

Light a fire and dry it. མེ་བཏང་ནས་སྐམ། *me-tang-ne kam.*

How much a day are you paying each cooly? ཁྱོད་རས་ཉིན་མ་རེ་ལ་མི་ཧྲང་རེ་ལ་གླ་ག་ཚོད་སྤྲོད་ཀྱི་ཡོད། *khyö-re nyi-ma-re-la mi-hrang re-la la ka-tshö trö-kyi yö?*

Eight annas each a day; they would not come for less. ཉིན་མ་རེ་ལ་གླ་ཨ་ན་བརྒྱད་བརྒྱད་སྤྲོད་ཀྱི་ཡོད། དེ་མ་སྤྲད་པ་ཁོ་ཚོ་ཡོང་གི་མི་འདུག *nyi-ma-re-la la anna gye-gye trö-kyi yö; te ma-tre-pa khon-tsho yong-gi min-du.*

What time shall we start to-morrow? སང་ང་ཚོ་ཆུ་ཚོད་ག་ཚོད་ལ་འཐོན་ག། *sang ngan-tsho chhu-tshö ka-tshö la thön-ga?*

Let us start very early before the snow becomes soft. ཞོགས་གས་སྔ་པོ་གངས་མ་བཞུ་གོང་ནས་ང་ཚོ་འགྲོ་དོ། *shok-ke nga-po kang ma-shü kong-ne ngan-tsho dro-to.*

---

12. *The same continued.*

Have my baggage mules arrived? ངའི་ཁལ་དྲེལ་ཚོ་བསླེབས་བྱུང་ངས། *nge khe-tre-tsho lep chung-nge?*

What must I pay for each riding mule from here to Phari? འདི་ནས་ཕག་རི་ཐུག་ངས་བཞོན་དྲེལ་རེ་ལ་ཏ་གླ་ག་ཚོད་སྤྲད་དགོས་ཀྱི་རེད། *di-ne pha-ri thuk nge shön-tre re-la tap-la ka-tshö tre gö-kyi re?*

Is it safe to ride over this bridge? ཟམ་པ་འདིའི་སྒང་ལ་རྟ་བཞོན་ནས་ཕྱིན་ན་གའི་བྱས་མི་ཡོང་ངས། *śam-pa di-ï gang-la ta shön-ne chhin-na kai che mi yong-nge?*

I am going on ahead. ང་སྔོན་ལ་འགྲོ་གི་ཡིན། *nga ngen-la dro-kyi-yin.*

I am returning in a few days. ང་ཉི་མ་ཁ་ཤས་གཅིག་ལ་ལོག་ཡོང་གི་ཡིན། *nga nyi-ma kha-she-chi-la lok yong-gi-yin.*

I have forgotten to bring any money with me. ངས་དངུལ་འཁྱེར་ཡོང་རྒྱུ་རྗེད་ནས་མི་འདུག *nge ngü khe-yong-gyu je-ne min-du.*

Is this the road for Pemionchi? པདྨ་དབྱངས་རྩེ་འགྲོ་སའི་ལམ་འགག་འདི་རེད་པས། *pe-ma-yang-tse dro-se lang-ga di re-pe?*

My pony is limping; see whether it has a stone in any of its shoes (*lit.* in its hoof). ངའི་རྟ་འདིའི་རྐང་པ་འཁྱོག་གི་འདུག། རྨིག་པ་ལ་རྡོ་ཡོད་མེད་ལྟོས། *nge ta di-ï kang-pa khyo-ki du; mik-pa la do yö-me-tö.*

Go slowly; the road is slippery *hon.* (*lit.* there will be a slipping on the road). ག་ལེ་ག་ལེ་བྱས་ནས་ཕེབས། ཕེབ་ལམ་ལ་ཞབས་འདྲེད་ཤོར་ཡོང་། *ka-le ka-le che-ne phe; phep-lam la shap-dre sho-yong.*

Please tell my syce to hurry and catch me up (*lit.* to catch my tracks quickly and come). ངའི་ཆིབས་དཔོན་མགྱོགས་པོ་རྗེས་ཟིན་པ་ཤོག་གསུང་རོགས་གནང་། *nge chhik-pön gyok-po je-śim-pa sho sung-ro-nang.*

I am going to halt here a short time and rest our ponies. ང་མདས་ཏོག་ཙ་བསྡད་ནས་རྟ་ཚོ་ངལ་གསོ་རྒྱག་རུ་བཅུག་གི་ཡིན། *nga de tok-tsa de-ne ta-tsho nge-so gyak-ru chuk-ki-yin.*

Bring me one of those flowers to look at! (*lit.* pluck and bring one of those flowers; I will look at it). ཕ་གི་མེ་ཏོག་དེ་ཚོའི་ནང་ནས་གཅིག་གཏོག་ནས་འཁྱེར་ཤོག་དང་། ང་མིག་ལྟ་གི་ཡིན། *pha-gi me-to te-tshö nang-ne chi tok-ne khye-sho-tang, nga mik ta-kyi-yin.*

Cut me a switch from the road-side bushes, as I have not got a whip. ང་ལ་རྟ་ལྕག་མེད་ཙང་། ལམ་གྱི་ཟུར་གྱི་ཤིང་ཆུང་ཆུང་ཕ་ནས་ལྕང་སྨྱུག་གཅིག་བཅད་ནས་འཁྱེར་ཤོག *nga-la te-cha me-tsang, lam-kyi sur-kyi shing chhung-chhung pha-ne chang-nyuk chi che-ne khye-sho.*

I will call on you when I return from Mongolia. ང་སོག་ཡུལ་ནས་འཁོར་མཚམས་ཁྱེད་དང་མཇལ་ཆོག་ག་ཞུ་དགོས། *nga sok-yul ne khor-tsham khye tang je chhok-ka shu-go.*

---

13. *The same continued.*

Is there much snow on the pass? ལ་ལ་གངས་ཞེ་པོ་འདུག་གས། *la lă kang she-po duk-ke?*

There is not much on the pass itself, but there is rather more on the way up to it (*lit.* before arriving). ལ་རང་ལ་ཞེ་པོ་རང་མི་འདུག། སླེབ་སླེབ་གོང་ལ་* ཏོག་ཙ་ཆེ་བ་འདུག *la rang lă she-po-rang min-du; lep-lep kong-la tok-tsa chhe-a du.*

How far (*lit.* how much to go) is the nearest village from here? འདི་ནས་གྲོང་གསེབ་ཐག་ཉེ་ཤོས་ལ་འགྲོ་རྒྱུ་ག་ཚོད་ཡོད། *di-ne trong-se thak-nye-shö-lă dro-gyu ka tshö yö?*

---

* སླེབ་སླེབ་གོང་ལ་=མ་སླེབ་གོང་ལ

It is quite near, Sir. ལགས་ཐག་ཉེ་ཐག་ཚོད་ཡོད། *lā thak-nye thak-chhö yö.*

It is a long way, Sir. ལགས་ཐག་རིང་པོ་ཡོད། *lā tha-ring-po yö.*

It is a moderate distance, Sir. ལགས་འབྲིང་ཅིག་* ཡོད། *lā dring-chi yö.*

It is a day's journey, Sir. ལགས་ཞག་པོ་ཅིག་གི་ས་ཡོད། *lā shak-po chik-ki sa yö.*

It is a three or four hours' journey, Sir. ལགས་ཚ་འཕོག་ཅིག་གི་ས་ཡོད། *lā tsa-pho chik-ki sa-yö.*

How many houses are there in the village? གྲོང་གསེབ་དེའི་ནང་ལ་གྲོང་པ་ག་ཚོད་ཡོད། *trong-se te-ï nang-la trong-pa ka-tshö yö?*

I cannot say exactly, Sir. ལགས་ང་ཏྲེན་ལྡན་ཤུ་ཡ་མེད་†། *lā nga ten-den shu-ya me.*

How many approximately (*lit.* by guess)? ཚོད་བྱེད་ན་ག་ཚོད་ཡོད། *tshö-che-na ka-tshö yö?*

How many adult men and women are there in the village? གྲོང་གསེབ་དེ་ལ་གཞོན་པ་དང་གཞོན་མ་ག་ཚོད་ཡོད། *trong-se te-la shöm-pa tang shön-ma ka-tshö yö?*

How many monks are there in that monastery up there? ཡ་གི་དགོན་པ་དེ་ལ་གྲྭ་པ་ག་ཚོད་ཡོད། *ya-gi gom-pa te-la tra-pa ka-tshö yö?*

---

*གང་མཚམས་ཅིག་ may be substituted for འབྲིང་ཅིག་ Both are commonly used.

† *Lit.* There is not to me the saying accurately. Note the use of ཤུ་བ (Cap. VI, para. 24).

What provisions are obtainable in this place? ལུང་པ་མདས་ (འདི་རུ་) ཟ་ཡ་ག་རེ་ག་རེ་འབྱོར་ཡོང་*། *lung-pa de sa-ya ka-re ka-re jor-yong?*

Yak's flesh, Sir, mutton, pork, fowls, eggs, wheat, barley, barley flour, potatoes, turnips, radishes are all obtainable. ཚག་ཤ་ལུག་ཤ་ཕག་ཤ་བྱ་ཏེ་སྒོ་ང་གྲོ་ནས་རྩམ་པ་ཞོ་ཀོག་ཉུང་མ་ལ་ཕུག་བྱུས་ལགས† དེ་རྒྱུས་འབྱོར་ཡོང་‡། *tshak-sha luk-sha phak-sha cha-te go-nga tro ne tsam-pa sho-ko nyung-ma la-phu che lā te-gye jor-yong.*

What is the road like from here to Gyantse? འདི་ནས་རྒྱལ་རྩེ་བར་ལམ་ཀ་བདེ་ལོས་ག་འདྲས་ཡོད§། *di-ne gyan-tse par lang-ga de-lö kan-dre yö?*

Can laden ponies and laden mules travel over it? ཁལ་མ་རྟ་དང་དྲེ་འགྲོ་ཐུབ་ཀྱི་རེད་པས། *khe-ma ta-tang tre dro thup-kyi re-pe?*

Is there any short cut? མགྱོགས་ལམ་འགྲོ་ས་ཡོང་ངས།། *gyok-lam dro-sa yong-nge?*

---

* *Lit.* What provisions will be obtained in the country here?

† ལགས་ is often spoken inside the sentence instead of at the beginning.

‡ These are the kinds of provisions commonly obtainable in the Ü (Lhasa) and Tsang (Shigatse) provinces.

§ *Lit.* from here as far as Gyantse what kind of goodness has the road? བདེ་པོ་ is somewhat commoner than ཡག་པོ་ in the sense of *good* as applied to a road, but ཡག་པོ་ can also be used.

14. *Crossing a river.*

How broad is that stream over there? ཕ་གི་ཆུ་དེའི་ཞང་ (ཞེང་) ཆེ་ལོས་ག་འདྲས་འདུག། *pha-gi chhu te-ī shang chhe-lö kan-dre du?*

It is not very broad, Sir. ལགས་ཞང་ (ཞེང་) ཆེན་པོ་རང་* མི་འདུག། *la shang-chhem-po-rang min-du.*

Are there any boats where the road meets it? (*Lit.* the road and stream meeting-place, there are boats?) ཆུ་དང་ལམ་ཐུག་ས་དད་ (དེར་) ཀོ་བ་† ཡོད་པས། *chhu tang lam thuk-sa te ko-wa yö-pe?*

No, Sir. ལགས་ཡོད་པ་མ་རེད། *la yo-wa-ma-re.*

How do people get across? (*Lit.* how does one cross the stream and arrive at the farther side?) ཆུ་དེའི་ཕར་ཕྱོགས་ལ་ག་འདྲ་བྱས་ནས་སླེབ་ཀྱི་རེད། *chhu te-ï pha-chho-la kan-dre che-ne lep-kyi-re?*

There is a ford if you go a little lower down. མར་ཙུ་ (ཙམ་) ད་ག་ཕེབ་ན་‡ རབ་ཅིག་ཡོད། *ma-tsa ta-ka phep-na rap-chi-yö.*

---

*རང་ joined to a negative means *not very* and is very commonly used in this way. So also མང་པོ་རང་མི་འདུག། *there are not very many.*

†ཀོ་བ་ means a boat made of hide. For a boat made of wood use གྲུ་

‡Note the *hon.* ཕེབ་ན་ instead of ཕྱིན་ན་ If the Tibetan is a townsman or has any education he will use the higher *hon.* འཆིབ་ཀྱུ་གནང་ན།

Whose foot-prints are these? འདི་སུའི་ཀང་རྗེས་རེད། *di sü kang-je re?*

I do not know, Sir. ལགས་ཤེས་ཀྱི་མེད། *la shing-gi me.*

If you speak the truth, I will give you bakshish; if you tell (me) a lie, you will get into trouble (*lit.* it will not be good for you). དངོས་ནས་བཤད་ན་ངས་ཁྱོད་ལ་ངན་པ་སྟེར་གྱི་ཡིན། ཧམ་པ་* བཤད་ན་ཁྱོད་ལ་ཡག་པོ་མི་ཡོང་། *ngö-ne she-na nge khyö-la ngem-pa te-kyi-yin; ham-pa she-na khyö-la yak-po mi-yong.*

They are only the foot-prints of traders coming from Shigatse. འདི་གཞིས་ཀ་རྩེ་ནས་ཡོང་མཁན་གྱི་ཚོང་པའི་ཀང་རྗེས་ཤ་སྟག་རེད། *di shi-ga-tse-ne yong-khen-kyi tshong-pe kang-je sha-ta re.*

How deep is this water? (*Lit.* this water depth how much is.) ཆུ་འདི་གཏིང་རིང་ཐུང་ག་ཚོད་འདུག *chhu-di ting ring-thung ka-tshö-du?*

It is about (up to one's) waist, Sir. ལགས་སྐེད་པ་ཙ་ (ཙམ་) རྒྱག་གི་འདུག། *lā ke-pa tsa gyak-ki-du.*

What sort of a road is there by the ford (*lit.* at the ford-existing-place)? རབ་ཡོད་ས་ལ་ལམ་ཀ་ག་འདྲ་ཡོད་པ། *rab yö-sa-la lang-ga kan-dre yö-pa?*

On this side it is rock; on the other side it is all mud. ཚུར་ཕྱོགས་ལ་བྲག་ཡོད་པར་ཕྱོགས་ལ་འདམ་ཤ་སྟག་ཡོད། *Tshu-chho-la tra yö pha-chho-la dam sha-ta yö.*

---

* ཀུག་རྫུན་ may be used instead of ཧམ་པ་

Is there a bridge across that stream over there ? ཕ་གི་ཆུ་ལ་ཟམ་པ་ཡོད་པས། *pha-gi chhu-la śam-pa yö-pe ?*

Yes, Sir. ལགས་ཡོད། *lā yö.*

Is it a good one ? ཡག་པོ་ཡོད་པས། *yak-po yö-pe ?*

It is shaky and narrow (*lit.* it shakes and its breadth is small). Ponies cannot cross by it (*lit.* there is no passage for ponies.) ལགས་ཧྲེམ་ཧྲེམ་བྱེད་ཀྱི་ཡོད་ཞང་ (ཞིང་) ཀ་ཡང་ཆུང་ཆུང་ཡིན། ཆིབས་པ་ཐར་ས*མེད། *lā dem-dem che kyi-yö ; shang-ka yang chhung-chhung yin ; chhik-pa thar-sa me.*

---

15. *Talking to persons on the road.*

Where have you come from ? ཁྱོད་ག་ནས་ཡོང་ང་། *khyö ka-ne yong-nga ?*

I have come from Rhenok. ང་རི་ནས་ཡོན་ང་ (བ་) ཡིན། *nga ri-nak ne yong-nga yin.*

What is there in those loads ? དོག་ཁྲེད་དེ་ཚོའི་ནང་ལ་ག་རེ་ཡོད་པ། *dok-thre te-tshö nang-la ka-re yö-pa ?*

Cotton cloth in these sacks and cups, soap, matches and miscellaneous goods in those boxes. ཕད་ཀོག་འདི་ཚོའི་ནང་ལ་རས་ཆ་དང་། སྒམ་དེ་ཚོའི་ནང་ལ་དཀར་ཡོལ་དང་ཡི་རྩེ་སྨུ་ཟི་དང་ཅ་ལག་སྣ་ཚོགས་ཡོད། *phe-ko di-tshö nang-la re-chha tang, gam te-tshö nang-la ka-yö tang yi-tse mu-śi tang cha-la na-tsho yö.*

---

* ཐར་བ་ is commonly used in the sense of "to be passable," e.g., ལམ་ཀ་ཐར་གྱི་མི་འདུག། *the road is not passable* (i.e., too rough to march along, or blocked by snow, boulders, etc.).

No, I am not a Tibetan, Sir, I am a Bhutanese. ལགས་སྐུ་གཞོགས་ང་བོད་པ་མིན། ང་འབྲུག་པ་ཡིན། *lā hu-sho nga pö-pa min, nga druk-pa yin.*

Where are you going to? ཁྱོད་ག་པ་འགྲོ་གི་ཡིང་པ། *khyö ka-pa dro-ki-yim-pa?*

I am going on pilgrimage to India. ང་རྒྱ་གར་གནས་སྐོར་ལ་འགྲོ་གི་ཡིན། *nga gya-ka ne-kor-la dro-ki yin.*

What places will you visit? ཁྱོད་གནས་ག་རེ་སྐོར་ག་འགྲོ་གི་ཡིན། *khyo ne ka-re ko-ga dro-ki yin?*

I shall go to Bodh Gaya and Benares. ང་རྒྱ་གར་རྡོ་རྗེ་གདན་དང་ཝ་ར་ན་སི་ལ་འགྲོ་གི་ཡིན། *nga gya-ka dor-je-den tang wa-ra-na-si la dro-ki yin.*

Please give me some bakshish, Sir. སྐུ་གཞོགས། ང་ལ་གསོལ་རས་ཏོག་ཙ་གནང་རོགས་གནང་། *ku-sho nga-la sö-re tok-tsa nang-ro nang.*

Are you taking those sheep to Darjeeling? ཁྱོད་ལུག་དེ་ཚོ་རྡོ་རྗེ་གླིང་ལ་དེད་* འགྲོ་གི་ཡིན་པས། *khyö luk te-tsho Dor-je-ling la te dro-ki yim-pe?*

Is this one of the halting places for mules carrying wool to Kalimpong? བཀའ་བློན་སྤུང་ལ་བལ་འཁྱེར་འགྲོ་མཁན་† དྲེ་ཚོ་སྡོད་ས་ས་ཆ་གཅིག་འདི་རེད་པས། *ka-lön-pung la pe khye-dro-khen tre-tsho dö-sa sa-cha chi di re-pe?*

Who lives in that house? ནང་ཕ་གས་སུ་བསྡད་ཀྱི་ཡོད་པ་རེད། *nang pha-ge su de-kyi yo-wa-re?*

---

* For one or two sheep འཁྲིད་འགྲོ་བ་ *to lead*, would be used; for a larger number དེད་འགྲོ་བ *to drive*, as above.

† The postposition ཀྱི་ denoting the genitive, is sometimes dropped for the sake of brevity.

16. *General enquiries by an Interpreter in the field.*

Are there any soldiers behind that hill? ཕ་གི་རིའི་རྒྱབ་ལ་དམག་མི་ཡོད་པས། *pha-gi ri-ï gyap-la mak-mi yö-pe?*

Have they all got guns? ཁོ་ཚོ་སྒང་ཁ་ལ་མེ་མདའ་ཡོད་པས། *khon-tsho gang-kha-la men-da yö-pe?*

The majority of them have got swords and spears only. མང་ང་ (བ་) ལ་གྲི་དང་མདུང་ཤ་སྟག་ཡོད། *mang-nga la tri-tang dung sha-ta yö.*

Some of them have bows and arrows. ཁ་ཤས་ལ་མདའ་གཞུ་ཡོད། *kha-she la da-shu yö.*

Will the arrows be poisoned? མདའ་ལ་དུག་རྒྱབ་ཡོད་པ་རེད་པས། *da-la tuk gyap yo-wa re-pe?*

Yes, with aconite poison. ལགས་རེད་བཙན་དུག་རྒྱབ་ཡོད་པ་རེད། *lā-re tsen-tuk gyap yo-wa-re.*

Have they any cavalry with them? ཁོ་ཚོ་ལ་རྟ་དམག་ཡོད་པས། *khon-tsho-la ta-ma yö-pe?*

Not at present, but I heard a noise like that of ponies coming in the distance. ལགས་ད་ལྟ་མེད། རྟ་ཐག་རིང་པོ་གཅིག་ནས་ཡོང་གི་ཡོད་པ་འདྲ་པོ་གཅིག་གོ་བྱུང་། *lā tan-da me; ta tha-ring-po chi-ne yong-gi yö-pa dra-po chi ko-chung.*

Have the soldiers built a wall? དམག་མི་དེ་ཚོས་རྫིང་ར་* བཟོས་སོང་ངས། *mak-mi te-tshö dzing-ra sö song-nge?*

Yes, about so high (indicating his breast). ལགས་དག་་ག་ཙ་ (ཙམ་) བང་ (བྲང་) ཁོག་མཐོ་ལོས་ཙ་ (ཙམ་) བཟོས་སོང་། *lā tak-ka-tsa pang-kho tho-lö-tsa sö-song.*

---

*A fortified wall. རྩིག་པ་ is not used for wall in this sense.

How far does the wall extend to the east of the road? ལམ་ཀ་ཤར་ཕྱོགས་ཀྱི་འཛིང་ར་ག་རེ་*བར་དུ་འདུག། *lang-ga shar-chho kyi dzing-ra ka-re par-tu du?*

About as far as that mule over there carrying shovels. ཕ་གི་དྲེ་འཇག་མ་འཁུར་ཡོང་མཁན་དག་ག་ཙ་ (ཙམ་) གཅིག་ལ་ཡོད།། *pha-gi tre ja-ma khur-yong-khen tuk-ka-tsa chi-la yö.*

---

17. *The same continued.*

Is it the custom of the Tibetans to attack at night? བོད་པས་མཚན་ཐེག་†རྒྱབ་པའི་ལུགས་སྲོལ་ཡོད་པ་རེད་པས། *po-pe tshen-thi gyap-ye luk-sö yo-wa re-pe?*

Yes, Sir. ལགས་ལུགས་སྲོལ་ཡོད་པ་རེད། *lā luk-sö yo-wa-re.*

What sort of cannon have they got? ཁོ་ཚོའི་མེ་སྒྱོགས་ག་འདྲ་ཡོད། *khon-tshö me-gyo kan-dre yö?*

About how far will they carry? (*lit.* to about what distance will the cannon-balls arrive?) མེ་སྒྱོགས་ཀྱི་བདེའུ་ཐག་རིང་ལོས་ག་ག་ཙ་ (ཙམ་) སླེབ་ཡོང་། *me-gyo kyi di-u thak-ring-lö ka-ka-tsa lep-yong?*

How did they get their cannon across the river? མེ་སྒྱོགས་དེ་ཚོ་ཆུ་ལ་ ག་འདྲ་བྱས་ ནས་འཁྱེར་ཡོང་ང་ (བ་) རེད། *me-gyo te-tsho chhu-la kan-dre che-ne khe yong-nga-re?*

---

*Here ག་རེ་ has the sense of ག་པ་ Either may be used.

†མཚན་ཐེག་ (མཚན་རྡེབ་) = night-attack.

All arms must be handed in to me (*lit.* bring all arms to me) before noon to-morrow. ཁྱོད་རང་ཚོ་མཚོན་ཆ་སྔང་ཁ་སང་ཉིན་གུང་གོང་ལ་ངའི་རྩ་ལ་འཁྱེར་ཤོག། *khyö-rang-tsho tshön-chha gang-kha sang nyin-kung kong-la nge tsa-la khe-sho.*

Anybody who is found in possession of arms after that will be severely punished. གཞུག་ལ་སུའི་རྩ་ནས་མཚོན་ཆ་འཐོན་ན་ཉེས་པ་ཆེན་པོ་བཏང་ (གཏོང་) གི་ཡིན། *sku-la sü tsa-ne tshön-chha thön-na nye-pa chhem-po tang-gi-yin.*

18. *Buying supplies for troops.*

Have you any grain and grass to sell? འབྲུ་* དང་རྩྭ་འཚོང་རྒྱུ་ཡོད་པས། *dru tang tsa tshong-gyu yö-pe?*

I will pay you two-and-a-half trang-kas per bo for it. I have brought the money with me (showing it). འབྲུ་འབོ་† རེ་ལ་རིན་ཏྲཾ་ཀ་ཕྱེད་དང་གསུམ་སྤྲོད་ཀྱི་ཡིན། ངས་དངུལ་མདམ་ (འདི་རུ་) འཁྱེར་ཡོད། *dru bo re-la ring trang-ka chhe-tang sum-sum trö-kyi-yin ; nge ngü de khe-yö.*

The grain and grass are in that village up there. I cannot bring it down. ལགས་འབྲུ་དང་རྩྭ་ཡ་གི་གྲོང་པ་ལ་ཡོད་པ་རེད། ངས་མར་འཁྱེར་ཡོང་ཐུབ་ཀྱི་མ་རེད། *lā dru tang tsa ya-ki trong-pa lă yo-wa-re ; nge ma khe-yong thup-kyi ma-re.*

---

* Grain for animals=ཆག་ ; that for men=འབྲུ་

† 1 bo=about $\frac{1}{3}$ of a maund ; 1 trang-ka=$\frac{1}{4}$ of a rupee. The *maund* (pronounced in Tibetan *mön*) is not generally understood by Tibetans other than those that trade in British territory.

Never mind! I can have it fetched. (*Lit.* I can send the carriers). ཨའུ་ཙེ་འཁྱེར་མཁན་ངས་བཏང་ (གཏོང་) ཆོག་ *au-tse khe-khen nge tang-chho.*

No violence will be shown to anybody སུ་ལ་ཡང་དབང་ཡོད་* བྱེད་མི་ཡོང་། *su-la-yang wang-yö che-mi-yong.*

Please, Sir, pay me for the fodder now. སྐུ་གཞོགས་རྩྭ་ཆག་†གི་རིན་ད་ལྟ་གནང་རོགས་གནང་། *ku-sho tsa-chha-ki ring tan-da nang-ro-nang.*

No! I will pay you when I get the fodder. ད་ལྟ་སྤྲོད་ཀྱི་མིན་ (མིན།) རྩྭ་ཆག་མདས་ (འདི་རུ་) འབྱོར་ནས་སྤྲོད་ཀྱི་ཡིན།། *tan-da trö-kyi-men; tsa-chha de jor-ne trö-kyi-yin.*

---

19. *The same continued.*

Can I get any fuel here? མདས་ (འདི་རུ་) མེ་ཤིང་འབྱོར་གྱི་རེད་པས། *de me-shing jor-kyi re-pe?*

Not even yak-dung? ལྕོ་ (ལྕི་བ་) ཡང་འབྱོར་མི་ཡོང་ངས། *cho-yang jor mi-yong-nge?*

There is a little yak-dung, but we shall burn it ourselves; it is not for sale. ལྕོ་(ལྕི་བ)ཏོག་ཙ་ཡོད་དེ་ ‡ངར་རང་ཚོའི་མེ་གཏོང་ཡ་ མ་གཏོགས་ལགས་ §འཚོང་ཡ་མེད་**། *cho tok-tsa yö-te nga-rang-tshö me tong-ya ma-to lā tshong-ya me.*

---

*དབང་ཡོད་ = *Hind.* Zabardasti.

†རྩྭ་ཆག་ = *lit.* grass and grain.

‡དེ་ has here the sense of *but, in spite of.*

§Note the second ལགས་ It is put in because this is really a second sentence.

***Lit.* Apart from what we burn ourselves there is none for sale.

If you do not tell me where it is I shall search your house. ཁྱོ་ (ཁྱེ་བ་) ག་པ་ཡོད་མ་ལབ་ན་ངས་ཁང་པའི་ནང་ལ་འཚོལ་ (འཚོལ་) ཀྱི་ཡིན། *cho ka-pa yö ma-lap-na nge khang-pe nang-la tshe-kyi yin.*

I shall pay you for it in any case. ག་རེ་བྱས་ན་ *ཡང་རིན་སྤྲོད་ཀྱི་ཡིན། *ka-re che-na-yang ring trö-kyi-yin.*

It is against our orders to take things without paying for them. རིན་མ་སྤྲད་པ་ལ་ལེན་ཆོག་གའི་ (པའི་) བཀའ་མེད་†། *ring ma-tre-pa-la len chhok-ke ka me.*

You will make a large profit, and will be able to live in comfort without working. ཁྱོད་རང་ལ་ཁེ་བཟང་ཆེན་པོ་ཡོང་གི་རེད། ལས་ཀ་བྱེད་མི་དགོས་པ་ལ་སྐྱིད་པོ་བྱས་ནས་སྡོད་རྒྱུ་ཡོང་གི་རེད།། *khyö-rang-la khep-śang chhem-po yong-gi-re; le-ka che mi-go-wa-la kyi-po che-ne dö-gyu yong-gi-re.*

---

20. *The same continued.*

I want to buy fifty donkeys. They must all be sound and strong. བུང་གུ་. (བོང་བུ་) སྐྱོན་མེད་པ་ཤེད་མོ་ཡག་པོ་ཤ་སྟག་ལྔ་བཅུ་ཐམ་པ་ངས་ཉོ་གི་ཡིན། *pung-gu kyön-me-pa she-mo yak-po sha-ta ngap-chu tham-pa nge nyo-ki-yin.*

**Lit.* *Whatever be done*, i.e., whether you sell willingly or I take forcibly.

†*Lit.* There is no order allowing to take on the nonpayment of the price.

Only twenty of these are fit to carry loads. འདིའི་ནང་ནས་ཉི་ཤུ་མ་གཏོགས་ཁལ་འཁུར་ཐུབ་པ་མི་འདུག །* *di-i nang-ne nyi-shu ma-to khe khur thup-pa min-du.*

How old is that sheep? ལུག་དེ་ཀད་གཞོན་† ག་འདྲ་རེད། *luk-te gen-shön kan-dre re?*

I will pick out thirty of them and give you ninety rupees for the lot. ང་ཚོ་ འི་ནང་ནས་སུམ་ཅུ་འདབས་ནས་རིན་སྣང་ཁ་བསྡམས་ནས་‡ སྒོར་མོ་དགུ་བཅུ་ཐམ་པ་སྤྲོད་ཀྱི་ཡིན། *te-tshö nang-ne sum-chu dam-ne ring gang-kha dom-ne gor-mo gup-chu tham-pa trö-kyi-yin.*

Go and bring all the grain and vegetables that you can get hold of. འབྲུ་དང་ཚས་གཙོད་ཁྱུང་ན་མདས་ (འདི་རུ་) འཁྱེར་ཤོག། *dru tang tshe ka-tshö chung-na de khe-sho.*

The owners will be well paid. བདག་པོ་ཚོ་ལ་རིན་ཡག་པོ་སྤྲོད་ཀྱི་ཡིན༎ *dak-po tsho-la ring yak-po trö-kyi-yin.*

---

21. *Buying meat in the bazaar.*

How far is it from here to the bazaar? འདི་ནས་ཁྲོམ་ལ་ཐག་རིང་ཐོས་ག་ཚོད་ཡོད། *di-ne throm-la tha-ring-lö ka-tshö yo?*

---

* Or ཐུབ་ཀྱི་མ་རེད་

†ཀད་གཞོན་ =age; *lit* old-young. See Cap. III, para 1.

‡སྣང་ཁ་བསྡམས་ནས་ = *lit.* having added all together, i.e., in the total.

It is close by. ལགས་ཕེབ་ཐག་ཉེ་པོ་* ཡོད། *lā phep-tha nye-po yö.*

(*On arrival.*) Here is the bazaar. ལགས་ཁྲོམ་མདངས་ (འདི་དུ་)རེད། *lā throm de re.*

Is there no other bazaar besides this one? ཁྲོམ་འདི་མན་པ་གཞན་ཡོད་པ་མ་རེད་པས། *throm di mem-pa sh̃en yo wa ma-re-pe?*

There is no other. ལགས་གཞན་པ་ཡོད་པ་མ་རེད། *lā sh̃em-pa yo-wa ma-re.*

Where is the butcher? ཤ་ཚོང་མཁན† ག་པ་ཡོད་བ་རེད། *sha-tshong-khen k̃a-pa yo-wa-re?*

He is just over there. ལགས་ཕ་གི་རེད། *lā pha-gi re.*

(*To the butcher.*) What meat have you for sale? ཁྱོད་‡ཤ་ག་རེ་འཚོང་རྒྱུ་ཡོད་པ། *khyö sha k̃a-re tshong-gyu yö-pa?*

I have mutton and yak's meat. ལགས་ལུག་ཤ་དང་ཡག་ཤ་ཡོད། *lā luk̃-sha t̃ang tshak̃-sha yö.*

What is the price of a leg of mutton? ལུག་ཤ་བཞི་གླིང་ལ་གོང་ག་ཚོད་ཡིན་པ། *luk̃-sha sh̃i-ling-la k̃ong k̃a-tshö yim-pa?*

Two sh'o (i.e., five annas, four pies). ལགས་ཞོ་ དོ་ཡིན། *lā sh̃o-t̃o yin.*

Very well, I will buy a leg of mutton. འོ་ན་ངས་བཞི་གླིང་ཅིག་ཉོ་གི་ཡིན༎ *O-na nge sh̃i-ling chi nyo-k̃i-yin.*

---

* *Hon.* for ཐག་ཉེ་པོ་ So also ཕེབ་ལམ་ for ལམ་ཀ་ *road* and several others.

† ཤན་པ་ the actual word for *butcher* is avoided as far as possible since it involves some opprobrium. Similarly མགར་ར་ (བ་) for *blacksmith* which should not be used in a blacksmith's presence, but དབུ་མཛོད་ (*lit.* head-man) substituted for it.

‡ The ལ་ after ཁྱོད་ is omitted (See Cap. V, para. 15).

22. *Buying a turquoise.*

Have you any turquoises for sale? ཁྱོད་གཡུ་འཚོང་རྒྱུ་ *ཡོད་པས། *khyö yu tshong-gyu yö-pe?*

Yes, Sir. ལགས་ཡོད། *lā yö.*

Have you any good ones? ཡག་པོ་ཡོད་པས། *yak-po yö-pe?*

Yes, Sir; I have excellent ones. ལགས་ཡག་ཐག་ཆོད་† ཡོད། *lā ya-thak-chhö yö.*

What is the price of this one? འདིའི་གོང་ག་ཚོད་ཡིན་པ། *di-i kong ka-tshö yim-pa?*

Three sang, Sir (five rupees). ལགས་སྲང་‡ གསུམ་ཡིན། *lā sang-sum yin.*

Tell the correct price. ཏན་ཏན་ལབ། *ten-den lap.*

How much will you give, Sir? སྐུ་གཞོགས་ཀྱིས་ག་ཚོད་གསོལ་རས་གནང་ཡོང་ང།§ *ku-sho-kyi ka-tshö sö-re nang-yong-nga?*

Make it ten trang-kas (two rupees, eight annas). ཊྃ་ཀ་བཅུ་ཕྱིས་ (ཕྱིད།) *trang-ka chu chi.*

---

* Lit. *to be sold.*

† ཐག་ཆོད་ is added to many adjectives to denote *very*; e.g., ཆེ་ཐག་ཆོད་ *very great.*

‡ One sang=six trang-kas and one sh'o= one rupee, ten annas, eight pies.

§ གསོལ་རས་གནང་བ་ is *h. hon.* of སྟེར་བ་ *to give.* The ordinary *hon.* is གནང་བ་

That price does not quite suit. Please give me a little more than that. ཕྱགས་གོང་*དེ་ཏོག་ཙ་ (ཙམ་) ཡོང་ང་ (བ་) མི་འདུག། དེ་ནས་ཏོག་ཙ་སྤར†རོགས་གནང་། *ja-gong te tok-tsa yong-nga min-du ; te-ne tok-tsa pa-ro-nang.*

Well, make it two sang (three rupees, five annas, four pies). ད་འོ་ན་སྲང་དོ་བྱེས་ (བྱེད །)‡ *ta o-na sang-to-chi.*

As you, Sir, give the order, I must sell it you for that. སྐུ་གཞོགས་ཀྱིས་བཀའ་གནང་ང་ (བ་) ཡིན་ཙང་དག་ག་རང་ཕུལ་§ དགོ་ (དགོས་) ‖ *ku-sho-kyi ka-nang-nga yin-tsang tak-ka-rang phü-go.*

---

23. *Buying silk.*

By a gentleman of the middle class (6th or 7th grade).

G.=Gentleman. S.=Shopkeeper.

G. (*Coming to the door of the shop.*) Is the merchant in? ཚོང་དཔོན་ལགས་བཞུགས་ཡོད་པས། *tshong-pön-la shu yö-pe?*

S. Yes, Sir. Please come in. ལགས་ཡོད། སྐུ་གཞོགས་ཡར་འཆིབ་རྒྱུ་གནང་དགོ་ (དགོས་)། *lā yö ; ku-sho ya chhip-gyu nang-go.*

---

* *Hon.* of གོང་

† སྤར་བ=*to raise.*

‡ Note that དོ་ is used instead of གཉིས་ So also སྲང་གང་=one sang. For three and more than three the ordinary numerals are used.

§ ཕུལ་བ་ (འབུལ་བ)=lit. *to offer* ; therefore *to give* or *sell* to a superior.

S. (*After G. has come in.*) Please sit down. བཞུགས་གདན་འཇག་དགོ་ (དགོས་) *sh̄u-den ja-go.*

G. Thank you. Have you got any silk of the best quality for making a dress? ལགས་སོ། ཁྱེད་རང་ལ་ཆུ་པ་བཟོ་ཡའི་གོས་ཆེན་ཨང་གི་དང་པོ་ཡོད་པ་གནང་ངས། *les, khye-rang-la chhu-pa so-ya k̄ö-chhen ang-gi tang-po yö-pa nang-nge?*

S. Of what colour do you require it, Sir? ལགས་ཚོས་མདོག་གང་འདྲས་དགོ་བ (དགོས་པ་) གནང་གི་ཡོད་དང་། *lā tshön-do k̄an-dre go-wa nang-gi yö tang?*

G. Have you any dark yellow? སྙུགས་སེ་ (སེར་) ཡོད་པ་གནང་ངས། *nyuk̄-se yö-pa nang-nge?*

S. (*Showing some.*) Will this suit you, Sir? ལགས་འདིས་འགྲིག་ག་ (པ་) གནང་གི་ཨ་ཡོད། *lā di drik̄-k̄a nang-gi a-yö?*

G. That will do. What is the price? དག་གས་ཡོང་ང་།* ཇལ་གས་གོང་ག་ཚོད་ཡིན་པ་གནང་ང་། *tak̄-k̄e yong-nga; ja-k̄ong k̄a-tshö yim-pa nang-nga?*

S. The price, Sir, is four ngü-sang (six rupees, ten annas, eight pies). ལགས་གོང་དངུལ་སྲང་བཞི་ཡིན། *lā k̄ong ngü-sang sh̄i-yin.*

G. Tell me the real price. ཡང་ཏིག་གསུང་། *yang-tik̄ sung.*

S. How much will you give, Sir? སྐུ་གཞོགས་ཀྱིས་ཇལ་གས་གོང་ག་ཚོད་གསོལ་རས་གནང་ཡོང་ང་། *ku-sh̄o-kyi ja-k̄ong k̄a-tshö sö-re nang-yong-nga?*

---

*ཡོང་ང་ = will do. So also when a servant is filling a glass, cup, etc., ད་ཡོང་ང་། means *that will do*=*bas* in Hindustani.

G. Give it me for two sang (three rupees, five annas, four pies). སྲང་དོ་གནང་། *sang-to nang.*

S. I cannot give it you for that. Please give me two sang and five sh'o (four rupees, two annas, eight pies). དེ་ལ་ཏོག་ཙ་འབུལ་ནུས་པ་མི་འདུག། སྲང་དོ་ཞོ་ལྔ་གསོལ་རས་གནང་རོགས་གནང་། *te-la tok-tsa bü nü-pa min-du; sang-to sho-nga sö-re nang-ro-nang.*

G. Very well, then, that price will suit. ལགས་སོ། ཨོ་ན་དག་གས་ཡོང་ང་། *les, o-na tak-ke yong-nga.*

S. In future whatever you require, Sir, is here. གཞུག་ལ་སྐུ་གཞོགས་ལ་ཐུགས་འཁོ་ག་རེ་ཡོད་པ་གནང་ང་མདངས་ (འདི་རུ་) ཡོད། *shu-la ku-sho-la thung-kho ka-re yö-pa nang-nga de yö.*

G. Thank you. If I require anything, I will get it here. ལགས་སོ། དགོས་པ་བྱུང་ན་ལེན་གྱི་ཡིན། *les, go-wa chung-na len-kyi-yin.*

S. Thank you, Sir. ལ་ལགས་སོ། *lā les.*

G. Good-day. ཨོ་ན་བཞུགས་ཨ། *o-na shu-a.*

S. Thank you, Good-day, Sir. ལ་ལགས་སོ། ག་ལེ་འཆིབ་རྒྱུ་གནང་།། *la les, ka-le chhip-gyu-nang.*

24. *A small trader calls at a gentleman's house with some wares.*

M.=Master. T.=Trader. S.=Servant.

T. to S. Please ask if I may see the master. ང་སྐུ་མདུན་ལ་བཅར་ཆོག་ག་ཞུ་རོགས་གནང་། *nga kun-dün-la cha chhok-ka shu-ro-nang.*

S. to T. Very good. ལགས་སོ། *les.*

S. to M. A trader wants to know if he may see you, Sir. ཚོང་པ་ཅིག་སྐུ་མདུན་ལ་བཅར་ཆོག་ག་ཞུ་གི་འདུག། *tshong-pa chi kun-dün-la cha-chhok-ka shu-ki-du.*

M. to S. Very well, let him come in. འོང་། ཤོག་ཁྲིས་ (ཁྲིད་)། *wong sho chhi.*

S. to T. The merchant may come in. ཚོང་དཔོན་སྐུ་མདུན་ལ་ཕེབ་ཆོག་ག། *tshong-pön kun-dün-la phe-chhok-ka.*

(*Then the trader comes in before the master of the house, takes off his hat, bows, and puts out his tongue according to the regular salutation.*)

M. to T. The merchant has arrived. Sit down. ཡ། ཚོང་དཔོན་བསླེབས་བྱུང་། སྡོད། *ya tshong-pön le-chung ; dö.*

T. to M. Thank you, Sir. ལ་ལགས་སོ། *la les.*

M. to S. Pour out some tea for the merchant. ཚོང་དཔོན་ལ་ཇ་ལྡུག། *tshong-pön la chha lu.*

M. to T. What have you got for sale? ཚོང་རྒྱུ་ག་རེ་འཁྱེར་ཡོད། *tshong-gyu ka-re khe yö?*

T. to M. I have brought some turquoises to show you. མགུལ་གཡུ་སྟོན་ཕེབ་ཞུ་རྒྱུ་འཁྱེར་ཡོད། *gü-yu chem-phe shu-gyu khe yö.*

M. to T. (*picking up a turquoise.*) What is the price of this one? མདས་ (འདི་ལ་) གོང་ག་ཚོད་ཡིན་པ། *de kong ka-tshö yim-pa?*

T. to M. Sir, the price of this one is three sang (five rupees). ལགས། མདས་ (འདི་ལ་) གོང་སྲང་གསུམ་ཡིན། *lā, de kong sang-sum yin.*

M. to T. Tell the real price. ཡང་ཏིག་ལབ། *yang-ti lap.*

T. to M. How much will Your Honour give? སྐུ་གཞོགས་ཀྱིས་ག་ཚོད་གསོལ་རས་གནང་ཡོང་ང་། *ku-sho-kyi ka-tshö sö-re nang yong-nga?*

M. to T. Make it one sang and five sh'o (two rupees, eight annas). སྲང་གང་ཞོ་ལྔ་བྱིས་ (བྱེད་)། *sang-kang sho-nga chi.*

T. to M. Please give me two sang (three rupees, five annas, four pies). སྲང་དོ་གསོལ་རས་གནང་རོགས་གནང་། *sang-to sö-re nang-ro-nang.*

M. to T. Very well, I will. འོ་ན་ཡོང་ང་། *o-na yong-nga.*

M. to T. Now-a-days is the business of you traders fairly good? ད་རིང་སང་ཁྱེད་ཚོང་པ་ཚོ་ལ་ཚོང་ཨའུ་ཙེ་འདུག་གས། *te-ring-sang khye tshong-pa-tsho-la tshong au-tse duk-ke?*

T. to M. Yes, fairly good. ལགས། དགའ་རོ་འདུག། *lā, ga-ro-du.*

M. to T. In future if I want anything, I will send word to you to bring it. གཞུག་ལ་འགོ་བྱེད་ག་རེ་ཡོད་པ་འཁྱེར་ཤོག་ཟེ་ལན་བཏང་ (གཏོང་) གི་ཡིན། *shu-lă kho-che ka-re yö-pa khe-sho-se len tang-gi-yin.*

T. to M. Thank you, Sir. ལ་ལགས་སོ། *la les.*

M. to. T. Take tea, don't be in a hurry. ཨ་ལས་ཇ་འཐུང་། བྲེལ་བ་མ་བྱེད། *a-le cha-thung, trel-la ma-che.*

T. to M. Thank you, Sir, I won't have any more (tea). ལགས་ཐུགས་ཆེ། ཞུ་གི་མེན། *lā thu-chhe, shu-ki-men.*

M. to T. Have another cup. གང་འཐུང་། *kang thung.*

T. to M. No more, thank you, Sir. ལགས་མེན། ལགས་མེན། *lā-men, lā-men.*

M. to T. Very well. འོ་ན་ཡོང་ང་།། *o-na yong-nga.*

(*Then the trader makes the same salutation as at entering and goes out.*)

---

25. *Deciding a dispute.*

Which is the complainant? སྙན་ཞུ་ཞུ་མཁན་སུ་རེད། *nyen-shu shu-khen su re?*

Which is the accused? ཁ་ཐེག་སུ་རེད། *khap-the su re?*

Put the witnesses outside. I will call them in presently one by one. དཔང་པོ་ཕྱི་ལོགས་ལ་སྐྱོད་ཕྱིས་ (ཕྱིད་)། གཅིག་ལ་རེ་རེ་བྱས་ནས་སྐད་བཏང་ (གཏོང་) གི་ཡིན། *pang-po chhi-lo-la dö-chi; shu-la re-re che-ne ke-tang-gi-yin.*

What is your complaint? ཁྱོད་ཀ་རེ་ཞུ་རྒྱུ་ཡོད་པ། *khyö ka-re shu-gyu yö-pa?*

Yesterday evening a Tibetan named Wang-dü beat me in the bazaar without any reason. མདང་དགོང་ཁྲོམ་ལ་བོད་པ་དབང་འདུས་ཟེར་མཁན་གྱིས་ང་དོན་དག་ཙ་ནས་མེད་པ་* བརྡུངས་བྱུང་། *dang-gong throm-la ṗö-pa wang-dü ṡe-khen-ḱyi nga ṫön-ṫa tsa-ne me-pa dung cḣung.*

He would not (*lit.* would not know to) beat you without some reason. What actually happened? (*Lit.* What is it?) ཁྱོད་དོན་དག་ཙ་ནས་མེད་པ་རྡུང་ཤེས་ཀྱི་མ་རེད། དེ་ག་རེ་རེད། *khyö ṫön-ṫa tsa-ne me-pa dung shing-gi ma-re. ṫe ḱa-re re?*

He was coming drunk down (the hill), and I was going up. When he reached me he assaulted me. ཁོ་ར་བཟི་ནས་མར་ཡོང་གི་འདུག། ང་ཡར་འགྲོ་གི་ཡོད། ངའི་ཙ་ལ་སླེབས་པ་དང་ང་བརྡུངས་བྱུང་། *kho ra-ṡi-ne ma yong-gi du nga ya dro-ḱi yö, nge tsa-la leṗ-pa ṫang nga dung cḣung.*

(*To the accused.*) Why did you beat him? (*Lit.* What is the meaning of beating by you?) ཁྱོད་རེས་རྡུང་བའི་དོན་དག་ག་རེ་རེད། *khyö-re dung-we ṫön-ṫa ḱa-re re?*

Yesterday I drank a little beer † at a friend's house, and consequently I have no idea what I did. ཁས་ས་ང་རེས་དགའ་

---

* དོན་དག་ཙ་ནས་མེད་པ་ is an adverb and as usual takes the adjectival form.

† Beer is brewed from barley in Tibet, and from marwa (eleusine coracana) in Darjeeling and Sikkim.

ཕོ་ཉེ་ཕོ་གཅིག་གི་རྩ་ལ་ཆང་ཏོག་ཙ་གཅིག་འཐུངས་ང་ (པ་) ཡིན་པས་* ག་རེ་བྱས་ཡོད་རྩ་ནས་ཞུ་རྒྱུ་མི་འདུག། *khe-sa nga-re ga-po nye-po chik-ki tsa-la chhang tok-tsa-chi thung-nga yim-pe ka-re che yö tsa-ne shu-gyu min-du.*

You must pay a fine of five rupees; in default (*lit.* if that does not happen) I shall send you to jail for a week. སྒོར་མོ་ལྔ་ཉེས་པ་སྒྲུབ་† དེ་མ་བྱུང་ན་བདུན་ཕྲག་གཅིག་བཙོན་ལ་བཅུག་(འཇུག་)གི་ཡིན༎ *gor-mo nya nye-pa drup te ma chung na dün-thra chi tsön-lă chuk-ki-yim.*

---

26. *Paying a visit.*

V. = Visitor. H. = Host.

V. How do you do? སྐུ་གཞོགས་བཞུགས་གདན་འཇག་ཡོད་པ‡། *ku-sho shu-den ja yö-pa?*

H. Very well. Please come in and sit down. ལགས་ཡོད§། ཡར་འཆིབ་རྒྱུ་གནང་། བཞུགས་གདན་འཇག། *lā yö, ya chhip-gyu-nang, shu-den-ja.*

H. (*to servant*). Give this gentleman some tea. སྐུ་གཞོགས་ལ་གསོལ་ཇ་ཞུས། *ku-sho la sö-ja shü.*

---

*པས་ here means *because.*

† སྒྲུབ་པ་ means lit. *to accomplish*, and is used sometimes in the sense of *to give, to procure.*

‡ *Lit.*—Are you seated, Sir?

§ *Lit.*—Yes.

H. (*to visitor*). I never meet you now-a-days. བར་ལམ་ *ཅིག་སྐུ་དཞོགས་མ་ནས་† མཇལ་མ་བྱུང་། *par-lam-chi ku-sho ma-ne je-ma-chung.*

V. That is so. I have been a bit worried by some work lately, and so have been unable to call on you. བཀའ་གནང་རང་། བར་ལམ་ཅིག་བྲེལ་གཡེང་‡ འདྲ་པོ་གཅིག་གིས་བཙར་རྒྱུ་མ་ནས་མ་བྱུང་། *ka-nang-rang, par-lam-chi trel-yeng dra-po chik-ki char-gyu ma-ne ma-chung.*

H. You have now come from your house I suppose. ད་ལྟ་གཟིམ་ཤག་ནས་འཆིབ་རྒྱུ་གནང་ང་ (བ་) ཡིན་འགྲོ། *tan-da sim-sha ne chhip-g yu nang-nga yin dro.*

V. Yes, after finishing my committee work I have come straight here. ལགས་ཡིན། ལྷན་རྒྱས་§ གྲོལ་ནས་ལམ་སང་མདངས་ (འདི་རུ་) བཅར་ར་ (བ་) ཡིན། *lā yin hlen-gye trö-ne lam-sang de cha-ra-yin.*

H. Well, stay here to-day and take it easy. ཨོ་ན་དེ་རིང་སྐུ་ལྷོད་ལྷོད་གནང་ནས་བཞུགས་གདན་འཇག་དགོ་ (དགོས་)། *O-na te-ring ku hlö-hlö nang-ne shu-den-ja go.*

V. Many thanks. ལ་ལགས་སེ།། *lā les.*

---

* བར་ལམ་ཅིག་ a literary word. The ordinary colloquial word would be ད་རིང་སང་ In conversation between gentlemen a good many literary words are used.

† Or ཚ་ནས་

‡ བྲེལ་བ་ = business, གཡེང་བ་ (literary word) = to agitate.

§ ལྷན་རྒྱས་ཚོགས་ས་ = a place where officials attend for work = cutchery, committee-room, etc.

27. *The same continued.*

V. Now the night is far advanced; I must be going. ད་ཏོ་དགོང་ཕྱི་པོ་ཕྱིན་ཀྱི་འདུག། དགོངས་པ་ཞུ་དགོ་ (དགོས་*)། *ta to-gong chhi-po chi-kyi-du ; gong-pa shu-go.*

H. Very well, you must come and see me sometimes, when free from work. ལ་ལགས་སོ། ཐུགས་སངས་ཐུགས་སངས་ལ་ † འཆིབ་ཀྱུ་གནང་དགོ་ (ནགོས་) *lā les, thuk-sang thuk-sang lă chhip-gyu nang-go.*

V. Many thanks. You too must come and see me when you are not busy. ལ་ལགས་སོ། སྐུ་གཞོགས་ཡང་ཐུགས་བྲེལ་ ‡ མེད་པའི་སྐང་ལ་ངའི་ཙ་ལ་འཆིབ་ཀྱུ་གནང་དགོ་ (དགོས་)། *lā les, ku-sho yang thu-tre me-pe gang-la nge tsa-la chhip-ggu nang-go.*

H. Well, Good-bye. ད་ག་ལེ་འཆིབ་ཀྱུ་གནང་དགོ་ (དགོས་)། *ta ka-le chhip-gyu nang-go.*

V. Good-bye. ལ་ལགས་སོ་ §། ག་ལེ་བཞུགས་གདན་འཇག། *lā les, ka-le shu-den-ja.*

---

* *Lit.* I must ask for leave.

† ཐུགས་སངས་ཐུགས་སངས་ལ་ *Hon.* for མཚམས་མཚམས་

‡ *Hon.* for བྲེལ་བ་

§ ལ་ལགས་སོ། Note the different senses in which this very frequent expression is used, e.g., "Thank you," "Yes," "Very well," etc. Here no translation is necessary.

28. *Receiving a visit from a Tibetan Official.* (*Conversation about Tibet.*)

T. = Tibetan. E. = Englishman.

T. How do you do ? སྐུ་གཞོགས་བཞུགས་གདན་འཛག་ཡོད་པ། *ku-sho shu-den-ja yö-pa ?*

E. Very well. Welcome. ལགས་ཡོད། ཕྱག་ཕེབས་གནང་བྱུང་། *lā yö, chha-phe nang-chung.*

T. (*Polite reply.*) ལགས་ཡོད། *lā yö.*

E. Please sit down. སྐུ་གཞོགས་བཞུགས་གདན་འཛག། *ku-sho shu-den-ja.*

T. Thank you. ལ་ལགས་སེ། *lā les.*

E. (*to his servant.*) Offer the gentleman some tea. སྐུ་གཞོགས་ལ་གསོལ་ཇ་ཞུས། *ku-sho-la sö-ja shü.*

E. In what part of Tibet do you live ? སྐུ་གཞོགས་བོད་ལ་བཞུགས་གདན་འཛག་ས་ག་པ་རེད། *ku-sho pö-la shu-den ja-sa ka-pa re ?*

T. I live in Lhasa. ང་སྡོད་ས་ལྷ་ས་ལ་ཡིན། *nga dö-sa lha-sa la yin.*

E. What Government post do you hold ? སྐུ་གཞོགས་གཞུང་གི་ཕྱག་ལས་ག་རེ་གནང་གི་ཡོད་པ། *ku-sho shung-gi chha-le ka-re nan-gi yö-pa ?*

T. I am a Tsi-pön (i.e., in charge of an accounts office). ང་རྩིས་དཔོན་གྱི་ལས་ཀ་བྱེད་ཀྱི་ཡོད། *nga tsi-pön-kyi le-ka chi-kyi-yö.*

E. What work do you have to do as a Tsi-pön ? སྐུ་གཞོགས་རྩིས་དཔོན་གྱི་ཕྱག་ལས་ག་རེ་གནང་དགོས་རེད། *ku-sho tsi-pön-kyi chha-le ka-re nang-go-re ?*

T. We have a lot of work to do in connection with the accounts of the Government revenues and the like. ལགས་ང་ཚོ་གཞུང་གི་འབབ་ཀྱི་རྩིས་ལས་ལ་སོགས་པ་མང་པོ་བྱེད་དགོས་ཀྱི་ཡོད། *lā ngan-tsho shung-gi bap-kyi tsi-le la-sok-pa mang-po che go-kyi-yö.*

E. Now-a-days who exercises supreme power in Tibet? ད་རིང་སང་བོད་ཀྱི་རྒྱལ་པོ་སུས་གནང་གི་ཡོད་པ་རེད། *te-ring-sang pö-kyi gye-po sü nang-gi yo-wa-re?*

T. The Dalai Lama has taken up the secular and spiritual Government, and exercises the supreme power. སྐྱབས་མགོན་རིན་པོ་ཆེ་གིས་རྒྱལ་སྲིད་ཆོས་སྲིད་བཞེས་ནས་སྐྱབས་མགོན་རིན་པོ་ཆེ་གིས་གནང་ང་ (བ་) རེད། *kyam-gön Rim-po-chhe-ki gye-si chhö-si she-ne kyam-gön Rim-po-chhe-ki nang-nga-re.*

E. I see. Is Tibet a very large country? ལ་ལགས་སེ། བོད་ལུང་པ་རྒྱ་ཆེན་པོ་ཡོང་ངས། *lā les, pö lung-pa gya-chhem-po yong-nge?*

T. It is of middling size. ལགས་ཨ་ཙུ་ཙོ་འདྲ་པོ་ཡོད*། *lā au-tse dra-po yö.*

E. Which is the pleasantest part of Tibet? བོད་ཀྱི་དཀྱིལ་ནས་ག་པ་སྐྱི་བ་ཡོང་། *pö kyi kyil ne ka-pa tro-wa-yong?*

T. Lhasa is about the pleasantest. ཏོག་ཙ་ལྷ་ས་སྐྱི་བ་ཡོང་། *tok-tsa hle-sa tro-wa yong.*

E. I see. Tibet must be, I fancy, a nice country. ལ་ལགས་སེ། བྱས་ན་བོད་དེ་ཡག་པོ་དེ་ཡག་པོ་ཡིན་པ་རེད། *lā les, che-na pö te yak-po yö-pa yim-pa-re.*

---

* He means that it is very large, but it is not considered etiquette among Tibetan gentlemen to praise one's own possessions, not even one's own country.

T. Now I must be going for to-day. ད་དེ་རིང་དགོངས་པ་ཞུ་གི་ཡིན། *ta te-ring gong-pa sh̄u-k̄i-yin.*

E. Won't you stay a little longer? ཏོག་ཙ་བཞུགས་གདན་འཇག་དགོས། *tok̄-tsa sh̄u-den ja-go?*

T. To-day I have some work to do, so I must be going. I will call on you later on. དེ་རིང་ང་བྲེལ་བ་ཏོག་ཙ་ཡོད་དགོངས་པ་ཞུ་གི་ཡིན། གཞུག་ལ་བཅར་གྱི་ཡིན། *te-ring nga trel-la tok̄-tsa yö gong-pa sh̄u-k̄i-yin; sh̄u-la char-k̄yi-yin.*

E. Very good. You must come and see me when you are not busy. ལ་ལགས་སེ། ཐུགས་བྲེལ་མེད་པའི་སྐང་ལ་ངའི་རྩ་ལ་འཆིབ་གྱུ་གནང་དགོས། *lā les, thuk̄-trel me-pe gang lă nge tsa-la chhip̄-gyu nang-go.*

T. Many thanks. Well, good-bye. ལ་ལགས་སེ། འོ་ན་ག་ལེ་བཞུགས་གདན་འཇག། *la les, o-na k̄a-le sh̄u-den-ja.*

E. Good-bye, then. ལ་ལགས་སེ། ག་ལེ་འཆིབ་གྱུ་གནང་།། *la-les, k̄a-le chhip̄-gyu nang.*

---

29. *The same continued (discussing travelling arrangements).*

T.=Tibetan. E.=Englishman.

E. According to Tibetan custom when a gentleman goes on a journey does he give all his servants ponies to ride? བོད་ཀྱི་ལུགས་སྲོལ་ལ་དཔོན་པོ་ཕྱུགས་ཕེབས་གནང་ངའི་ (བའི་) སྐང་ལ་ཞབས་ཕྱི་སྐང་ཁ་ལ་ཆིབས་པ་གནང་ཡོང་ངས། *pö-k̄yi luk̄-sö la pöm-po chho-phe nang-nge gang-lă sh̄ap̄-chhi gang-kha lă chhik̄-pa nang-yong nge?*

T. Yes, he provides them all with ponies. ལགས་སྐང་ཁ་ལ་རྟ་གནང་ཡོང་། *lā gang-kha la ta nang-yong.*

E. After what manner do they proceed on their journey? འཆིབ་རྒྱུ་གནང་ངའི་ (བའི་) སྒང་ལ་ག་འདྲས་ཟེ་འཆིབ་རྒྱུ་གནང་ཡོང་། *chhip-gyu nang-nge gang-lă ka̋n-dre-śe chhip-gyu nang-yong?*

T. He puts half in front of him and half behind him, and rides himself in the middle. ཞབས་ཕྱི་ཕྱེད་ཀ་སྔོན་ལ་གཏོང་ང་ (བ་) གནང་ཡོང་། ཕྱེད་ཀ་གཞུག་ལ་གཤོག་ག་ (འཛོག་པ་) གནང་ནས་དཔོན་པོ་དེ་དཀྱིལ་ལ་འཆིབ་རྒྱུ་གནང་ཡོང་། *sk̄ap-chhi chhe-ka ngen-la tong-nga nang-yong; chhe-ka sk̄uk-la shok-k̄a-nang-ne pöm-po kyil-la chhip-gyu nang-yong.*

E. I understand. Do all the servants travel with their master? ལ་ལགས་སོ། དཔོན་པོ་དང་ལྷན་རྒྱས་ཞབས་ཕྱི་སྒང་ཁ་ཕེབ་ཡོང་ང་། *lā les; pöm-po tang hlen-gye sk̄ap-chhi gang-kha phe yong-nga?*

T. He sends his butler and cook on ahead; then after his muleteers have started, he starts himself with his servants in single file. ལགས་གཉེར་པ་དང་མ་ཆེན་གཉིས་སྔོན་འགྲོད་ལ་གཏོང་ང་ (བ་) གནང་ནས་དེའི་གཞུག་ལ་ཏྲལ་པ་ཕྱིན་ཚར་ར་ (བ་) དང་དེ་ཕྱིང་ཞབས་ཕྱི་སྒང་ཁ་དཔོན་པོ་དང་ལྷན་རྒྱས་ཆིབས་རགས་བསྒྲིགས་ནས་འཆིབ་རྒྱུ་གནང་ཡོང་། *lā nyer-pa tang ma-chhen nyi ngen-drö lă tong-nga nang-ne te-ï-sk̄uk-la tre-pa chhin tshar-ra tang te-ch̄ing sk̄ap-chhi gang-kha pöm-po tang hlen-gye chhip-ra drik-ne chhip-gyu nang-yong.*

E. To do what does he send the butler and cook on ahead? གཉེར་པ་དང་མ་ཆེན་གཉིས་སྔོན་ལ་ག་རེ་བྱེད་ལ་གཏོང་ང་ (བ་) གནང་ང་ (བ་) རེད། *nyer-pa tang ma-chhen nyi ngen-la k̄a-re ch̄e-la tong-nga nang-nga-re?*

T. He sends the two servants in advance in order to have things ready and prepare food before he arrives. སྔོན་འགྲོད་གཉིས་པོ་དཔོན་པོ་འཆིབ་རྒྱུ་མ་གནང་གོང་ལ་ཕེབས་བསྒྲིགས་ཞུ་བ་དང་ཞལ་ལག་བཟོ་བ་གཏོང་ང་ (བ་) གནང་ང་ (བ་) རེད། *ngen-drö nyi-po pöm-po chhip-gyu ma nang kong-lă phep-drik shu-wa tang she-la so-wa tong-nga nang-nga re.*

E. I understand. ཨོང་། ལ་ལགས་སོ།། *wong, lā les.*

---

30. *The same continued (discussing the agricultural and mineral products of Tibet).*

T.=Tibetan. E.=Englishman.

E. What crops are grown in Tibet? ལགས་བོད་ལ་སྟོན་ཐོག་ག་རེ་སྐྱེ་ཡོང་། *lā pö-lă tön-tho ka-re kye-yong?*

T. In Tibet itself, wheat, barely, peas and mustard are the chief crops. In Kong-po maize, buck-wheat and various other crops grow. Kong-po is warmer than Lhasa. Besides bamboos, apricots, apples, walnuts, and all kinds of food are grown. ལགས་བོད་རང་ལ་གྲོ་ནས་སྲན་ (tren) གསུམ་དང་པེ་གང་ཤུགས་ཆེ་བ་སྐྱེ་ཡོང་། ཀོང་པོ་ལ་ཀན་རྫོམ་དང་བྲའུ་ (བྲ་བོ་) ལ་སོགས་པ་སྟོན་ཐོག་སྣ་ཚོགས་སྐྱེ་ཡོང་། ལྷ་ས་ལས་ཀོང་པོ་དྲོ་གི་རེད། སྨྱུང་ (སྨྱུག་) མ་དང་ཁམ་བུ་ཀུ་ཤུ་སྟར་ཀ་ཟས་གང་ཡང་སྐྱེ་ཡོང་། *lā pö rang-lă tro ne tren sum tang pe-kang shuk-chhe-wa kye-yong; kong-po lă ken-dzom tang trau la-sok-pa tön-tho na-tsho kye-yong; hla-sa le kong-po tro-ki-re; nyung-ma tang kham-pu ku-shu tar-ka se kang-yang kye-yong.*

E. I see. How many days' journey is it from Lhasa to Kong-po? ལ་ལགས་སོ། ལྷ་ས་ནས་ཀོང་པོ་བར་ལ་ཞག་* མ་ག་ཚོད་ཀྱི་ས་རེད། *lā les, hla-sa ne kong-po pa-la shak-ma ka-tshö-kyi sa re?*

T. One reaches Upper Kong-po in fifteen days. To Lower Kong-po the journey takes one month. ལགས་ཀོང་སྟོད་ལ་ཞག་མ་བཅོ་ལྔ་ལ་ཕེབ་ཀྱི་རེད། ཀོང་སྨད་† བར་དུ་ཟླ་བ་གཅིག་ཙམ་ཕེབ་དགོས་ཀྱི་རེད། *lā kong-tö lă shak-ma chö-nga la phe-kyi-re; kong-me par-tu da-wa chi tsam phe go-kyi-re.*

E. Is wood plentiful in Tibet? བོད་ལ་ཤིང་འཕེལ་པོ་ཡོང་ངས་ལགས། *pö-lă shing be-po yong-nge-lā?*

T. There is a certain amount of wood; but for fires cattle-dung is mostly used. ལགས་ཤིང་ཏོག་ཙ་ཡོང་ཏེ་ཤུགས་ཆེ་བ་མེ་གཏོང་ཡ་ལ་སྤྱོ་བ (སྤྱི་བ) འབུས་ (འབུ་) ཡོང་། *lā shing tok-tsa yong-te shuk-chhe-wa me tong-ya lă cho-wa bü yong.*

E. Are gold, silver and coal to be had in Tibet by mining? བོད་ལ་གསེར་དང་དངུལ་རྡོ་སོལ་ས་ནས་འདོན་རྒྱུ་‡ ཡོང་ངས་ལགས། *pö-lă ser tang ngü do-sö sa-ne dön-gyu yong-nge lā?*

T. Yes, in Tibet itself gold, silver and coal are to be had by mining, but it is not customary to mine for them. ལགས་ བོད་ རང་ ལ་ གསེར་དང་དངུལ་རྡོ་སོལ་འདོན་རྒྱུ་ཡོང་ཏེ་འདོན་པའི་ལུགས་སྲོལ་མི་ཡོང་། *lā pö rang-lă ser tang ngü do-sö dön-gyu yong-te dön-pe luk-sö mi-yong.*

---

*ཞག་མ་ is often used colloquially for ཞག་པོ་

† Note method of describing the upper and lower parts of a country. It is often used.

‡ འདོན་ In conversation between ordinary people བཏོན་ is used, but the higher classes affect literary forms in their conversation.

E. Is that so? What harm is there in mining? ལ་ལགས་སེ། འདོན་པ་གནང་ང་ལ་སྐྱོན་ག་རེ་ཡོད་པ་རེད། *la-les; dön-pa-nang-nga la kyön ka-re yo-wa-re?*

T. If they are mined the soil-essence of the country is damaged, and good crops are not produced. ལགས་བཏོན་ན་ལུང་པའི་ས་བཅུད་ཉམས་ཀྱི་རེད། སྟོན་ཐོག་ཡང་ཡག་པོ་སྐྱེ་ཀྱི་མ་རེད*།། *la; tön-na lung-pe sa-chü nyam-kyi-re; tön-tho yang yak-po kye-kyi ma-re.*

---

31. *A visit to the Dalai Lama by a Tibetan General (De-pön).*

T.=Tibetan. E.=Englishman.

E. In Tibet when a general goes to pay his respects to the Dalai Lama, what does he have to do? པོད་ལ་སྐྱབས་མགོན་རིན་པོ་ཆེའི་སྐུ་མདུན་ལ་མདའ་དཔོན་སྐུ་གཞོགས་གཅིག་མཇལ་ག་ (བར་) བཅར་ར་ (བ་) གནང་ན་ག་འདྲས་གནང་དགོས་ཀྱི་རེད་ལགས། *pö-la kyam-gön Rim-po-chhe kum-dün-la De-pön ku-sho chi je-ka char-ra nang-na kan-dre nang go-kyi-re la?*

T. After sitting for a while in the ante-room, the chief drö-nyer† says to him, "You can come." After going up, he must make three obeisances‡; offer the Dalai Lama a ceremonial scarf, take off his hat, and ask for a blessing. གཟིམ་ཆུང་འགག་ལ་ཏོག་ཙ་འདུགས་ གདན་ འཛག་ནས་དེ་ནས་མགྲོན་གཉེར་

---

* A prevalent Tibetan idea.

† An official of the fourth grade. Under him in the Dalai Lama's household are eight drö-nyers, who are fifth grade. All nine are monks. Besides these, there are four drö-nyers, one for each Shap-pe, these drö-nyers being laymen and of sixth grade.

‡ Knees and forehead touch the ground at each obeisance.

ཆེན་པོས་འཆིབ་རྒྱུ་གནང་ཆོག་ག་བཀའ་གནང་ཡོང་། ཡར་ཕེབས་པ་དང་སྐུ་ཕྱག་གསུམ་འཚལ་ར་ (བ་) གནང་ནས་སྐྱབས་མགོན་རིན་པོ་ཆེ་ལ་མཇལ་དར་དབུལ་ར་ (བ) གནང་ནས་འབུ་ཞྭ་ཕྱིས་ (ཕུད་) ནས་ཕྱག་དབང་ཞུ་བ་གནང་དགོས་ཀྱི་རེད། *śim-chhung gaḱ-la toḱ-tsa sḱu-den ja-ne ṫe-ne drön-nyer chhem-pö chhiṗ-gyu-nang chhoḱ-ḱa ka-nang-yong ; yar-phep-pa ṫang ku-chha sum tshe-ra nang-ne kyam-gön Rim-po-chhe la je-dar bü-ra-nang-ne wu-sḱa pi-ne chhaḱ-wang sḱu-wa nang go-kyi-re.*

Then a silk cushion is placed below the throne. The De-pön having sat down on it, tea is brought. དེ་ནས་བཞུགས་ཁྲིའི་གཤམ་དུ་བཞུགས་གདན་གོས་ཁ་གཅིག་སྐྱོན་ཡོང་། དེའི་སྟེང་ལ་མདའ་དཔོན་སྐུ་གཞོགས་བཞུགས་གདན་འཇག་ཚར་ར་ (བ་) དང་གསོལ་ཇ་འཆིབ་རྒྱུ་གནང་ཡོང་།* *ṫe-ne sḱuḱ-thri sham ṫe sḱuḱ-den kö-kha chi kyön-yong : ṫe-ï gang lā De-pön ku-sḱo sḱuḱ-den ja tshar-ra-ṫang, sö-cḱa chhiṗ-gyu nang-yong.*

After tea has been offered to the Dalai Lama, some is laid before the De-pön. སྐྱབས་མགོན་རིན་པོ་ཆེ་ལ་གསོལ་ཇ་ཀྱག་ (འཁྱུག་) གྲུབ་པ་དང་མདའ་དཔོན་སྐུ་གཞོགས་ལ་གསོལ་ཇ་ཞུ་བ་གནང་ཡོང་། *Kyam-gön Rim-po-chhe lā sö-cḱa kya ṫrup-pa-ṫang De-pön ku-sḱo lā sö-cḱa sḱu-wa nang-yong.*

After that rice-pudding is brought. དེའི་གཞུག་ལ་བཞེས་འབྲས་སིལ་† འཆིབ་རྒྱུ་གནང་ཡོང་། *ṫe-ï sḱuk-lā sḱen-dre dre-si chhiṗ-gyu nang-yong.*

---

* Note the *hon.* given to the verb by which the tea of the Dalai Lama is brought in. It is not used in similar cases for officials even of high rank.

† Made of rice, butter and sugar.

Then after this has been offered to the Dalai Lama, and to the De-pön, the Dalai Lama inquires after his health saying "Tsha-rong De-pön, are you in good health?" དེ་ནས་སྐྱབས་མགོན་སྦུགས་ལ་* ཀྱག་ (འཁྱག་) སྒྲུབ་པ་དང་མདའ་དཔོན་སྐུ་གཞོགས་ལ་ཞུ་བ་གནང་ནས་སྐྱབས་མགོན་རིན་པོ་ཆེ་ནས་མཚམས་དྲི་† (འདྲི་) གནང་ང་ (བ་) ལ་ཚ་རོང་‡ མདའ་དཔོན་གཟུགས་པོ་བདེ་པོ་བྱུང་ངས་བཀའ་གནང་ཡོང་།། *te-ne Kyam-gön Buk lā kya trup-pa ang De-pön ku-sho la shu-wa nang-ne kyam-gön Rim-po-chhe ne tsham-tri nang-nga lā Tsha-rong De-pön suk-po de-po chung-nge ka-nang-yong.*

---

32. *Diplomatic intercourse*, hon.

The British Government is not responsible. དབྱིན་གཞུང་ལ་ཐུགས་ཁག་ཡོད་པ་མ་རེད། *in-shung-la thu-kha yo-wa ma re.*

It will be a source of friction. འཁྲུགས་གཞིའི་རྐྱེན་ཡོང་གི་རེད། *thruk-shi kyen yong-gi-re.*

Our subjects will refuse to pay taxes or obey the laws. ང་ཚོའི་མི་སེར་གྱིས་ཁྲལ་ འཇལ་ ཐུབ་ མི་ ཡོང་།§ ཁྲིམས་ཡང་འཁྱེར་མི་ཡོང་། *ngan-tsho mi-ser kyi thre je thup mi-yong; thrim yang khye-mi-yong.*

---

* *Lit.* "Inner or real protector."

† *Lit.* "Intermediate question," i.e., the first question of the new interview some time having elapsed since the last.

‡ The family name or surname of the De-pön, with estates in the Ü province.

§ *Lit.* "will be unable," i.e., "will profess inability," "will refuse."

It is probably not finally decided. ཐད་རང་ངེས་མེད་པ་འདྲ། *Be-rang nge me-pa dra.*

It will be referred for equitable adjustment. འདྲ་དྲང་བར་འདུམ་ཡོང་ང་སྐུ་གི་རེད། *Dra-trang-ṕar-dum yong-nga sk̄u-k̄i-re.*

The British Government desire to maintain amicable relations with other governments. དབྱིན་ གཞུང་གིས་རྒྱལ་ཁབ་ གཞན་ དང་ མཐུན་ ལམ་ ཡོང་ བའི་ ཐུགས་ འདོད་ གནང་གི་ཡོད་པ་རེད། *in-sk̄ung-gi gye-khaṕ sk̄en t́ang thün-lam yong-nge thuk̄-dö nang-gi yo-wa-re.*

They will make every endeavour to pick a quarrel with the Tibetan Government. ཁོང་ཚོས་བོད་གཞུང་ལ་སྙད་ཉེས་ཀྱུའི་ཐབས་གང་ཐུབ་བྱས་ཡོང་། *khon-tshö ṕö-sk̄ung-la nye kö-gyü thaṕ k̄ang-thuṕ ch̄e-yong.*

Although China is divided into parties, she can raise soldiers to meet aggression on her territory. རྒྱ་ནག་ནང་ཚག་ཁ་ཁག་བྱས་ སྡད་ན་ ཡང་སོ་སོའི་ ས་ ཆ་ སྲུང་ རྒྱུ་ དམག་ མི་ སྐུལ་ ཐུབ་ ཡོང་། *gya-na nang-tsa 'cha-kha ch̄e de-na-yang, so-sö sa-cha sung-gyu mak̄-mi kü-thuṕ-yong.*

It will be difficult for us to hold out much longer, for you know how much more powerful the one nation is than the other (*lit.* the great difference in the extent of the power of the two nations). དགོངས་མངགས་ནང་བཞིན་རྒྱལ་ཁབ་གཉིས་པོ་སྟོབས་ཆེ་ཆུང་ཧེ་བག་ཆེན་པོ་ཤོར་བ་ཡིན་ཙང་ང་ཚོས་རྒྱུན་རིང་དཀག་ཐུབ་པ་དཀའ་ལས་ཆེན་པོ་ཡོང་གི་རེད། *gong-ngak̄ nang-sk̄in gye-khaṕ nyi-po toṕ chhe-chhung he-bak̄ chhem-po shor-wa yin-tsang ngan-tshö gyün-ring kak̄ thuṕ-pa ka-le-chhem-po yong-gi-re.*

I fear that serious complications may arise, for the majority of the people are already beginning to complain of the situation. མི་ཕལ་ཆེར་ལས་ཀ་འདིའི་བཟོ་ལ་བརྟས་ནས་ད་ལྟ་ནས་སྐད་ཤོར་ཀྱི་འདུག་དགེ་སྐྱོན་གང་མེན་ཡོང་ཉེན་ཆེན་པོ་རེད། *mi phe-chhe le-ka di-ï so-la te-ne tan-da-ne ke-sho kyi-du; ge-kyön kang-men yong-nyen chhem-po-re.*

I shall be held responsible if the negotiations fail. བཀའ་མོལ་དོན་སྨིན་མ་བྱུང་ན་མ་བྱུང་མ་འཐུས་པའི་ཁག་ང་ལ་ཡོང་གི་རེད། *ka-mön tön-min ma-chung-na ma-chung ma-thü-pe kha nga-la yong-gi-re.*

Our government has no aim other than the maintenance of the *status quo.* ང་ཚོའི་གཞུང་གི་ཐུགས་འདོད་ལ་ཆབ་སྲིད་སྔོན་ཡོད་རང་འཇགས་བཞགས་རྒྱུ་མ་གཏོགས་གཞན་གྱི་དགོངས་པ་ཡོད་པ་མ་རེད། *ngan-tshö shung-gi thung-dö-la chhap-si ngön-yö rang-ja shak-gyu ma-to shen-kyi gong-pa yo-wa ma-re.*

GBPress—631Y—1,000B—16-9-193